T0305066

A New Model of Socialism

A New Model of Socialism

Democratising Economic Production

Bruno Jossa

Professor of Political Economy, University 'Federico II' of Naples, Italy

 Edward Elgar
PUBLISHING

Cheltenham, UK • Northampton, MA, USA

Published by
Edward Elgar Publishing Limited
The Lypiatts
15 Lansdown Road
Cheltenham
Glos GL50 2JA
UK

Edward Elgar Publishing, Inc.
William Pratt House
9 Dewey Court
Northampton
Massachusetts 01060
USA

A catalogue record for this book
is available from the British Library

Library of Congress Control Number: 2017960000

This book is available electronically in the **Elgar**online
Economics subject collection
DOI 10.4337/9781788117838

MIX
Paper from
responsible sources
FSC   FSC® C013056
www.fsc.org

ISBN 978 1 78811 782 1 (cased)
ISBN 978 1 78811 783 8 (eBook)

Typeset by Columns Design XML Ltd, Reading
Printed and bound in Great Britain by TJ International Ltd, Padstow

Contents

Acknowledgements

This book is conceived as a blend which combines new text with excerpts and fragments from earlier writings. Specifically, the Introduction is the English version of a book dating from 2015, *Un socialism possibile* (Il Mulino, Bologna); Chapter 2 reproduces the text of a paper, *Production Modes: Marx's Method and the Feasible Revolution*, which appeared in the October 2016 issue of the *European Scientific Journal*; Chapter 3 is the English translation of *Cooperativismo, capitalismo e socialismo* (Novalogos, Aprilia, 2012); Chapter 4 reports pages from 'On the Advantages of a System of Labour-Managed Firms' (*Journal of Entrepreneurial and Organizational Diversity*, vol. 5, no. 1); Chapter 5 reproduces, with some additions, the text of the paper 'Marx, Marxism and the Cooperative Movement' (*Cambridge Journal of Economics*, 2005, no. 1); Chapter 6 analyses cooperation in connection with the labour theory of value; Chapter 7 offers a closer look at the links between Marxism and producer cooperatives; Chapter 8 is about criticism of labour-managed firms, Chapter 9 reprints excerpts from 'On Producer Cooperatives and Socialism', a paper published in *International Critical Thought* (2014, vol. 4, no. 3); Chapter 10 offers an outline of the evolution of socialism from its utopian stage to the emergence of producer cooperation theory; Chapter 11 is about the democratic firm in the estimation of intellectuals; Chapter 12 analyses the actions and attitudes of trade unions as involuntary antagonists of history and progress.

I owe a special debt of gratitude to Professor Cuomo, from the University of Naples, for his valuable advice and collaboration.

The texts have been translated into English by Aloisia Rigotti.

1. Introduction

This book revolves around the research hypotheses that capitalism is not a democratic system and that a system of producer cooperatives, or democratically managed enterprises, gives rise to a new mode of production which is genuinely socialist in essence and fully consistent with the ultimate rationale underlying Marx's theoretical approach.[1] In essence, these arguments reflect the ideas at the basis of a much praised book by Lewis Mumford, *Technics and Civilization*, viz., the conviction that the precondition for ensuring the survival of such priceless instruments of progress as science and technology is rescuing man from his enslavement to the tools he himself has created and overrated (see Mumford 1934, p. 15).

The proposition that 'those who work in the mills should own them', which is tantamount to arguing that firms should be run by the workers on their own, was endorsed by John Dewey, the greatest social thinker of the twentieth century, but is also shared by Marxists such as Anton Pannekoek, Karl Korsch, Angelo Tasca, Antonio Gramsci, Richard Wolff and Ernesto Screpanti, as well as by socialist thinkers including Pierre Proudhon, John Stuart Mill, Karl Polanyi, G.D.H. Cole, Lucio Libertini, Raniero Panzieri and Franco Ferrarotti[2] – to mention just a few. According to Hobsbawm 2011 (p. 37), it was the strong impression of the experience of the French Revolution 'as a class struggle between nobility, bourgeois and propertyless masses' that led Marx to conclude that it was time to liberate the proletarian from his subjugation to the bourgeoisie and even in Marx's own lifetime a great many workers thought of socialism as the cooperation of producers (p. 54).

In times nearer to us, when two champions of a democratic transition to self-management socialism spelt out that 'the institutions of proletarian power' were to be established even before the revolutionary leap proper, i.e. over '*the very course of the whole struggle of the workers' movement for power*', and were to 'arise from the economic sphere ... the real

---

[1] The argument that a cooperative firm system coincides with socialism was first set forth in Jossa 1978.

[2] See, inter alia, Ferrarotti 1960.

source of power' (Libertini & Panzieri 1969, pp. 41–4), they gave expression to the idea that this book is ultimately intended to advance.

The need to democratise first and foremost the economic sphere is suggested by the finding that the true and sole source of all power is economic action. Marx himself taught that democracy was incomplete unless political democracy was combined with economic democracy and that the latter was therefore the precondition for the evolution of formal into full democracy.

This means I cannot subscribe to Sartori's (1995, p. 40) statement that

> the role of social democracy as the vital prerequisite for the existence of a democratic State or the need to work towards such vital goals as economic equality and industrial democracy can barely be called into question, but there is little denying that these are but secondary forms of democracy whose necessary precondition is political democracy. Indeed, it is a fact that these are subordinated, not *sovereign* aspects of democracy overall.

From my perspective, Sartori's argument should altogether be reversed: industrial democracy is the primary form and the precondition for the attainment of full-fledged political democracy. As mentioned before, Marx himself made it absolutely clear that political democracy is incomplete unless it is complemented by economic democracy.

John Stuart Mill described a cooperative firm system as 'the nearest approach to social justice' and 'the most beneficial ordering of industrial affairs for the universal good which it is possible at present to foresee' (Mill 1871, p. 792). Ever since, economic theorists have been analysing the organisational aspects of worker-controlled firm systems and have reached the conclusion that a system of this kind can both operate at high levels of efficiency and ensure major improvements over capitalism. Sartre, for his part, rightly argued that such obviously democratic institutions as workers' committees may act as 'the founding stones of the future socialist society' (see Sartre 1960, p. 29) and Landauer looked upon a cooperative firm system as 'the first true step towards a strong stand against capitalism' (see Landauer 1985, as quoted in Candela 2014, p. 210). The Italian patriot Giuseppe Mazzini contended that 'acquiring title in the fruits of our labour is the goal that lies ahead' and is to be pursued by any means since 'the combination of capital and productive work in the same hands will result in immense advantages not only for workers, but for society at large' (Mazzini 1862, p. 233). Much in the same vein, R. Tawney argued that the preconditions for attaining full freedom are absence of repression and, most importantly, opportunities for self-advancement through the extension of representative institutions to industry (see Tawney 1918, p. 103), and Marković suggested that no theoretical approach could be categorised as truly radical or revolutionary unless it was ultimately aimed to create conditions under which producers in association would be able to freely dispose of the output of their work (Marković 1969, p. 143).[3]

Despite these authoritative endorsements, the idea of furthering the access to workers to the self-management of their firms, especially medium–large enterprises,[4] hardly features on the agendas of any scholars, be they Marxists or non-Marxists. Cole has written (1920, p. 14): 'theoretical "democrats" totally ignore the effects of undemocratic organization and convention in non-political spheres of social action, not only upon the lives which men lead in those spheres, but also in perverting and annihilating in practice the theoretical democracy of modern politics'.

Today, the idea of changing society by creating a system of democratically run enterprises is likely to gain fresh momentum due to the dramatic crisis of capitalism, the collapse of the Soviet-type centralised planning model and, even more generally, the decline of statism and kingship. In this connection, Bobbio wrote that 'the leading actors in political affairs are invariably groups, i.e. associations, unions of various trades and professions, as well as political parties rooted in a gamut of different ideologies'. Consequently – he concluded – 'it is groups, rather than individuals, that loom large in the political agenda of a democratic society without a king' (for this argument of Bobbio's, see Bolaffi 2002, p. 156). All the same, the proposal to establish a system of democratically managed firms features on the research agendas of just a few (Marxist and non-Marxist) theorists.

The claim that workers' councils are nothing but a means of creating new forms of power or that the council movement, far from striving to abolish the State, is poised to create an ideal 'society of producers' as an alternative power model has been forcefully refuted by the well-known Marx scholar Valentino Gerratana (1972, p. 26). Those authors who describe a system of producer cooperatives as a new production mode do so on the assumption that a well-structured system of this kind will

---

[3] According to Chomsky, it is still a matter for debate whether, and to what extent, State tyranny in the USSR was to be blamed on the Bolshevik doctrine or the circumstances under which the State arose and grew, but the contention that the Soviet state model was a socialist system is nothing but a cruel joke (see Chomsky 1971, p. 79).

[4] In his *Guild Socialism* model Cole tends to restrict worker management to medium–large-scale organisations only (see Cole 1920, pp. 63ff.).

ensure effective control of production without interfering with the working of markets and is consistent with the ideals of the Marxian socialist tradition notwithstanding its market orientation.

At first sight, the decision to discuss a market system against the background of Marxian theory may strike the reader as surprising. In fact, it will appear quite obvious to anyone thinking that Marx's revolution in social science can compare with Copernicus's revolution in astronomy (see Plechanov 1911, p. 2) or that Marxist thought 'will never die' (Gramsci 1917, p. 43) and will be heartily welcomed by anyone thinking of revolution as a change of the current mode of production. Some authors have gone so far as to contend that cross-references to Marx's thought constitute the sole mode of scholarly reflection that any social scientist is expected to adopt. According to Wright Mills, for instance, no one can think of himself as a modern social thinker if he fails to concern himself earnestly with Marx's theoretical approach (see Wright Mills 1962, p. 7) and Bloom has argued that 'each great cultural era of the globe seems to be fated to live through an absorbing and usually bitter controversy over the merits and relevance of the doctrines of Karl Marx' (Bloom 1943, p. 53).[5]

The equally unwarranted notion that the scientific gist of Marx's method can only be brought into focus by expunging its mystico-religious dialectical kernel (see, inter alia, Sombart, Weber, Pareto, Schumpeter, Mannheim and Gurvich) and Pellicani's clear-cut distinction between Marx the Enlightenment thinker and Marx the prophet of millennial communism (see Pellicani 1987, p. 186) will be addressed further on.

The question to be raised at this point is what Marx meant by socialism.[6]

Before I attempt an answer, let me specify that ever since the close of the nineteenth century the ongoing debate over the comparative merits of

---

[5] From Pivetti 2006 (p. 82) we learn that Sraffa, aware of the scant regard in which Marx was held by mainstream economists and desirous to arouse the interest that his critique of economic theory deserved, did not mention that the true underpinning of his approach was Marxian theory. Since my target audience is principally formed of Marxists, such an overly cautious attitude is unnecessary in this book (on this point, see also Sylos Labini 2006, pp. 34–5).

[6] With reference to this point in the preface to the first edition of *Capital*, Marx wrote: 'In the domain of Political Economy, free scientific inquiry meets not merely the same enemies as in all other domains. The peculiar nature of the materials it deals with, summons as foes into the field of battle the most violent, mean and malignant passions of the human breast, the Furies of private interest' (Marx 1867, p. 34).

capitalism versus socialism has always been revolving around a model of socialism typified by centralised planning.[7] It is common knowledge that Marx and Engels strongly argued against Bakuninism on account of its failure to acknowledge the State and abstentionism in politics. 'The call for suppressing the State' – Engels wrote to Cafiero in 1871 – 'is an old slogan we used to spout as young men, but it would be stupid to include it in our programme for the International' (see Engels 1871).

A great many academics, including Pareto, have criticised the European model of socialism because of its allegedly statist overtones. Specifically, both Pareto and Hayek argued that the common starting point for any scientific approach to the essence of socialism is a comparative analysis of two antithetical systems such as free competition and state-controlled production.

It is well known that Marx flatly refused to concern himself with what he termed 'the cook-shops of the future'. As indicated by Wright Mills (1962, p. 90), Marx thought it beyond our power to predict the organisational structure of the post-capitalist society and dismissed detailed scenarios of the future as nothing but the mental constructs of utopians and dreamers. Just as Marx hated indulging in daydreams, Wright Mills concluded, so he shrank from going into details about the future.[8]

Hence, although quite a lot of Marxists are 'cynical about the prospects of creating a system of worker-controlled firms', the contention that socialism does not coincide with either statism or social democracy is not at odds with Marx's theoretical approach (see Mellor et al. 1988, p. 72).

Getting back to this point later, I will be arguing that within a socialist system founded on democratic firm management the State, far from suffering an eclipse, would be free to perform its function, i.e. to intervene in the economy in an effort to serve the interests of society at large.

---

[7] Bidet (2004, p. 83) holds that the basic ingredients of socialism are the principles that production means are jointly owned and that production is to be organised in accordance with a democratically developed plan. Much to the same effect, Kouvélakis has argued (2005, p. 203) that the abolition of class property and the management of national production by all cooperative associations according to a common plan are the only means to keep cooperative production from reaching a dead end or falling into a trap. These, he went on to conclude, are two pillars of what is clearly characterised as 'communism'.

[8] This same idea is at the basis of the argument that 'it rests with the revolutionary movement to flesh out the best possible forms of production and distribution models' (Kramer-Badoni 1972, p. 60).

The idea that what is termed socialism is a system founded on democratic firm management (rather than centralised planning) is gradually gaining ground thanks to advancements in scientific speculation.

One of the mainstays of self-management is the idea that 'capitalism's pathology cannot be imputed to the market' (Bidet 2004, p. 82). According to Bobbio (1984, p. 136), the 'goalposts' of modern democracy are majority rule and the associated principle that each head is entitled to one vote, and it is hard to see why this principle should hold good for politics and not for economic life as well. The precondition for extending the ambit of democracy today, Bobbio argued, is proceeding from the political to the social domain, i.e. from the sphere where people are reckoned with as individuals, to the context in which their multiple roles in society come into play (Bobbio 1985, p. 147).[9]

The idea that socialism boils down to economic democracy arises in connection with the distinction between two different cooperative enterprise models, worker-managed firms (WMFs) versus labour-managed firms (LMFs), and the classification of the latter as 'pure' cooperatives. An LMF, or labour-managed firm, keeps capital incomes strictly segregated from labour incomes and pays its members labour incomes only: for this reason the worker-members of a cooperative of this kind cannot be described (in the words of John Stuart Mill) as 'their own capitalists'. And further on it will be demonstrated that a system of 'pure' LMF cooperatives literally reverses the current relation between capital and labour and thereby strips capital of all its power (the distinction between LMF and WMF will be discussed in detail further on).

In this connection, let me emphasise that a system of democratic firms is compatible with a flexible type of planning which fixes even more than the broad outlines of a possible product mix (see, for instance, Wolff 2012, pp. 142–4) and that the market socialism model upheld in this book assigns a major role to State intervention.

All the same – let this be re-emphasised – there is sufficient evidence that Marx did think of producer cooperatives as a possible new mode of production.

Today, some authors look upon the global worker movement as split into two main groups (recalling those in Russia after the Bolshevik

---

[9] Proof of the fact that this view is not generally shared is provided, inter alia, by some of the writings of Beatrice Webb and Gibson-Graham, in which the Marxist affiliation of the movement for democratic firm control is flatly denied (see Webb 1891 and Gibson-Graham, 2003) and by the tendency of the French pro-cooperation trade union movement CFDT to vindicate its independence from Marxism (see Rosanvallon 1976).

Revolution) which respectively advocate a Jacobin-fashion mass struggle similar to the Russian Revolution and a parliamentary transition to socialism (see, for instance, Mayer 1994, pp. 281ff.; Bolaffi 2002, p. 139).[10] According to Massimo Salvadori (1979, pp. 549–50), the confrontation between these two groups recalls the debate over the first Russian Revolution that raged in Germany from 1905 to about 1907.

In this connection, there is an important consideration that those calling for a parliamentary transition to socialism have to bear in mind. As the representatives of the workers are a majority in all economically advanced countries, they might be expected to create a system of democratically managed firms by passing a parliamentary vote to this effect. Actually, such a development is impeded by the fact that 'hegemony' (in Gramsci's definition) in today's society is firmly in the hands of capitalists and that these use their control of the media in order to avert the attainment of full democracy.

According to Richard Wolff (2012, ch. 9), probably the most influential American Marxist today, what strikes us as absurd is that politicians pay lip service to democracy but fail to encourage any material steps in this direction: and it is this that explains why people have lost all interest in politics to the point of staying away from the ballot box en masse.

One of the key ideas underlying this book was well expressed by Lange (1957, p. 169), when he argued that the need for markets and economic incentives were important factors in support of the establishment of socially owned cooperative firms as constituent elements of a socialist system and that this was probably one of the reasons why Marx did not hold on to the idea of democratic firm management. Accordingly,

---

[10] The characteristics of political economy just mentioned have induced even qualified scholars to make incredibly false statements. An example in point is Antonio Martino, a full professor in economics who countered Schumpeter's appreciative arguments that 'nothing in Marx's economics can be accounted for by any want of scholarship or training in the technique of theoretical analysis' and his description of Marx as 'the first economist of top rank to see and to teach systematically how economic theory may be turned into historical analysis' with the scathing statement that Marx 'commands our respect for his pathos, but not for his theoretical approach to political economy, of which he was absolutely ignorant' (see Favilli 2001, p. 379, note 21, and p. 382).

With reference to Volume II of *Capital*, de Paula has recently argued that 'the amount of notes that Marx took down with respect to each of the points touched upon in his book' is evidence of 'a degree of modesty and rigour which is unparalleled by any contemporary academic standards' (de Paula et al. 2013, p. 173).

it is worth spelling out that the equation of socialism with democratic firm management requires a change in perspective on Marxian theory.[11]

As 'Marxism develops and changes at every single step in the advancement of science' (see Lenin, as quoted in Lombardo Radice 1972, p. 162), according to Schaff (1965, p. 256), it will hardly come as a surprise that different shades should be read into Marx's texts upon each change in the prevailing conditions. In other words, provided it is true that 'any stride forward taken by the revolutionary movement is enabled by the insight gained following a previous defeat' (Mordenti 2007, p. 43), there are grounds for believing that the demise of the Soviet planning model leads us to read Marxism and socialism from a different perspective.[12] The undeniable fact that Marx did not flesh out a detailed producer cooperative model may explain why the view of democratic firm management as the crowning achievement of scientific socialism requires a different focus on some of Marx's key concepts.

A great many Marxists hold that violence, far from being dethroned by legality, has turned, as it were, into its supporting pillar. And as the law bears the indelible mark of the violent sway of the bourgeoisie, any attempt to make use of it as a weapon to eradicate violence from society must necessarily prove ineffectual (Frölich 1967, p. 84). All the same, it is my conviction that socialism can be established by peaceful means.

According to many, one still unsolved query is why the broad consensus for the values and culture of the left that shaped the sentiment of the general public right across Italy from 1968 onwards and throughout the 1970s has broken down (Finelli 2004, p. 7). As far as I can see, the answer is that even after the collapse of the Soviet model of society the Italian left held on to the idea of socialism as founded on centralised planning (rather than democratic firm management). In the opinion of Salvadori (2015), the current crisis of the left is caused by the globalisation of the economy, i.e. by the fact that the political and economic agendas are dictated by supranational oligarchies which are capable of controlling the media, influencing the opinions of electors and the general public and forcing the left into a corner. As a result, the left is 'seriously ill and must gain an awareness that idle protest leads nowhere'.

---

[11]   Some economists hold that the post-capitalistic system will neither be socialism nor communism, but a peer-to-peer production model envisaging the production of socially owned goods made available for free use according to need (see Benkler 2006; Kleiner 2010; Rigi 2013).

[12]   'Painstaking theoretical work' – Natoli writes (2008, p. 32) – 'went into the making of Marxism, which is the ultimate source of the "lexis of revolution"'.

Moreover, statism is on the wane because of its inability to 'steer the economy and offer satisfactory welfare' (Bauman & Bordoni 2014, p. 22) in a globalised world and because historical experience has taught that it tends to generate inefficiencies and corruption. This conclusion is effectively summed up in Hobsbawm's concept of the death of the State and its organisational structure (see Hobsbawm 2005).

One of the founding assumptions of this book, let this be repeated, is that the establishment of a system of democratic firms is the precondition for enabling the State to perform its ultimate function, that is to say serving the public interest. Hence, those who think of socialism as a system of self-managed firms are called upon to emphasise the view that, contrary to capitalism, self-management is not a system which prioritises the interests of one class over those of another.

The idea that socialism boils down to worker management has featured prominently in most of my scientific work since 1978 (see, for instance, Jossa 1978, 1981, 1982, 1985, 1986, 1988, 1989, 1992, 1993, 1994, 1997, 2004, 2005a, 2005b, 2010, 2014a, 2014b and a few more recent writings) and in well-known contributions by theorists of great renown such as Ward (1958), Vanek (1972), Meade (1972, 1979), Schweickart (1992, 1993, 2002, 2005) as well as Wolff (2012), to mention but one of the best-known British Marxists active today.

2. Production modes, Marx's method and the feasible revolution

1 INTRODUCTION

It is not from scientific advancements – Gramsci argued – that we are to expect solutions to the issues on the traditional agenda of philosophical research. Fresh inputs for philosophical speculation have rather come from notions such as 'social production relations' and 'modes of production', which are Marx's paramount contributions to science.[13] In a well-known 1935 essay weighing the merits and shortcomings of Marxian political economy against those of mainstream economics, the Polish economist Oskar Lange expressed a comparable view when he wrote that the former, while arguably coming short of the latter in areas such as pricing and resource allocation, had the superior merit of spotlighting the way economic life is organised, the division of society into classes and the existence of different modes of production and principally aimed to identify the laws governing the development of human society in the long term (see Lange 1935). In a few words, this strong point of Marxian theory can be summed up as follows: (a) it highlights a sequence of different production modes that arose at various steps in history (the mode of the ancients, feudalism, capitalism, etc.) and thereby suggests that capitalism can barely be the last link in this chain; (b) it shows that the mechanisms governing the development of each production mode

---

[13] For quite a long time, Marxists used to look upon the value theory as Marx's most important contribution to science: only when the newly published second and third books of *Capital* revealed that Marx had tried to reconcile his value theory with the doctrine of prices as determined by the interplay of demand and supply did they gain a correct appreciation of the importance of the materialist conception of history. Detractors include Brewer, who controverts that Marx's approach offers few, if any, insights into the far-reaching issues with which mainstream economists concern themselves and thinks this explains why they hold him in scant esteem (see Brewer 1995).

obey specific laws and rules and that individual behaviour is greatly affected by the way production is organised.[14]

The prominence of production modes in Marx's overall approach provides clues to the identification of the correct scientific method of Marxism and, probably, of Marx himself.[15]

The main aim of this chapter is to define this method and to discuss a type of socialist revolution which appears feasible in this day and age.

2 THE NOTION OF PRODUCTION MODES

In Marx, the production mode is defined as a social organisation mode which is typified by one dominant production model which confers significance on the system at large.[16] The idea that society is shaped by its production methods is often rated as Marx's most pregnant scientific finding (see Bloom 1943, p. 58). Stedman Jones (1978, p. 341), e.g. rates modes of production as 'the decisive concept around which the materialist conception of history was to crystallize between 1845 and 1847'.

The relevance of the notion of production modes was first emphasised in Engels's review of the *Contribution to the Critique of Political Economy*: 'the proposition that the process of social, political and intellectual life is altogether necessitated by the mode of production of material life', he argued, 'was a revolutionary discovery not only for

---

[14] Curiously, yet interestingly enough, in the four-square breakdown used by U. Pagano to illustrate the four economic organisation models he rates as the most prominent of all (Marxian socialism, the rational expectations model, Lange's 1936 model and Hayek's market economy model) we would expect market socialism to be associated with Hayek, but Pagano remarks that despite the traditional contrast between the Marxian and Austrian schools, a combination of the two would probably carry us much further (see Pagano 2006, p. 116). As mentioned before, it strikes us as surprising that Hayek never as much as attempted to explain why he thought it necessary to have business enterprises run by capitalists, rather than by worker-appointed managers.

[15] Unlike O'Boyle, I do not think that the description of history as a sequence of modes of production results in downscaling the role of human action (see O'Boyle 2013, p. 1024).

[16] The idea that Marx's concept of modes of production resulted in an epistemological break within the traditional approach to the philosophy of history is widely shared. For the changes the notion of Marxism underwent over time, see, inter alia, Haupt 1978, pp. 115–45.

economics but also for all historical sciences – and all branches of science which are not natural sciences are historical' (Marx 1859, p. 203).

The notion of production modes is both inextricably intertwined with the materialist conception of history and one of its principal constituents and corollaries.[17] From the idea that the economic mechanisms governing a society are not consciously or wilfully contrived by the people – the core assumption behind historical materialism – it follows, by way of corollary, that the existing production mode is a direct offshoot of the level of development of the productive forces. Moreover, thanks to a distinct focus on the production relations prevailing at the corresponding historical stage, this notion highlights parallel trends under way in a plurality of countries and shows that economic life develops in accordance with laws comparable to those of material life.

3 PRODUCTION MODES AND 'TOTALITY' IN MARX'S APPROACH

In Marx's theoretical framework, production modes are closely associated with the notion of totality.[18] In the *Grundrisse* Marx wrote that production, distribution, exchange and consumption are not identical, but members of a totality, distinctions within a unity (Marx 1857–58, vol. 1, p. 25), and that no concept, however general, can exist 'except as an abstract, *one-sided* relation within an already given, concrete, living whole' (Marx 1859, p. 189).

These and comparable statements may explain the generalised assumption that Marxists reject any one-sided descriptions of capitalism and prioritise an approach founded on the notion of totality.

According to Marcuse, 'for Marx, as for Hegel, "the truth" lies only in the whole, the "negative totality"' (Marcuse 1954, p. 347); and Wolff et al.

---

[17]   On the subject of historical materialism, Hobsbawm wrote (2011, p. 209): 'George Unwin, perhaps the most impressive English economic historian of his generation, took to his subject through Marx, or at any rate to confute Marx', but he did not doubt that 'Marx was trying to get at the right kinds of history' and that 'orthodox historians ignore all the most significant factors in human development'.

[18]   According to Arthur, the ultimate subject under investigation in *Capital* is a totality, which means that the complementariness of the constituent parts of this totality is the precondition for an object to be what it is (see Arthur 2001, p. 240).

(1982) have laid stress on the paramount place of the totality notion in Marx's approach.[19]

The prominence of the totality notion in some authors' approach is associated with the dynamic view of historical development, specifically the claim that the structure of the whole must be conceived before any discussion of temporal sequence.

In an attempt to help appraise the role of totality in Marx's approach and underscore his valuable contribution to science, Veblen argued that 'taken in detail, the constituent elements of the system are neither novel nor iconoclastic, but the system as a whole has an air of originality such as is rarely met with among the sciences dealing with any phase of human culture' (for a similar view, see Bronfenbrenner 1967, p. 625).

The reasons why the notion of production modes and totality may help shed light on Marx's dialectical method[20] are implied in the description

---

[19]   In the estimation of Adorno, it is principally in analyses of bourgeois society that the totality notion is found to be particularly rich in valuable insights; MacGregor (1984, p. 174) held that the idea of capitalism as a living system and an organic whole was one of the key elements of the dialectical method that Marx took over from Hegel; Proudhon described capitalism as a systematic totality which generates a complex tangle of contradictions (see Proudhon 1846, but also Ansart 1969, pp. 159ff.).

[20]   The assumption that Marx was always a dialectical reasoner is supported by the following passage from Marx's letter to Kugelmann (dated 6 March 1868): 'Hegel's dialectic is the basic form of all dialectics, but only after being stripped of its mystical form, and it is precisely this which distinguishes my method' (Marx 1868, p. 544). In fact, Marx also wrote: 'if ever the time comes when such work is again possible, I should very much like to write two or three sheets making accessible to the common reader the rational aspect of the method which Hegel not only discovered but also mystified' (Marx 1858, p. 155). As this plan was never put into practice, it can barely come as a surprise that Marx's dialectical method is still being construed in a variety of different ways or that Heilbroner has dismissed dialectics as 'a term without a clear or univocal meaning' (Heilbroner 1980, p. 28).

Irrespective of the unmistakable Hegelian colouring of all Marx's writings, Schumpeter warned, to think of Hegelism as the keystone of Marxism would amount to debasing the scientific standing of Marx's overall theoretical edifice. Marx, he added, delighted in 'coquetting' with Hegelian phrasing, but did not go any further (see Schumpeter 1954, p. 9). Studies aimed to show that Marx gradually scaled down his use of dialectical reasoning and that dialectics cannot help us understand Marx include Bernstein (1899, ch. 2), Rosenthal 1988 and Bidet 1998 (p. 225). Analytical Marxists rate dialectical reasoning as altogether misleading and, hence, barely more helpful than formal logic in constructing a social theory (see Meyer 1994, p. 1). Setting the long string of cross-references to Hegel (especially his *Logic*) appearing in the recently published *Grundrisse*

of dialectics as 'a theory of both the unity and exclusion of opposites' (Ilyenkov 1960, p. vii) and a method which uses the concept of totality as a tool for determining the truth (Bell 1995, p. 112), as well as in the remark that 'for Hegel and Marx, the notion of a living organism expresses the essence of dialectics in history' (see MacGregor 1984, p. 111).[21]

Hence, it is also possible to argue that the application of the dialectical method to economic research thrusts into the foreground 'an endless intertwining of mutually connected forces, a picture in which nothing remains either what, where or as it was, but in which everything moves, changes, is in process of formation or dissolution' (Engels 1891a, pp. 35–6); it shows that dialectics is 'research into the many ways in which entities are internally related' (Ollman 1976, p. 61).[22]

Marxism draws on Hegel for the theory that reason is in essence relational, that is to say that it necessitates a simultaneous focus on co-existing antithetical elements – i.e. 'unity of opposites'. Indeed,

---

against the sparse Hegelian overtones resounding in just a handful of footnotes in *Capital*, Rosdolsky argued that no academic could dare to address Marxian economics unless he had concerned himself earnestly both with Marx's method and its links with Hegel's (see Rosdolsky 1955, p. 8).

In a well-reasoned study, Colletti provided evidence that Marx's dialectical method was not identical with Hegel's (Colletti 1969). What is needed, he added elsewhere (Colletti 1958, pp. 92–3), is 'purging today's Marxism of all the remnants of *Hegelian* dialectical thinking – not of all its *dialectical* overtones, but just of passages with an *idealistic* colouring. In other words, what needs to be done is *not* rectifying Marx's theoretical edifice, but just rephrasing parts of it in an effort to bring to the fore all its extraordinary complexity' (see, also, Croce 1899, pp. 4–9; Hyppolite 1969, pp. 300–3; Garaudy 1969, pp. 312–14; and Hofmann 1971, pp. 80–4). In later years, though, Colletti did reconsider this position (see Colletti 1974).

In Althusser (1965, pp. 18–20) we read that 'young Marx was never strictly speaking a Hegelian', that he was moderately inspired by Hegel when he wrote the *Manuscripts of 1844*, but that by 1845 he had broken free from all Hegelian influence.

Musto's intellectual biography of Marx offers an intriguing glimpse into the interrelations between Marx and Hegel (see Musto 2011).

[21] Vidoni remarks that dialectical reasoning 'looms large in Marx's analyses of organisms, their relationship with the environment and their social relations, that is to say in passages which address highly complex processes entailing a wealth of interrelations between different actors' (see Vidoni 2007, p. 260).

The Italian poet Giacomo Leopardi argued that non-dialectical thinking 'obliterates vastness and grandeur and prevents us from grasping the totality of the natural world' (see Citati 2010, p. 53).

[22] For different views see Severino 1978 and Napoleoni 1985, part III.

Hegel's ideas of reason and 'the negative' constitute the celebrated 'rational kernel' of his dialectical method.[23] There is general agreement that Marx's dialectic method is not Hegel's.[24]

The Marxian form of dialectical thinking is even observed in a comparatively early work such as the *Criticism of Hegel's Philosophy of Right* (1843), which Screpanti explains as an attack on idealism mounted by Marx in full sync with Feuerbach's rejection of Hegel's hypostases, as an attempt to validate the Aristotelian view that the non-contradiction principle is a necessary prerequisite for logical thinking, and as Marx's first attempt to lay the foundations for the materialist conception of history (see Screpanti 2011, p. 7).

These reflections call to mind Gramsci's conception of dialectics. 'The ability to detect identity in seemingly different things and far-reaching diversity behind a seeming identity is the subtlest, least understood, and yet greatest virtue of a critic of ideas or analyst of historical evolution' (Gramsci 1975, p. 2268).[25] Commenting on this passage, Finocchiaro remarked that 'this ability of the critic-historian is dialectical thinking par excellence, or dialectics in a narrow and very special sense' (1988, p. 157).[26,27]

---

[23] In Hegel's dialectical approach, 'the individual terms are *inseparably* conjoined' (Hegel 1831, p. 14). For a correct appreciation of the sheer magnitude of Hegel's speculative powers it is worth bearing in mind that Hegel was the only philosopher who rose to the challenge of offering consistent definitions of reason and thought as immaterial, rather than positive processes and even of the infinite. All pre-Hegelian philosophers, be they Schelling or Spinoza, Leibniz or Descartes, thought of the infinite as what lies beside, above or beyond the finite; in other words, as but one extreme of an opposition, a unilateral term (Ilyenkov 1960, p. VIII).

[24] For a demonstration that Marx's investigation of truth is consistent with the basics of the Aristotelian principle of non-contradiction, see Schaff 1974, pp. 26ff. and 171ff.

[25] For Gramsci's use of dialectics, see Bobbio 1958, where Gramsci is shown to have used both the form of dialectical thinking that focuses on mutual interactions between opposed elements and the form using the thesis-antithesis-synthesis triad.

[26] As my approach may actually entail attempts at attenuation and reconciliation of the type that Naville holds to distort Marx's masterly dialectical method and reduce it to a pale cast for use by more or less eclectic philosophers (see Naville 1948, p. 12), let me re-emphasise my pledge to be always true to the spirit of Marx's approach.

[27] For an analysis of the subjects touched upon in this section, see Habermas 1969, ch. 4.

4 MARX'S METHOD

Coming to the method of Marx and Marxism as originally defined in the preface to *A Contribution to the Critique of Political Economy*, let me mention, right from the start, that this text dates from 1857, but did not go to press since Marx, rating it as nothing but a fragmentary attempt, refused to offer solutions that were not backed up by adequate demonstrations. Upon its appearance in 1903, the preface showed that by the autumn of 1875 Marx had fleshed out the methodological foundations of his economic theory to the full and that the continuing debate over the correct interpretation of his work is just to be blamed on the fact that his method remained hidden in the folds of *Capital*.

Marx held that contrary to all appearances, the procedure that starts from the real and concrete actually 'proves false' (Marx 1857–58, vol. 1, p. 26), because within the process of thinking the concrete appears 'as a process of concentration and, as a result, not as a point of departure' (p. 27). Accordingly, he recommended beginning with the abstract on the assumption that 'the method of rising from the abstract to the concrete is the only way in which thought appropriates the concrete, reproduces it as the concrete in the mind' (p. 27).[28] This begs the question if beginning with the abstract means using as starting points the simplest possible categories, for example commodities and value, or complex categories such as the mode of production.

As far as I can see, the use of abstractions as a starting point does not necessitate starting out from the simplest categories; on the contrary,

---

[28] Analysing Marx's methodological approach to the study of political economy, Althusser acutely remarked that there were two methods, one starting from the real itself, the other from abstractions. With reference to the *Grundrisse* (Marx 1857–58, p. 27), he asked himself which of these two methods was the correct one and drew the following conclusion: 'it seems to be correct to start with the real and concrete ... but on closer inspection it is clear that this is false'. The second 'is manifestly the correct scientific method' (Althusser & Balibar 1965, p. 94).

Not unlike him, Rosa Luxemburg was persuaded that Marx tended to gravitate from the abstract to the concrete, but she also spelt out that this procedure was antithetical to the European mode of speculation which in her opinion had been

more often than not the correct procedure is to start from such an abstract key notion of Marxism as the mode of production.[29]

In Marx 1857 (p. 188) and Marx 1857–58 (vol. 1, p. 26) we read: 'It seems to be correct to begin with the real and the concrete, with the real precondition'. In economics, therefore, it seems correct to begin, by way of example, 'with the population, which is the foundation and the subject of the entire social act of production'. On closer analysis, though, he continues,

> this proves false. The population is an abstraction if I leave out, for example, the classes of which it is composed. These classes in turn are an empty phrase if I am not familiar with the elements on which they rest, e.g. wage labour, capital, etc. The latter in turn presuppose exchange, division of labour, prices, etc. For example, capital is nothing without wage labour, prices, etc.[30]

'The simplest economic category, say e.g. exchange value', Marx wrote (1857, p. 189 and 1857–58, pp. 27–8), 'presupposes population; moreover, a population producing in specific relations, as well as a certain

---

revived by the European social democrats and by Lenin's party (see Negt 1979, pp. 329–30). This view is also shared by Aron (1969, pp. 159–60).

The reflections just developed should not make us forget that Marx consistently contrasted the Kantian-Feuerbachian approach with Hegel's. The former, which he rejected, theorised the separation of the ideal from the real and looked upon reality as irrational. In a letter to his father written in November 1837, he set this approach against Hegel's thesis that 'the real is rational and the rational is real' (see Cingoli 2001, pp. 44–5).

[29]   In a recently published review of the new Mega2 edition of Marx's works, Marcello Musto tries to make out what picture of Marx emerges from this new historical-critical edition of work. His conclusion is that Marx appears to be a polymorphous thinker and that the differences between this picture and that traditionally painted by Marx commentators (be they supporters or critics) are clear evidence that Marxian research still has a long way to go (Musto 2011, pp. 215–16). The aim of this paper is just to analyse the method that emerges from Marx's 1857 preface and the *Grundrisse* and, based on relevant passages, it attempts to show that despite Marx's failure to offer conclusive methodological indications, the Marxist method is one that starts out from determined abstractions, specifically from the mode of production.

[30]   A critical perusal of the 1857 preface shows that Marx not only considered the option of moving from the abstract to the concrete, but finally described this procedure as the only properly scientific method. Consequently, Fineschi argues, whereas the method he had been using up to then had been as mystical in essence as Hegel's logic, 'from that time on it became not mystical *tout court*, but just to the extent it purported to reflect the way reality is created' (Fineschi 2006, p. 47).

kind of family or commune, or state, etc. It can never exist other than as an abstract, one-sided relation within an already given, concrete, living whole'.

Further on (see Marx 1857, p. 191 and Marx 1857–58, vol. 1, p. 30), Marx offered the following clarifications:

> Although the simplest category may have existed historically before the more concrete, it can achieve its full (intensive and extensive) development precisely in a combined form of society, while the more concrete category was more fully developed in a less developed form of society. Labour seems a quite simple category. The conception of labour in this general form – as labour as such – is also immeasurably old. Nevertheless, when it is economically conceived in this simplicity, 'labour' is as modern a category, as are the relations which create this simple abstraction.

The following passage is no less relevant: 'Bourgeois society is the most developed and the most complex historic organisation of production. The categories which express its relations, the comprehension of its structure, thereby also allow insights into the structure and the relations of production of all the vanished social formations' (Marx 1857, p. 193 and Marx 1857–58, pp. 32–3).[31]

My line of reasoning so far goes to clarify that the correct procedure is generally one that starts from the whole, i.e. from totality or the abstract notion of the production mode, and then moves downward in order to bring to the fore the individual constituents of this whole.

This conclusion is fully in line with the importance Marx attached to the notion of determined abstractions. From Marx's perspective, the severest shortcomings of his favourite field of study, political economy, were caused by the tendency of economists to focus on the concrete

---

[31]   In the opinion of Vinci (2008, p. 56), the method which starts from the concrete extracts from it general abstract ideas and re-examines the concrete in the light of the latter can be compared to a Copernican revolution. As the concrete starting point is fixed within historical time, he explains, the abstractions that Marx draws from it are determined, i.e. specifically applicable to capitalistic society. In a capitalistic society, a determined abstraction such as abstract labour is deduced from a concrete phenomenon, i.e. the existing labour organisation model, and is used to bring to the foreground an antithesis: in this case the contrast between a natural physical phenomenon such as concrete labour and a social phenomenon such as abstract labour. Let me mention that the concrete-to-abstract procedure (which he termed the 'analytical' method) was ascribed by Hegel to seventeenth-century economists and the opposite, abstract/ simple-to-concrete/complex procedure (termed the 'synthetic' method) to eighteenth-century economists.

based on abstractions which were unrelated to a specified production mode and, hence, not 'determined'.

In his review of the *Contribution to the Critique of Political Economy* Engels wrote that Marx adopted 'the only correct mode of conceptual evolution' because he divested Hegel's dialectical method of all its idealistic echoes. The method that Marx worked out for his critique of political economy, he added, was 'hardly less significant than the basic materialist conception' (Engels 1859, p. 208).[32]

Engels's argument requires a reasoned analysis (see Carver 1984). As noted above, the key element of Marx's dialectical method is a focus on totality, the production mode, and we also know that he criticised earlier economists for failing to work out the notion of modes of production and for a naive conviction that capitalism was bound to last forever.[33]

The logical thread followed by Meek in a 1956 study leads to basically the same conclusion. According to this author, not unlike other great theoreticians Marx starts out from what Schumpeter termed the 'vision' of the economic process. The reason why Marx defers the analysis of details is that 'to quite large an extent they are dependent upon the nature of the model-builder's vision' and upon 'the nature of the *general* method of analysis which he decides to adopt' (Meek 1956, p. 277). Lenin also, he argued, pointed out that Marx's first step was to select from all social relations the 'production relations' because it is these that are the basic and prime relations that determine all the others (p. 279).

Hence, it is clear that also from Meek's perspective the proper Marxist method is one that starts out from an abstract notion such as the production mode, proceeds to focus on simpler categories and finally reverts to the concrete – the 'synthesis of many determinations'.[34]

With reference to Marx's position in and around 1957, Musto remarks:

---

[32] Moving from abstract to concrete is a method whereby thought is made to reflect material reality, not (as Hegel claimed) to create it.

[33] In this connection, Althusser wrote (1973, p. 42) that Marxism-Leninism cannot start from man. It starts from the economically given social period and this is why once this analysis has been completed it can reach a knowledge of real men.

[34] In Lukàcs we read: 'Abstraction is never fragmentary, that is to say no single element is ever presented, by way of abstraction, as segregated from the rest. Rather, it is the whole sector of the economy that is presented as an abstract realm in which the temporary exclusion of precise links between broader categories allows the categories that come into focus to act themselves out to the full' (Lukàcs 1976, p. 290).

Unlike evolutionary theorists, who used to describe simple organisms first and then to progress to more and more complex ones along a simplistic ascending ladder of sorts, Marx chose to proceed in the opposite direction, and the resulting, much more complex method led him to theorise a notion of history as the sequence of different modes of production ... Ultimately, it was the bourgeois economic system that offered valuable clues to a correct appreciation of the salient traits of the economic systems of earlier ages. (Musto 2011, pp. 139–40)

Much to the same effect, Sgrò argues (2016, p. 177) that

the text of the first part of *Chapter Six* in which commodities are discussed as the specific output of the capitalistic production progress is clear evidence that the type of commodity that Marx chose as his starting point is already a capitalistic one, viz., a capitalistically determined commodity which is both the precondition for, and the *output* of, the capitalistic production process.

In short, Marx held it necessary to take as a starting point determined abstractions founded on the production mode.

In this connection, it is worth emphasising that Marx rated production modes and capitalism as abstract notions which offered the preliminary knowledge required to analyse, by way of example, a concrete production note such as British capitalism in the nineteenth century. The capitalistic mode of production, Fineschi explains (2006, p. 9), is 'a sophisticated abstract reconstruction of the working mode of bourgeois society in a given period of history' and the far from simple concept of the production mode is therefore itself an abstract notion.

5   A DIFFERENT APPROACH

The way the method of Marx and Marxism is being analysed in this chapter has little in common with the traditional approach. A recurring question is whether Marx's recommendation to begin with the abstract and move to the concrete entails taking as a starting point simple notions and working out complex notions based on these. Marx wrote, 'The concrete is concrete because it is the concentration of many determinations, hence unity of the diverse' (1857, p. 189 and 1857–58, p. 27). The conclusion which seems implied in this statement is that abstract notions are simple.

Further on in the same text, Marx made it clear that a simple concept such as population is an abstraction and that the division of labour, money, value, which are 'individual moments', are general, hence abstract determinations. Also the *Grundrisse* include a passage which recommends beginning with the simple and proceeding to the complex, and this may obviously account for the above-mentioned misconception. The passage concerned runs as follows:

> The economists of the seventeenth century, e.g., always begin with the living whole, with population, nation, state, several states, etc.; but they always conclude by discovering through analysis a small number of determined, abstract, general relations such as division of labour, money, value, etc. As soon as these individual moments had been more or less firmly established and abstracted, there began the economic systems, which ascended from the simple relations, such as labour, division of labour, need, exchange value, to the level of the state, exchange between nations and the world market. The latter is obviously the scientifically correct method. The concrete is concrete because it is the concentration of many determinations, hence unity of the diverse. It appears in the process of thinking, therefore, as a process of concentration, as a result, not as a point of departure, even though it is the point of departure in reality and hence also the point of departure for observation and conception. Along the first path the full conception was evaporated to yield an abstract determination; along the second, the abstract determinations lead towards a reproduction of the concrete by way of thought. (Marx 1857–58, p. 27)

These and similar passages induced Marx commentators to argue that whenever we take as starting points abstract notions we have to begin with simple concepts and, from these, rise to the level of the concrete (which, let this be repeated, Marx held to be complex).

As far as I can see, this wrong conclusion can both be traced to Marx's failure to define or discuss such starting abstractions and to the undeniable fact that the method he proposed in 1857 (rising from abstract to concrete) was reversed but two years later, in *Contribution to the Critique of Political Economy*, where Marx recommended 'rising from the particular to the general' (see Marx 1859, p. 3).

An additional explanation for the misconception that the method upheld in the 1857 preface is rising from the particular to the general, from simple to complex, and may be the use of a simple notion such as commodities as the starting point for *Capital*. On closer analysis, however, those who reached this conclusion failed to give due consideration to Marx's explicit statement, in both the *Contribution to the Critique of Political Economy* and *Capital*, that the use of a simple starting concept in these works was necessitated by his decision to follow a sequence exactly *opposite* to that typical of mainstream scientific research:

> It would be unfeasible and wrong to let the economic categories follow one another in the same sequence as that in which they were historically decisive.

Their sequence is determined, rather, by their relation to one another in modern bourgeois society, which is precisely the *opposite* of that which seems to be their natural order or which corresponds to historical development. (Marx 1857, p. 196 and Marx 1857–58, p. 35)

Reverting to this point years later, Marx added: 'Of course, the method of presentation must differ in form from that of inquiry' (see Marx 1873, p. 44).

In part, the blame for this misconception can also be laid on a passage from the already mentioned 1859 review of the *Contribution to the Critique of Political Economy*, in which Engels (irrespective of Marx's declared intention to reverse the traditional method) spelt out that Marx, contrary to his own recommendation to use as starting points logical categories, made use of the traditional method on the assumption that 'the point where this history begins must also be the starting point of the train of thought and its further progress will be simply the reflection, in abstract and theoretically consistent form, of the historical course' (Engels 1859, p. 208).

Still another explanation for the wrong assumption that the abstract starting point must be a simple concept is probably the general belief that abstract notions are simple by their very nature.

This assumption is implied, for instance, in the following excerpt from Wetter 1948 (p. 386):

> By unity of analysis and synthesis we do not mean that the first step must be an analytical procedure designed to identify the simpler categories by way of abstraction and that the second step should solely be their concentration into a synthesis. Actually, analysis and synthesis must be inextricably intertwined over the whole process which starts from abstract determinations and rises to the concrete. The process whereby the categories rise from abstract to concrete (synthesis) requires an ongoing effort at differentiation within each of the less abstract categories (analysis) and, lastly, an additional synthesis to work out a less abstract category.[35]

Although the first and most obvious objection that comes to mind is that the passage concerned features in a work which was never published, it is probably necessary to admit that Marx's approach to this methodological point is contradictory.

---

[35]   The same misconception underlies the following excerpt from Ilyenkov 1960 (p. 7): 'Each of the definitions forming part of a system naturally reflects only a part, a fragment, and records only one of the particular moments of concrete reality in its entirety. Hence, when it is considered separately from the others, it is abstract.'

Let me re-emphasise that quite a lot of Marxists rated the simple-to-complex procedure as the correct scientific method on the assumption that this was the method that Marx and Engels themselves recommended. In a much praised monograph on Marx's method, Dal Pra wrote that 'our mind reconstructs its representation of reality by combining together a number of simple determinations' (Dal Pra 1972, p. 316) and that the procedure entailing the rise from simple to concrete must consequently be looked upon as the appropriate scientific method.

Discussing a point analysed in *Capital*, Lukàcs wrote that this key problem alone was sufficient evidence that the method of rising from individual sub-processes to the all-embracing process required not only a major effort at abstraction consistent with our modern thought processes, but the attempt to transcend certain limitations of abstract ideas in an effort to gain a correct appreciation of totality (see Lukàcs 1976, p. 303). Here Lukàcs seems to assume that the notion of totality, that is to say the production mode, is not an abstract concept, but a material reality. As a result, he argues that economic analysis must take as its point of departure a simple concept such as the notion of value (see Lukàcs 1976, pp. 290–6).

Much in the same vein, Marković maintained that the technical and methodological innovation introduced within the framework of Marx's conception of history was a method which starts from simple universal abstract notions such as commodities, labour, money, capital, surplus value, etc., and rises from these to aspects of material reality (see Marković 1969, p. 133); Some authors argued that the Marxist method was to rise from simpler to ever more complex aspects of the object of our inquiry; and Fineschi (2006, p. 136) described Marx's research method as positing 'the starting category, that is to say commodities, with all the determinations highlighted before' (see, also, Fineschi 2006, pp. 139–46).[36]

6 MARX AND SOCIALISM

According to an authoritative commentator (see Abendroth 1958, p. 77), Marx and Engels struggled to come to terms with the finding that even human actions that have been autonomously devised tend to evolve in

---

[36] According to Bellofiore (2005, p. 265), 'As a whole, capital has to be known through a "systematic" exposition that begins from simple and abstract categories, developing into more and more *complex* and *concrete* categories'. On this point, see also Nicolaus 1973, p. 33.

directions other than those that had been – and could be – anticipated and end up by shaping the subsequent path of mankind. From Abendroth's perspective, this means that unless and until this situation is reversed, the aim of making men masters of their history is and remains out of reach. According to Marcuse, 'the control of "immediate producers" over the process of production is supposed to initiate the development that distinguishes the history of free man from the prehistory of man' (see Marcuse 1964, p. 61).[37]

As Abendroth held this to be the core problem behind Marxist thought, he concluded that Marxism was as timeless as that issue (1958, pp. 78–9). For my part, I fully agree with him on this point since I hold that Marxism as a theory of revolution has lost none of its topicality.

In an analysis of this point, Bloch argued that based on a misreading of Marx, scholars addressing Marxian theory from a merely empirical point of view end up by expunging two supposedly utopian visions of reality which actually draw their relevance from this utopian colouring: firstly the ideal and, secondly, the ultimately utopian component of the former. And while they do so on the assumption that these visions lack concreteness – he went on to argue – it remains that both of them are integral components of Marxism and will continue to be so (see Bloch 1968, p. 209).

Day after day, ever more people are developing an awareness that capitalism is a catastrophe from which humankind is unable to break free. An often quoted argument has it that unless and until critics of free enterprise capitalism succeed in working out a suitable alternative other than a better regulated free market capitalist system or state capitalism (the traditional socialist system), it is highly unlikely that people will join together to form a social movement capable of dismantling capitalism. Although this criticism is widely shared, it is fair to admit that the alarming tendency to stage protests without offering viable alternative options is probably the main vice of democratic citizenship today (see Bodei 2013, p. 163).

In my opinion, at this stage of history we have realised that shedding the fetters of capitalism without recourse to a violent revolution is no unrealistic prospect, i.e. that this goal can be attained through the peaceful enforcement of resolutions passed in parliament. Indeed, the findings reported in the producer cooperative literature since the appearance of Ward's seminal 1958 article have offered convincing evidence

---

[37] Lukàcs (1972, p. 38) laid stress both on Marx's argument that work was what turned primitive man into a human being proper and on his firm belief that history down to our days had been nothing but the prehistory of humanity.

that a system of worker-controlled firms, though evidently no cure-all, is sure to work at high levels of efficiency.

The question arising at this point is: what did Marx mean by socialism?

To answer this question, it is worth bearing in mind that Marx always refused to write recipes for what he termed the 'cook-shops of the future' and left it with the 'cooks' to work out solutions to the problems he had been pointing out (see Hudis 2013).

In the estimation of the Webbs, in matters of post-revolutionary economic policy Marxist theory is of no avail since Marx's theoretical approach, for all its depth and breadth, offers no indications concerning the way to address issues likely to emerge within a socialist economy. In support of this view they mentioned Lenin's explicit statement, following his seizure of power, that he did not know of any single socialist who had made it his task to investigate these issues.

The resulting theoretical void has been severely criticised by more than one author. Hutchinson, for instance, has emphasised that Marx and Engels did not realise that proclaiming themselves revolutionaries while failing to offer clues, however slight, to the possible organisational model of the proposed alternative society was, to say the least, an attitude of utter irresponsibility (see Hutchison 1978, p. 197).

For my part, I wish to point out that Marx and Engels, while doubtless failing to provide details of the organisation model of the future, spelt out in bold letters that the characteristics of the socialist model of society were to proceed from the successful supersession of all the contradictions they had pointed out in capitalism.

In this connection, let me mention that as Marx particularly emphasised two basic contradictions within the world in which we live (the plan-versus-market and capital-versus-labour oppositions), it is possible to envisage two production systems capable of guaranteeing the transition to communism: a system of publicly run and centrally planned enterprises and a system of workers' councils, that is to say a system of producer cooperatives run by the workers themselves.[38]

---

[38] Originally, Marx and Engels believed that the precondition for the establishment of a socialist system was centralising all powers firmly in the hands of the State. It was the Paris Commune that induced them to reconsider this stance and to think of socialism as mainly connoted by democratic production processes (see Screpanti 2007, pp. 145–6). This conclusion is prompted by a passage from *The Civil War in France*, dated 1871, where Marx wrote that the Paris Commune (which 'supplied the republic with the basis of really democratic institutions' and 'the political form, at last discovered, under which to work out the economic

Time and again, Settembrini emphasised that one of the two alternative transition scenarios sketched by Marx was a peaceful road to the establishment of a democratic form of evolutionary socialism (see also Avineri 1968). At the other end of the spectrum, Bakunin described Marx as a tyrannical centraliser who extolled the triumph of equality, but held on to the naive belief that this goal could be achieved through state action and the dictatorial rule of a possibly strong central government.

In my opinion, Marx's disregard for the cook-shops of the future gives us scope for arguing that either production system can have a place within his theoretical framework. In light of this, the question why Marx should deserve more credit as a theoretician of rational planning than an advocate of self-management and participative democracy is little more than a purely academic query (see Screpanti 2007, p. 146).

The call for the handover of factories to workers dates back to the Chartist movement in Britain and was translated into practice – albeit in non-democratic form – upon the establishment of a self-managed firm system in Yugoslavia. Its roots are in the notion that means of production are to be socialised.

In point of fact, self-management theorists draw a clear-cut distinction between nationalisation and socialisation. As the former, they claim, entails the retention of production means by the State and only the latter vests self-management powers in workers, this is only able to cancel the separation between the 'two factors of production' that Marx denounced.

As far as planning the first of the two above-mentioned systems is concerned, the model that Marx had in mind had little, if anything, in common with the top-down Soviet-type planning model that history has

---

emancipation of labour'; see Marx 1871, p. 85) had shattered the power of the modern state (pp. 82 and 83) to the point where the old centralised government had been obliged to give way to the self-government of producers even in the provinces (p. 82).

In contrast, Lichtheim (1965, p. 228) has argued that late in life Marx abandoned his temporary infatuation with the utopianism of the Paris Commune and reverted to statist stances. This opinion is shared by Lehning, who rates the 1871 text of *The Civil War in France* as that of a writer who was basically a non-Marxist, that is to say as a clear sign that Marx went through a spell of non-statist thinking (see Lehning 1969, p. 431).

Some Hegelian Marxists hold that Marx's theoretical speculation powers began to falter from his fortieth year of age onwards, specifically from the time he wrote the *Grundrisse* and published the first and second editions of Book I of *Capital* and the preface to its French edition, down to the second edition, in 1879, of *Notes on Adolph Wagner's 'Lehrbuch der politischen Ökonomie'* (see Backhaus 1997, p. 297 and Haug 2005, p. 293).

meanwhile proved wrong. The theoretical categories underlying twentieth-century socialism were principally defined by Lenin and then further developed by Stalin. And as the scant esteem in which Marx is held by many is doubtless to be blamed on his association with the USSR, today, following the collapse of the despotic state socialism model, the need to reconsider non-statist alternative options to liberal-democratic capitalism is becoming more urgent than ever.[39]

Although experience has taught that centralised planning is no solution, considering that Marxist policies today are moving further and further away from the principles of the Bolshevik model, this does not necessitate consigning socialism or Marxism to oblivion.

In the light of the fact that economic cooperation theorists have fleshed out an alternative to capitalism which would both ensure efficiency and not require central planning as a matter of course, there is scope for arguing that Marx has happily survived a spell of near hibernation, since his name will no longer be associated with the oppressive bureaucratic system of the past century.[40]

As Marxists clearly distinguish between socialism and communism and Marx and Engels themselves deemed it impossible to abolish markets at the earlier post-capitalist stages, a democratic firm system which vests management powers in workers can be said to be fully compatible with Marx's theoretical approach even if it fails to abolish markets.

According to Bernstein, the historical roots of revisionism are an aversion to the 'welfare state' and a supportive attitude towards the world of cooperation (see Bernstein 1918, p. 23 and Angel 1975, pp. 117–18). Conversely, I do not share Bernstein's view that class interests ebb away in direct proportion to advancements in democracy.

---

[39]   This is the rationale behind the argument that contrary to all appearances, the balance in Marx's polemic against Proudhon on this point is ultimately tilting in favour of the latter.

[40]   Lunghini and Cavallaro report an interesting statement by Keynes which runs as follows: 'The Republic of my imagination lies on the extreme left of the celestial spheres. Yet all the same I feel that my true home, so long as they offer a room and a floor, is with the Liberals' (Keynes 1926, p. 260). In their opinion, this quote is clear evidence that in 1926 even a person who thought of himself as an extreme radical rejected the system that had been established in post-revolutionary Russia as an inacceptable organisational model. An often heard objection is that those Marxists who call into question the labour theory of value and the Soviet model have generally failed to make it clear what they hold to be the true essence of Marxism (see, for instance, Rodinson 1969, pp. 9–13, who tries to reverse this tendency by offering his own definition of Marxism).

Those who hold that Marx's conception of socialism is difficult to reconcile with markets are hereby referred to a 'methodological' indication owed principally to Gramsci, i.e. an encouragement to reword any tenets of Marx (even basic ones) whenever this should appear to be necessitated by novel insights or historical developments. Such a practice would be perfectly in line with Derrida's argument that Marxism 'remains at once indispensable and structurally insufficient' and should therefore be 'transformed and adapted to new conditions and to a new thinking of the ideological' (see Derrida 1993, p. 78), and with Gramsci's own observation that the canons of historical materialism are applicable to history only *post factum* and should never become an obstacle to the analysis of the future (see Gramsci 1914–18, pp. 153–5 and Cacciatore 1987, pp. 255–6).[41]

7 CONCLUSION

The prominence of production modes in Marx's overall approach offers clues to the identification of the correct scientific method of Marxism and, probably, of Marx himself. Identifying both this method and a model of socialism feasible in this day and age have been the two main aims of this chapter.

In Tosel (1996, p. 147) we read that following the gigantic, yet incomplete effort to merge the high points of Western thought (Hegel + Ricardo + French Jacobinism) into a critically contrived synthesis, Marxism deteriorated into an orthodox creed that has doubtless helped socialise and politicise workers, but has failed to teach them how to secure a hegemonic position in economic life.

---

[41]   Bronfenbrenner traces the continuing topicality of Marx's thought in this day and age to a generalised feeling of dissatisfaction, rather than to its inherent scientific merits (see Bronfenbrenner 1970, pp. 137–40).

3. The cooperative firm as an alternative to the capital-owned business enterprise

1 INTRODUCTION

As mentioned in the Introduction, the precondition for abating unemployment and depriving capital of its power is allowing workers to manage firms (especially medium–large enterprises) on their own, viz., creating a system of cooperatives or democratically managed enterprises. As used in this book, the terms self-managed firm and producer cooperative are synonymous with the term democratically managed enterprise because a system composed of firms of this kind realises workplace democracy to the full. Although cooperatives may come in a variety of different organisational models, they have in common one main characteristic: the application of the cardinal rule of democracy dictating that decision powers are to be solely and entirely vested in the members (or partners) of the firm in line with the 'one head one vote' criterion. Other organisational characteristics are optional and should be selected with an eye to the need to ensure efficiency – as will be explained further on.

This chapter offers a broad outline of the principal organisational characteristics of our cooperative enterprises.

2 THE TWO FACETS OF COOPERATION

In a historical outline of the British cooperative movement, Beatrice Potter (better known as Beatrice Webb) highlighted a 'radical distinction' between the 'Creed of Universal Competition' shaping the strategies of capitalistic firms and the 'Co-operative Idea' at the basis of the newly established anti-capitalistic firms. The former, she explained, are governed by 'the biological law of the survival of the fittest through the struggle for existence', whereas the latter operate in line with a different biological law, the 'law of adaptation', which determines that 'the modification of structure is brought about by the modification of function' (Potter 1893, pp. 18–19). And as these biological laws are scientifically beyond question, she continued, anyone combating competition because of its emphasis on egoism and ruthlessness (with the consequential degradation of everyday life and adverse impact on character) simply cannot accept the idea that cooperators are motivated by a desire to make profits.

But is this true?

Two major points are worth discussing in connection with the inception of cooperativism. One, a motivational factor, is the determination of its founders to combat what they perceived as the evils of capitalism. The man to whom the origins of socialism and cooperativism are usually traced (see, for instance, Potter 1893, p. 17), Robert Owen (1771–1858),[42] had first-hand knowledge of industrial life in Manchester, of the race for wealth triggered by the ongoing Industrial Revolution in his day and the ruthless treatment of workers at the hands of manufacturers. His firm conviction that inhumanity, greed and the disintegration of all ethical principles were bred by the factory system and by free competition led him to plan new models of societal organisation in an effort to do away with a system designed to generate profits through cut-throat competition. Originally, Owen set up 'unity and cooperation villages' for the sole purpose of providing jobs to the unemployed, but later on he came to look upon them as 'a means of world regeneration through which the whole world could speedily be emancipated from the competitive profit system' (Cole 1953b, p. 105).

A major pioneer of cooperation and trade unionism was William Thompson, who advocated the establishment of unions as tools for cutting the profits of capitalists and furthering the gradual rise of cooperative firms intended to take the place of the existing system of capital-managed business enterprises. On the assumption that the co-operative mode of production was superior to capitalism, Thompson strove to set up producer cooperatives and to oust capital owners from production processes (see Thompson 1827).

In Italy, the development of cooperation was strongly advocated by the political activist Giuseppe Mazzini. The core idea behind Mazzini's approach was the need to free workers from the 'wage yoke', turn them into 'self-standing producers and allow them to appropriate the full value

---

[42]   The origin of the cooperative movement is usually made to coincide with the establishment of the Rochdale Society of Equitable Pioneers in 1844. In point of fact, British pre-Rochdale cooperativism spanned more than 80 years and falls into a pre-Owenite and post-Owenite period.

of the output produced by them'. From his perspective, the role of capital (described as the 'arbiter of a production system to which it is alien') was to be taken over by associated labour, viz., by associations of workers expected to ensure that 'their members would be given equal voting rights at elections of pro-tempore (i.e. revocable) managers' and would be paid profits commensurate with the quantity and quality of the work input contributed by each of them. This, he argued, would be 'the ideal revolution', since its effect would be to make labour 'the economic basis of human society' (see Mazzini 1935, pp. 109 and 132). Owen, Thompson and Mazzini looked upon cooperation as a viable alternative system to capitalism.

The second point to be discussed in connection with the rise of cooperativism is its descent from mutual aid societies, entities which were designed to provide a set of benefits, including health aid, to their members and were set up in Italy with some success in the mid-nineteenth century. Much like cooperatives, mutual aid societies were originally created in response to capitalist exploitation. Due to surges in unemployment caused by the introduction of machinery during the Industrial Revolution, the lifestyles of most people were changing dramatically, thus creating a need for solidarity and mutual aid as a shield against the competitive spirit, individualism and egotism of the entrepreneurial class. Along with aid to the sick and post-partum allowances for mothers, mutual aid societies granted their members death and unemployment benefits, inability and old-age pensions, as well as other kinds of aid.

The two factors characterising the cooperative movement from its inception were in part consistent and in part in contradiction with each other, in terms that the organisations advocated by Owen, Thompson and Mazzini, though doubtless anti-capitalistic in nature, pursued philanthropic aims which made them unsuited to supplant capital-managed business enterprises. Considering that human personality in general and the conduct of producers tends to be shaped by individualistic and egoistic drives, solidarity and mutualism must necessarily prove ineffectual when it comes to outperforming and gradually ousting capitalistic enterprises from the economy. In other words, a firm which is expected to operate at high levels of efficiency must necessarily leverage the individual profit motive 'until the ambit of men's altruism grows wider' and make 'an intense appeal to the money-making and money-loving instincts of individuals as the main motive force of the economic machine' (Keynes 1931, pp. 241 and 245).

This same conclusion is implied in the argument of Riguzzi and Porcari (1925, p. 191) which runs that in any regime the success of a cooperative, much like that of a privately owned enterprise,

> is a function of its ability to carry on production in accordance with the laws governing economic activity and the cost minimisation principle. Any co-operative firm aiming to put capital-owned enterprises out of play within a free competition environment has to apply these rules with utmost consistency. This is its true *raison d'être*.

A cooperative, I repeat, is faced with two antithetical options: if it resolves to shape its business policies in line with philanthropic and mutualistic aims, it will have to content itself with eking out a precarious existence and narrowly staying afloat within a capitalistic system where profit-earning enterprise rules the day; otherwise, if it resolves to turn its business into a success story, help free society from the 'wage yoke' and allow producers to appropriate their respective work outputs, it will have no option but to leverage the profit motive.

3 PRODUCER COOPERATIVES

Thanks to the rise of the earliest producer cooperatives, which Mill held to change workers into 'their own capitalists' (see Mill 1871, p. 739), a solution to the above-mentioned contradiction seemed to be at hand because these new firms could do without the intermediation of a person who organises production, takes all the associated risks and thereby acquires title to cash the surplus, i.e. the difference between cost and revenue. In a producer cooperative, production is run by the partners themselves and it is these that are consequently entitled to cash the surplus and apportion it among themselves. That is why Mill (1871, p. 744) remarked that the partners of a producer cooperative are 'in a relation to their work which would make it their principle and their interest – at present it is neither – to do the utmost, instead of the least possible, in exchange for their remuneration' and why Pantaleoni described cooperatives as *business enterprises* which pursue distinctively economic aims in line with economic criteria and whose partners, though partly committed to noble aims, are nevertheless motivated by *egoism* and the desire to make a *profit* (see Pantaleoni 1898, p. 133).

If cooperatives are analysed in abstract terms and without regard to historical experience, they can be described as enterprises in which 'the factors of production are rewarded by dividing up in agreed proportions the actual output of their cooperative efforts' (Keynes 1979, p. 66) and whose partners act rationally if they work towards maximising corporate revenues in an effort to add to their personal earnings (because by so doing they will maximise both their own incomes and those of their fellow partners). Accordingly, both personal utility calculations and solidarity feelings are aspects specific to worker-controlled enterprises.

Vilfredo Pareto was the first economist to emphasise the contradictoriness of the aims of cooperation (though he mentioned different aspects from those discussed in this chapter).[43] By a curious irony he wrote (Pareto 1926, pp. 382–3),

> cooperatives are thriving for reasons other than those that were expected to ensure their success. Originally established with the aim of putting an end to cut-throat inter-firm competition and promoting worker solidarity in its place, in actual fact, their entry into the market produced the effect of adding fresh competitors to those already in existence.

In other words, Pareto thought that cooperatives were able to engage in and even stand up to competition just because they were barely distinguishable from capitalistic firms. While paying lip service to solidarity, he argued, they actually leveraged the profit motive no less than their rivals. From his perspective, those economists who opposed cooperation in his day were grossly mistaken because they were missing the opportunity to welcome the rise of firms capable of vying with capitalistic companies and were hence 'implicitly endorsing the need to retain the role of intermediaries' in production (Pareto 1926, p. 384).

4 THE TRADITIONAL COOPERATIVE FIRM

The earliest cooperatives that got off the ground in Britain, including the Rochdale Society of Equitable Pioneers (set up by Owen in 1844), were 'consumer cooperatives', i.e. firms founded by groups of consumers for the purpose of maximising not revenue, but other types of benefits for their partners. Consumer cooperatives are sales outlets which do without capitalistic intermediaries and are consequently in a position to market goods at prices below those charged by other firms. This poses a need to establish the aspects that consumer cooperatives have in common with other cooperative models.

---

[43] Potter suggested that Owen himself was fully aware of this contradiction (see Potter 1893, pp. 24–8).

Traditionally, cooperators themselves and legal scholars, though not economists, have defined cooperatives as social organisation structures in which groups of workers or consumers join together with the aim of combating capitalistic exploitation by running business activities for their own account in a variety of sectors of the economy. Specifically, a consumer cooperative is a retail outlet whose partners jointly purchase goods at wholesale prices for resale to their fellow partners and manage to undercut other retailers because the prices they charge do not include the profit margin that is usually cashed by capitalistic outlets. Self-build housing cooperatives are set up in order to implement affordable housing projects. The partners use pooled resources to purchase and develop a building lot, i.e. to construct homes at low costs because they neither include the surplus value of the developed site, nor the profit margin that would have accrued to an external capitalistic developer. Producer or worker cooperatives operate in a variety of industries. The working partners run their firms for their own account and appropriate the output of their work without paying out part of the residual to a capitalistic employer. The same principle applies to cooperative banks, cooperative insurance companies and other types of cooperative firms.

The unifying factor common to all cooperatives is the determination to do without an intermediary and zero the earning potential of capitalists. In overall terms, a cooperative is a business enterprise which sets out to generate not profits, but other kinds of benefits associated with the fact that no part of the surplus has to be paid out to a capital owner.

These characteristics go to underscore the anti-capitalistic essence of cooperative firms, i.e. entities which are set up by members of the subaltern classes in an effort to evade the law of profit, the basic criterion of a capitalistic society which enables capital owners to hire workers, pay them a fixed income and appropriate the surplus notwithstanding the fact that this was actually generated by the workers. From this traditional perspective, producers', workers', consumers' and housing cooperatives are anti-capitalistic entities because the business activities of the former two are managed by their partners on their own and for their own account and because the partners of the others have access to goods, services or homes without paying out a 'surplus' to third parties.

In recent years, this traditional view has been called into question by some economists who object that only producer cooperatives are run in a manner that turns the partners into their own capitalists and employers (and hence overturn the worker-employee opposition). In other co-operatives, they argue, the partners pay their shares in the firm's capital, but then use hired workers to build their homes or market the goods purchased and, in general, adopt operational procedures that do not cancel the distinction between employers and employees.

In line with this widely shared objection, in the recent economic literature cooperation theory is ever more frequently identified with the economic theory of worker-controlled enterprises and the latter are usually made to coincide with producer, rather than consumer cooperatives.

5 WORKER-CONTROLLED ENTERPRISES

At this point, it is necessary to provide a more comprehensive picture of the worker-controlled enterprise. As mentioned, real-world cooperatives come in a variety of different models, which include not only producer and consumer cooperatives, but also pure labour and mixed capital-labour cooperatives, firms with state-owned production means (the Yugoslav model) and privately or group-owned production means (the Western model), cooperatives employing hired labour and firms exclusively formed of worker-members, and so forth.[44] Consequently, besides keeping producer cooperatives strictly distinct from consumer cooperatives, it is convenient to define specifics which are common to all worker-controlled enterprises. Above all, it is necessary to clarify if the term worker-controlled enterprise is synonymous with producer cooperative and decide if cooperatives are to be distinguished from self-managed firms.

As the crucial distinction is clearly between publicly and privately owned production means, one might be tempted to conclude that a cooperative is a worker-controlled enterprise with *privately* owned production means and that a self-managed system is a system of worker-controlled enterprises with *publicly* owned production means. In fact, today this distinction is held to restrict both the notion of cooperative and that of worker-controlled enterprise (since the term cooperative designates a variety of different firm models and the worker-controlled enterprises discussed in the current literature are often privately owned).

Major cues are offered by Sertel, who holds that the basic characteristic of a *workers' enterprise* is the double status of its members as partners and workers. In other words, in Sertel's approach a firm is defined as a

---

[44] Although Marx praised cooperation on several occasions, he held that workers should 'embark on co-operative production rather than on co-operative stores' because the latter 'touch only the surface of the economic system' and only the latter are suited to 'strike at its foundations' (Marx 1866, p. 190) – an argument to which Bernstein took exception (see Bernstein 1899, pp. 149–59).

workers' enterprise if its workforce is solely formed of its partners and, by contrast, as a capitalistic enterprise when it is not, that is to say when none of its partners work for the firm and none of its workers are, at the same time, partners of the firm (see Sertel 1982, p. 13). Although Sertel's 'radical distinction' between workers' and capital-owned enterprises just covers borderline cases, it offers an excellent opportunity for analysing the specific characteristics of a cooperative firm exactly because it reflects extreme and purely ideal cases. Whereas the core factor behind Sertel's definition appears to be the *ownership* issue (the 'workers' enterprise' is owned by those working for it), the preferential focus of mainstream economists is on the *management* issue, and this explains why they define producer cooperatives as worker-controlled enterprises regardless of whether they are owned by the workers, the State or private individuals.

At this point, we will focus simultaneously on Sertel's and Vanek's apparently antithetical stances and establish if, and to what extent, they can be reconciled. Although we do rate Vanek's as the basic distinction (the working modes of a firm segregating capital incomes from labour incomes differ greatly from those of firms that do not distinguish between these two income categories), on closer analysis there is evidence that the ownership issue is no less crucial to Vanek's distinction than it is to Sertel's because – in somewhat simplified terms – from the different investment funding practices of these firm models it follows that the LMF's capital goods are, for the most part, publicly owned while those of a WMF are usually the joint property of the partners.

And although this finding does not take us to the true heart of the matter, at this point it is possible to draw the provisional conclusion that a cooperative is a firm which is run by the workers themselves and may indifferently use privately or publicly owned capital goods and that a cooperative firm with publicly owned production means is tantamount to a self-managed firm.

In point of fact, even theorists who accept this definition of the cooperative firm tend to approach cooperation from diverging perspectives shaped by different cultural backgrounds. If they categorise the production means of a cooperative as the property of the workers' collective, they think of cooperation economics as the *third*, or *group property sector*, which operates alongside those of privately and publicly owned firms (see Jay 1980). If they hold a more modern view suggested by the approaches of Ward and Vanek, they tend to conceive of the capital goods of a cooperative as either owned by the workers' collective or the State (including public agencies) and to define a cooperative economy with publicly owned cooperatives as a system of self-managed firms, that is to say as market socialism.

6 MILL'S AND MARSHALL'S APPROACHES TO COOPERATION

Pareto's polemical description of coeval economists as enemies of producer cooperatives (see above) was just aimed at some mainstream scholars who did not see any viable alternatives to capital-owned enterprises. In fact, just a few years had elapsed since the time when economic scholars of renown greatly praised the cooperative movement. As mentioned above, Owen, Thompson and Mazzini looked upon cooperation as a viable alternative system to capitalism, and there are numerous other economists of considerable stature that do not fit within Pareto's description.

Among them was John Stuart Mill, whose critical attitude towards the typical capitalistic worldview is clearly revealed by the following quote:

> I confess I am not charmed with the ideal of life held out by those who think that the normal state of human beings is that of struggling to get on; that the trampling, crushing, elbowing, and treading on each other's heels, which form the existing type of social life, are the most desirable lot of humankind, or anything but the disagreeable symptoms of one of the phases of industrial progress. (Mill 1871, p. 20)

Mill looked upon work in association as the beachhead for the emancipation of the working class:

> The civilizing and improving influences of association and the efficiency and economy of production on a large scale may be obtained without dividing the producers into two parties with hostile interests and feelings, the many who do the work being mere servants under the command of the one who supplies the funds, and having no interest of their own in the enterprise except to earn their wages with as little labour as possible. (Mill 1871, p. 722)

More precisely, from Mill's perspective one major advantage of production in association was to transform human life 'from a conflict of classes struggling for opposite interests, to a friendly rivalry in the pursuit of a good common to all' (1871, p. 744).[45]

---

[45] Mill's theoretical approach to cooperation is analysed in depth by Pesciarelli (1981, ch. 6).

Authoritative supporters of the cooperative movement include Marshall, who claimed that cooperation 'does rest in a great measure on ethical motives' (Marshall 1890, p. 292), combines 'high inspirations with calm and strenuous action' and has the 'direct aim to improve the quality of man himself' more than any other movement with which it has points of affinity (Marshall 1925, p. 227).

Marshall is arguably the greatest and best known of all mainstream economists and his comments on cooperatives are not necessarily based on a misunderstanding of their true nature or his failure to realise that the partners of cooperative firms act in their personal interests.

All this said, Marshall's emphasis on the commitment of cooperators to collective aims can probably be explained if we bear in mind that the partners of a cooperative who strive to maximise corporate revenues simultaneously scale up the incomes of all their fellow partners.

Marx himself praised cooperatives on several occasions and thought of the rise of producer cooperatives as a new mode of production capable of leading to the demise of capitalism.

7 THE WANING CONSENSUS ON COOPERATION AMONG ECONOMISTS

From the late nineteenth century onwards, economic theorists became less and less supportive of cooperation and some of them turned their back on it (as mentioned by Pareto). In Italy, the heyday of cooperation lasted longer than elsewhere and reached a peak under the premiership of Giolitti. After the Paris Commune of 1870, Marx himself began to lose faith in a movement which he had rated as a potential new mode of production. In part, this change of focus among economists was caused by a downward trend in the overall performance levels of these firms and by the feeling that the movement had failed to live up to their expectations. Bernstein, for example, was convinced that producer cooperatives had no future and recommended establishing consumer cooperatives only.

A case apart was Italy during the premiership of Giolitti, when Gramsci's writings and the events of the so-called 'red biennium' induced the cooperative movement to propose the conversion of Fiat works into a cooperative enterprise.

In part, the decline of the cooperative movement in the early 1870s was caused by the rise of marginalism, a view of economics which revolutionised economic thinking and remained extremely critical of cooperation for many years. In many respects, marginalism can be described as a 'mechanical' theory because it postulates the existence of 'natural' economic equilibria which the spokesmen for this current of thought rate as bound to last forever. Utility calculus, the main focus point of marginalism, would suggest that provided a social system is organised in line with rational criteria the wage rates prevailing in it will always be commensurate with the marginal productivity of labour and that the same rule also applies to capital and to 'land'. The theory of general economic equilibrium which was fleshed out by marginalist thinkers (including Walras and Pareto) leads up to 'Pareto optimality', that is to say to the assumption that in perfect competition markets there is always one and only one equilibrium point which vouchsafes maximum social welfare and that this point is unrelated to the institutional context. This means that the equilibrium point of an efficient market economy is always the same, irrespective of whether the enterprises operating within it are capital- or worker-owned. In other words, in a perfectly competitive market economy it makes no difference if it is capital that hires labour or vice versa (i.e. if it is labour that manages enterprises with loan capital).

Marginalist theory is at the heart of an 1898 paper in which Matteo Pantaleoni stated that both consumer and producer cooperatives are *profit-making* entities and, as such, 'adopt business strategies geared towards making money ... engage in the production of goods with the aim of cutting costs as much as possible and strive to generate benefits for all their partners' (Pantaleoni 1898, pp. 132–3).

For the purposes of this book, the most interesting implication of the opinion of Pantaleoni is that aspects ostensibly specific to cooperatives only are actually common to all business enterprises. Insofar as it is true that 'each cooperator is exclusively concerned with making utility calculations' and that 'individuals engage in business for the sole purpose of gaining personal benefits', it follows that, given the absence of aspects specific to cooperatives only, 'the price formation model that would arise if the principles of cooperation were consistently and universally applied would by no means differ from the price formation model arising in free competition contexts whose operators are not committed to any of such principles' (Pantaleoni 1898, p. 142).[46]

In support of his arguments, Pantaleoni examined a number of principles and characteristics which were traditionally ascribed to cooperative

---

[46] Here, Pantaleoni seems to adopt the viewpoint of an economist in rewording the well-known saying of Hobbes that cooperation is not conceivable between individuals concerned with maximising their personal interests, i.e. between people he categorises as 'rational egoists'.

firms in order to argue that 'the so-called cooperative principles can only act themselves out in contexts characterised by the simultaneous existence of non-cooperative enterprises'. His ultimate conclusion was that the assumed specifics of cooperative firms were actually 'aspects common to any other enterprise operating for profit' and that, consequently, the rationale behind cooperation 'was not an autonomous principle' (Pantaleoni 1898, p. 145).

All this is clear evidence that marginalism was a major cause of the waning consensus on cooperation among economists.[47]

8 THE CONTRIBUTION OF BENJAMIN WARD

The first discordant note was struck as late as 1958, when the American economist Benjamin Ward challenged Pantaleoni's opinions by arguing that capitalistic enterprises differed from cooperatives or self-managed firms because the former strove to maximise profits (or the rate of return on their investment), while the latter were concerned with maximising the average income levels of their workers. The core point of Ward's argument became the starting point for the author's theory of the behaviour of firms and his 1958 paper is now rated as a classic. The publication of Ward's paper led to the emergence of the economic theory of producer cooperatives, a new research field founded on the assumption that cooperatives are enterprises aiming to maximise the average incomes of their workers. Considering the pace at which the scholarly literature on producer cooperatives has been expanding over the past decades, today it is possible to argue that the contemporary theory of the firm falls into two broad subdivisions: the traditional theory of the (capitalistic) enterprise as a firm model concerned with maximising its profits and the theory of the cooperative (or self-managed) firm founded on the assumption that this firm model strives to maximise the average income of its labourers.

This means that the criticisms of Pantaleoni and other neoclassical economists have been dismantled without being explicitly rebutted. In Ward's approach, cooperatives differ from capital-managed enterprises because they adopt a behavioural principle other than profit maximisation, but from 1958 onwards researchers highlighted and discussed an increasing number of differences between these two firm models.

---

[47] In Italy, Pantaleoni's paper was received with universal acclaim. Supporters of Pantaleoni's approach include Valenti (1902, p. 366), according to whom 'cooperation is not a new system of economic organisation'.

The partners of a cooperative can be categorised as 'rational egoists' because they are aware that any efforts to maximise the firm's total revenues will also drive up their own incomes. Accordingly, the motivational factor behind their efforts to boost the firm's average or total profits is not altruism, but a rational form of egoism which strips the cooperative movement of its utopian overtones and goes to refute the claim that cooperation requires of necessity 'the birth of a new man'.

Taking the cue from Ward's 1958 paper, Jaroslav Vanek made a pivotal contribution to the emerging theory of producer cooperatives by introducing the distinction between cooperatives that segregate labour incomes from capital incomes (LMFs) and cooperatives which self-finance their investments, do not keep distinct these two types of income and pay out to their partners mixed capital and wage labour incomes (WMFs) (see Vanek 1971a and 1971b).

9 THE MODERN ECONOMIC THEORY OF PRODUCER COOPERATIVES

The above reflections lead to the conclusion that the cooperative of which we speak is a worker-controlled (i.e. self-managed and democratic) enterprise whose residual (the difference between revenues and costs) is cashed by the worker-members. Economists' co-ops carry on business in the market with the aim of maximising the incomes of their members and are not subject to any restrictions, except for the ban on taking on hired workers (eventually, in numbers exceeding pre-fixed limits). In short, the 'pure' LMF type or economists' co-op can be said to reverse the relation between capital and labour specific to capitalism. Indeed, whereas the capitalistic investor-owned enterprise strives to maximise the income accruing to capital owners by taking on hired workers, paying out to them a fixed income (wage or salary) and appropriating the residual, in economists' co-ops it is the workers that operate in their own and their fellow partners' interests by operating with loan capital, paying capital providers a fixed income (interest) and keeping the surplus for themselves (see, for instance, Srinivasan & Phansalkar 2003, p. 366).

The capital–labour relation specific to capitalism is overturned because in the cooperative or self-managed firm the organisational model enabling capitalists to exercise control over labour is replaced by a model which transfers control powers to the workers. In the face of the ever tighter control that is being exercised by capitalists over their enterprises in consequence of rapid surges in the sheer amount of capital goods, the need to reverse the existing capital–labour relation is becoming ever more urgent. In a world which is characterised by escalating capital control, the time has come for workers to wrest themselves free from the resulting oppression.

Although economists' co-ops are not committed to the mutuality principle that legal theorists rate as essential, they operate in accordance with the cooperative principles originally laid down by Owen, Thompson and Mazzini and can therefore be rated not only as genuine cooperative firms, but as even more genuine than the jurists' co-ops that are currently operating in Italy and elsewhere. Like the earliest cooperatives, they are anti-capitalistic entities not because they reject the prospect of co-existing with capital-owned enterprises, but because thanks to the reversal of the capital–labour relation they are the opposite of capitalistic enterprises. And as they vest corporate decision powers in all their partners (and consequently substitute the 'one head, one vote' criterion for the 'one share, one vote' principle governing the exercise of corporate power in capital-owned enterprises), they can also be described as 'democratic firms'.[48]

Moreover, due to the above-mentioned anti-capitalistic essence and the tendency to upturn the existing capital–labour relation the cooperative can also be described as a 'socialist' entity. In a valuable historical outline of the cooperative movement Beatrice Webb offered an analysis of different cooperative firm models and drew the following conclusion:

> we should miss the national significance of the Co-operative movement, the spiritual meaning of the future grocer's shop, if we failed to realize that all these manifold forms of democratic association, with their various ways and different methods, had one aim and one motive – the same aim and the same motive, curiously enough, described as the cause of the mediaeval communes: the desire on the part of a majority to regulate and to limit the exploitation of their labour by a powerful and skilled minority. (Potter 1893, p. 39)

---

[48]   Potter described democracy as 'the distinct characteristic of the movement since its inception' (see Potter 1893, p. 63) and cooperation and legal theorists today concordantly hold that social functions of cooperation are exercised in accordance with the principle of economic democracy (see, inter alia, Galgano 1982, p. 81). As argued by Galgano, cooperatives differ from capitalistic enterprises because they apply the 'one head, one vote' principle and, hence, 'repudiate the plutocratic principle based on which power and control are vested in the wealthy at a scale which is proportional to the amount of wealth owned by an individual' (Galgano 1974, p. 174).

Let me add that the description of economists' co-ops as genuine cooperative firms is confirmed by a distinction that cooperators and legal theorists tend to draw between capitalistic and cooperative firms. Whereas Owen and other early theorists held that cooperatives had to self-finance all their investments, modern economists tend to maintain, with Vanek (1971a, 1971b), that they should rather opt for loan capital financing.

The implicit return of modern economists to the very origins of the cooperative movement and their endorsement of cooperation as an alternative to capitalistic enterprises are evidence that it is difficult to agree with Sapelli when he argues that the current debate on cooperation is unlikely to take us very far, that it is not by chance that this debate has mainly been involving economists of neoclassical extraction for several years now (specifically about 20 years or so), or that due to the 'sleep of reason' benumbing the minds of 'older' cooperation theorists the reductionist findings emerging from their research have been allowed to circulate freely to the point of becoming the received view. The latest literature, he adds, offers a chain of laughable, if not embarrassing research propositions. Among these are the tentative application of economic analysis methods to the study of producer cooperatives notwithstanding the fact that these are economic organisations only in part. In Sapelli's opinion, they are the materialisation of the desire of people to protect themselves and their values by working in association (and not based on individual contracts) and 'can be better understood against the background of the approach of Durkheim, rather than that of Jevons, of Mauss rather than Williamson' (Sapelli 1998, pp. 11–12).

Although there is little denying that until some time ago neoclassical economic speculation tended to proceed 'by way of reduction' and was marred by 'economistic overtones', it is fair to say that today things stand differently, which means that this criticism is probably applicable to earlier neoclassical scholars such as Pantaleoni, but much less so to the work of Meade or Sen in the field of cooperation theory. From my perspective, Sapelli's line of reasoning should be reversed, in terms that today the true reductionists are all those cooperators and legal theorists who categorise cooperation as the 'third sector' of the economy. In contrast, the cooperative firm system upheld in this book offers a rich array of non-economic benefits that justify its classification as a 'genuinely socialist' entity.

Lastly, it is a fact that modern professional economists are barely familiar with the modern economic theory of producer cooperatives. This means that cooperation theorists have probably failed to turn the spotlight on the true plus point of such a firm system: its potential for realising economic democracy. Consequently, the argument that the plan to establish 'worker control' has strangely 'antiquated' overtones that call to mind conditions and political movements of the past (which was set forth by Blumberg some 30 years ago – see Blumberg 1973, p. 150 and Nuti 2004, p. 201) does sound timely enough even today.

4. A few advantages of economic democracy

1 INTRODUCTION

This chapter is intended to discuss some of the main advantages of a system of employee-managed firms.[49]

As mentioned in the Introduction, the idea that the notion of economic activity as the source of all power necessitates categorising economic democracy as a basic component of democracy is one of the key assumptions underlying this book. Marx taught that political democracy could not be categorised as complete unless it was complemented by economic democracy and that the latter was therefore the precondition for the evolution of formal into full democracy.

In support of the generalised belief that cooperatives are potentially able to outpace capital-owned firms because the private profit motive induces the partners to work towards the success of their firms (see, inter alia, Pesciarelli 1981, p. 116), I wish to claim that this superiority over capitalistic enterprises is the direct effect of the potential of economic democracy to make political democracy a reality.

In this connection, Marcuse mentions Marx's prediction that with the progressive exacerbation of the anarchical character of the social process overall, the sway of capitalists over direct producers was bound to escalate into outright despotism (see Marcuse 1967, p. 111) and that the access of 'immediate producers' to the management of the production apparatus would lead to a *qualitative* process reconversion geared towards the production of commodities designed to meet individual needs as they were seen to freely arise (see Marcuse 1964, p. 43). Dworkin (2006, p. 147) explains that this is because 'democracy means self-government ... the form of government in which the people govern themselves' and in which 'it would compromise their dignity to submit themselves to the authority of others when they play no part in their

---

[49] This was the focus point of one of my earlier papers on the subject (Jossa 2010).

45

decisions'. Mill's theoretical approach to cooperation is analysed at length in chapter 6 of Pesciarelli 1981.[50]

This is also the opinion of many renowned theorists of socialism, who argued that if we want democracy, that is, if we want every man's voice to count for as much as it is intrinsically worth, irrespective of all extraneous consideration, we must abolish class distinctions by doing away with the huge inequalities of wealth and economic power on which they really depend.

In point of fact, humankind would draw a rich array of additional benefits from the establishment of a system of cooperative firms. Since most of these points are covered in a large body of literature, however, our analysis will be restricted to those advantages which can be rated as the true strong points of such a system: gains in labour productivity relative to capitalistic businesses; the production of finer human beings than those living in capitalistic systems; the abolition of external firm control; slower monopoly building; remote bankruptcy risks; a socially determined income distribution pattern and a reduced need for state intervention in the economy.

Economic democracy can be 'engineered' in dual fashion: through a parliamentary act suppressing wage labour by operation of law or, better still, by enforcing policies targeted towards furthering a gradual, but steady growth of the producer cooperative sector. In both these cases, economic democracy is a 'merit good' (see Musgrave 1958).

2   ON THE ADVANTAGES OF ECONOMIC DEMOCRACY

The following is a tentative list of the benefits ascribed to democratic firms in the literature:

(a)   the pleasure the partners derive from own-account work;
(b)   wresting power from capitalists;

---

[50]   In the organ of the one-time Italian party named Partito d'azione, the periodical *La Libertà*, we read that once the private profit motive of capitalists that helps perpetuate the absurd distinction between classes is cancelled, 'the corrupting influence of capitalism will be swept away, the firewall which seals off blue collars from high-profile managers and white collars in general will dissolve like mist and not only clerical workers, but even executives will at last realise that their own interests fall in with those of manual workers' (see Codignola 1944, p. 95).

(c)   a powerful impulse to political democracy;

(d)   major firm efficiency gains from worker involvement in production processes;

(e)   a stop to exploitation and degrading alienated labour;

(f)   the tendency of labour incomes to increase in proportion to boosts in labour and capital productivity;

(g)   more investments in human capital;

(h)   a positive influence on the characters of workers and stronger community feelings;

(i)   introduce softer competition and reduced insolvency risks;

(j)   the disappearance of classical and Keynesian unemployment and declines in structural unemployment;

(k)   marked downward trends in class conflict and wage hikes and the resulting slowdown in inflation;

(l)   improved income distribution;

(m)   an end to external firm control and, hence, to the sway of multinational corporations;

(n)   reduced monopoly building;

(o)   lower environment pollution levels and reduced production of hazardous materials;

(p)   lesser risks of power abuse and fraud;

(q)   economic efficiency gains from a lesser need for state intervention;

(r)   the eclipse of the current paramount role of the economic factor in the evolution of society.[51]

As mentioned above, since the first three advantages have already been analysed, in this chapter my analysis will be restricted to a few interrelated advantages of cooperation, specifically higher productivity levels, the different role of competition in a system of cooperative firms, lower bankruptcy risks, fairer income distribution patterns and a reduced need for State intervention in the economy. Additional advantages, including a sharp drop in unemployment, need not be dealt with here as they were addressed in sufficient depth in previous writings to which the reader may refer (for the unemployment issue, see Jossa 2001, 2005b, ch. 10, 2010, pp. 79–89, 2012b, ch. 10, 2014a, ch. 8, and 2016b, ch. 5).

---

[51]   On the subject of the advantages of cooperatives overall, see Birchall 2012. It is worth noting that Birchall's opinions on producer cooperatives strongly diverge from our approach in this book.

3 COMPETITION IN A SYSTEM OF DEMOCRATIC FIRMS

As far as competition is concerned, the Scottish eighteenth-century economists who first underscored its importance argued that due to its 'magic' effects people pursuing their personal interests would ultimately promote the interests of others as well and, hence, the overall interests of society. This idea is reflected in Adam Smith's well-known saying that

> it is not from the benevolence of the butcher, the brewer, or the baker that we expect our dinner, but from their regard to their own interests. We address ourselves, not to their humanity, but to their self-love, and never talk to them of our own necessities, but of their advantages. (Smith 1776, p. 17)

The extent to which competition will prove more or less tough depends on ethical, social and government-driven mechanisms. It is known that Max Weber tied competition to the Calvinistic ethic and that the general public are more supportive of the competitive race in the United States than in other parts of the world.

Marx (1857–58, p. 333) defined competition as 'the free development of the mode of production based upon capital; the free development of its conditions and of its process as constantly reproducing these conditions'. In free competition – he argued – 'it is capital that is set free, not the individuals. As long as production resting on capital is the necessary, hence the fittest form for the development of the force of social production, the movement of individuals within the pure conditions of capital appears as their freedom.'

Further on (1857–58, p. 335) he concluded:

> Thence, on the other hand, the absurdity of regarding free competition as the ultimate development of human freedom, and the negation of free competition as equivalent to the negation of individual freedom and of social production based upon individual freedom. It is merely the kind of free development possible on the limited basis of the domination of capital. This kind of individual freedom is therefore at the same time the most complete suspension of all individual freedom, and the most complete subjugation of individuality under social conditions which assume the form of objective powers, even of overpowering objects – of things independent of the relations among individuals themselves.

Taking the cue from Marx, then, it is possible to argue that the crux of the issue is not so much overly stiff competition, as the fact that competition today appears as 'the free development of the mode of production based upon capital'. In other words, insofar as it is true that competition in the service of capital is one thing and competition in the best interests of consumers and workers quite another, in a system of democratic firms competition would become a valuable mechanism and, as such, deserve effective protection.

According to Braverman (1974, p. 232), despite the progressive obsolescence of the division of labour, capitalists have a tendency to reconstitute it by exacerbating its worst aspects, with the effect that every leap forward in the development of capitalism widens the gulf between worker and machine and increases the worker's subjection to the yoke of the machine.

Hence, a major benefit of a producer cooperative system is its potential for reducing competition. As will be argued in more detail in Section 9, competition would be cooled off thanks to the fewer insolvency risks faced by cooperatives. A firm whose managers feel tolerably safe from bankruptcy are free to opt for less stiff competition, for instance by granting the partners more free time or reducing workloads in preference to scaling up earnings. No matter how keen, competition under such circumstances would be no ill since the partners might check its effects by deciding if they wish to stand up to it or opt for cuts on their earnings.

In part, the assumed softer competitive regime connoting a producer cooperative system can be traced to the practice of apportioning the surplus of a cooperative among all the partners. As a rule, the greater earnings flowing from the successful performance of a capitalistic business enterprise accrue to a small number of capitalists. In contrast, cooperatives apportion both earnings and losses among all the partners by definition and this, too, helps scale down competition.

Other authors lay emphasis on the importance of the finding that the pay rates of partners providing equal work inputs do not tend to level out (see Montias 1976, pp. 255–6). As the aim of cooperatives is to maximise per capita incomes, these firms have no incentive to recruit workers prepared to accept wage rates below the average pay rate accruing to the existing partners. It is a well-known fact that cooperatives are only interested in recruiting partners whose prospective marginal productivities are above the level corresponding to its average pay rate.

This is why workers in cooperatives enjoy a greater and, even more importantly, different freedom to choose between work and non-work. To clarify this point, it is worth considering that a firm which is not interested in replacing its workers with underbidders is one which knows all too well that even where its pay rates should fall below those of other firms it would barely be at risk of losing its existing workforce. As far as the partners are concerned, they are likely to use this circumstance to their advantage in terms of opting for more free time and fewer working hours.

The situation just described, though, is not devoid of drawbacks. As argued by Rothschild (1986, p. 190), anyone attaining the status of a capitalist and wishing to extend this newly acquired status in time will have no option but to accumulate. He is compelled to do so by the rules of competition governing the historically determined mode of production, and it is these that are the driving force behind his conduct. Accordingly, one adverse effect of a softer competitive regime is to interfere with the dynamic of the economic system and, probably, reduce its potential for growth.

With reference to my line of reasoning in this section, there are reasons for arguing that Marx was perfectly aware that markets are functional to the development of production forces and, therefore, acceptable to the extent they are non-capitalistic in nature. Consequently, this assumption authorises Marxists to lay in a comparable claim. Competition is to be upheld so long as it is not excessively tight; in other words, competition has its benefits and whenever it is kept bland its benefits are redoubled (as will be argued in more detail further on).

4 THE LABOUR PRODUCTIVITY EDGE ON CAPITALISTIC BUSINESSES

From Gramsci's perspective, for workers' councils to emerge, each worker

> must have gained an awareness of his place within the economy. First of all, he must have felt part of an elementary unit or team and must have realised that technical upgrades to machinery and equipment reshape relationships with engineers: less and less dependent on the engineer, his one-time master, the worker must have gained in autonomy and acquired the ability to self-govern himself. (Gramsci 1919–20, p. 81)[52]

The production modes that arose at various stages of world history, from slavery to capitalism, had one thing in common: workers were stripped of the output of their labour since the benefits of their effort were reaped by others. In other words, over the span of history the best energies of

---

[52] In Gramsci's mind, a social group aspiring to power must develop leadership abilities well before its takeover (Gramsci 1975, p. 2010).

workers have been 'wasted' for want of just those incentives that would have induced them to engage in work to the best of their abilities.

The same does not apply to the members of a producer cooperative, whose title to appropriate the earnings from their work and responsibility for the firm's operations are strong inducements to streamline production and increase output.

If Gintis is right when he argues that 'the labour forthcoming from a worker depends, in addition to his/her biology and skill, on states of consciousness, degree of solidarity with other workers, labour market conditions and the social organization of the work process' (see Gintis 1976, p. 37), an additional strong point of a cooperative system is a work organisation model which fosters mutual solidarity while allowing the partners to make their private utility calculations. And provided it is true that worker solidarity is a salient feature of cooperatives, it seems possible to argue that these firms will hardly be appreciably affected by problems arising in connection with the 'moral hazard in teams' issue.

Two additional reasons accounting for the higher labour productivity rates of cooperative firms include a greater focus on human capital building and less frequent dismissals. Indeed, risks of dismissal act as a disincentive to working towards the success of the firm and interfere with interpersonal relations.[53]

Other authors endorse the opposite view, i.e. that average work incomes in cooperatives fall short of those recorded in capitalistic business enterprises (see, for example, Zanotti 2016, p. 121). Their argument is that the powerful stimulus stemming from the link between the marginal inputs of workers in capitalistic firms and their pay rates is abated in cooperatives since incomes there are strictly dependent on the way the surplus is apportioned among the partners.

In addition to this, the assumed productivity edge of cooperatives is said to be backed up by insufficient evidence. Pointing to promotion as an additional powerful stimulus to dedication and to earning the employer's esteem, some theorists contrast this strong point of capital-managed systems with a major drawback of democratic firms: an incentive to shirk inherent in the fact that only a portion of the surplus revenue generated by a partner's greater work input accrues to that partner. In a cooperative of n partners assigned to equal tasks this portion is but $1/n$ – which

---

[53] Borrowing Hirschmann's terminology, it is possible to argue that positive productivity effects may flow from the prioritisation of 'voice' over 'exit' as the favourite mode of action (see Barreto 2011, pp. 202–203).

means that incentives to production increase in an inverse proportion to the size of a worker-controlled firm.

Even the above-mentioned impulse to worker solidarity is said to generate the awkward effect of inducing hard-working staff members to slow down their rates of work for fear of embarrassing their fellow workers (for this argument, see Prandergast's 1999 review of the literature on the perverse effects of incentives and Tortia 2008, pp. 87–8).

At the other end of the spectrum are authors such as Meade (1972, p. 403), Blumberg (1968), Conte (1982) and others who argue that worker involvement in corporate decision making may increase motivation even in larger cooperatives and, hence, lead to major productivity gains.

The productivity effect of worker involvement was confirmed by the findings of the well-known experimental project of the E. Mayo school and, more recently, by the empirical research of Jones and Backus (1977); Bellas (1972); Thomas and Logan (1982); Defourny et al. (1985); Estrin et al. (1987); Weitzman and Kruse (1990); Levine and Tyson (1990); Sterner (1990); Estrin and Jones (1992, 1995); Defourny (1992); Bartlett et al. (1992); Doucouliagos (1995); Levine (1995); Craig and Pencavel (1995); Gui (1996); Ben-Ner et al. (1996); Tseo et al. (2004) and Tortia (2008).

Conflicting results are reported in Hollas and Stansell (1988) and Faccioli and Fiorentini (1998). These two authors maintain that co-operatives are outperformed by capital-managed firms and a comparative analysis of capital- versus worker-controlled firms by Estrin points to a negligible productivity differential when headcount is used as a proxy of labour input and a considerable underperformance of cooperatives when the total hours worked by blue collars are used as a measure of labour input (see Estrin 1991).

For rather ambiguous results, see Fitzroy and Kraft (1987) and Berman and Berman (1989). Noticeable surveys of this research area include Jones and Pliskin (1991) and Bonin et al. (1993). On closer analysis, though, since the organisational patterns developed by cooperatives before the rise of economic worker control theory depart from the theoretical model to the point of impinging upon labour productivity, it is fair to admit that these surveys are not directly relevant to our approach in this book.

5 UNEMPLOYMENT IN A SYSTEM OF DEMOCRATIC FIRMS

By way of introduction, from the myriad benefits mentioned above, I will discuss only the main strong point of a system of worker-run firms, namely its potential for scaling down unemployment. And as I addressed this subject at some length in previous publications (see Jossa 2009 and 2014a, ch. 8), I will confine myself to a cursory analysis and refer the reader to scholarly monographs on this point by other authors.

It is common knowledge that unemployment is generally traced to three main causes: high labour costs, insufficient global demand and lack of employment opportunities. The corresponding types of unemployment will now be examined one by one.

Most economists are agreed that high labour costs are the main cause of unemployment in capitalistic systems. From the fact that the incomes of the partners of a worker-controlled firm are funded with the residual (the net income left after the firm has settled all its costs, to the exclusion of payroll expenses), it follows that a major plus point of a system of democratic firms is the cancellation of wage-hike unemployment. This conclusion is widely supported in the published literature to which the reader has been referred above.

As far as Keynesian unemployment is concerned, how would a cooperative firm respond to a fall in aggregate demand?

In every system where Say's law does not apply and where national income is determined in Keynesian terms, each fall in aggregate demand will reduce the aggregate number of hours worked. When layoff decisions are adopted by the workers themselves at meetings or, at any rate, in their interests, it is difficult to imagine that the workers will be prepared to fire each other. Indeed, especially in the event layoffs were decided by drawing lots, the fear of being drawn would induce the partners to vote against layoffs. Consequently, there is every reason to believe that in the case of a fall in aggregate demand, a democratic firm, instead of dismissing its workers, will opt for a shorter working week. No involuntary unemployment will ensue wherever this happens: all the workers already in employment will retain their jobs, though all of them will work fewer hours.

This argument receives confirmation from the debate on the Phillips curve. As a rule, a decreasing Phillips curve entails that unemployment and inflation are two antithetical ills and that there is no way of reducing one without increasing the other. And as inflation is always perceived as a danger, it has long been customary to shape monetary policies geared towards controlling inflation even at the cost of rises in unemployment. As a result, it is possible to argue that unemployment is often the effect of economic policies which drive up unemployment for the sake of inhibiting inflation.

From here it follows that one major advantage of a system of cooperative firms is the non-existence of a Phillips curve. In the absence of wages, any rise in incomes would reduce unemployment without driving up monetary wages and prices in their wake. And in a conflict-free context the government would be in a position to shape both expansionist monetary and fiscal measures and employment-boosting policies without igniting the social conflicts that trigger inflation.

With respect to structural unemployment, the question to be answered is whether the claim that due to the traditional investment problems of cooperatives the job-creation potential of a system of cooperatives would lag behind that of a capitalistic system is to be endorsed (see Pejovich 1975, pp. 262ff.; Furubotn & Pejovich 1970a, 1970b; Furubotn 1976, 1980). Addressing this point at some length in the above-mentioned publications, I reached the conclusion that the underinvestment hypothesis is unwarranted.

I gave a thorough analysis of the issue in the publications mentioned above and concluded that hypothesis of the investment deficit cannot be proven by any hard evidence. However, it is worth touching at least on one argument which can be dealt with in fairly simple terms. In situations where the prevailing technological standard is given and the two types of firms have comparable investment opportunities, worker-run firms would outperform their capitalistic twins even in terms of investment volumes since the absence of labour costs (or, rather, the fact that their labour costs are not posted to the accounts as payroll expenses, but only measured in terms of the partners' work inputs) would scale up their marginal efficiency to levels at which they would outperform their capitalistic twins even in terms of investment volumes. Hence, unemployment is expected to decline in a self-managed system (see, inter alia, Estrin 1985; Smith & Rothbaum 2013, pp. 4–7).

Insofar as these arguments are well grounded, it must come as a surprise that intellectuals give little attention to economic democracy despite such a great benefit as a steep decline in unemployment.

6 INCOME DISTRIBUTION IN DEMOCRATIC FIRMS

The productivity gains associated with cooperation are likely to boost worker incomes above the levels prevailing in capitalistic systems. The question is: will income distribution in democratic firms prove to be more or less fair?

As is known, in the theoretical producer cooperative model the profits reported by the firm are apportioned among the worker-partners based on 'coefficients', i.e. pre-fixed percentage shares which are centrally determined (and which in individual firms may be adjusted to remunerate some of the workers for more qualified production inputs). And there are reasons to assume that the socially determined distribution pattern substituted for the current market-determined pattern will bring about a fairer social order (see Castoriadis 1975).[54]

The 'sacrifice-based criterion' is a socially determined distribution method which was originally theorised by Albert and Hahnel in numerous essays and subsequently analysed and discussed, among others, by Panayotakis (2009). In our estimation, though, this criterion should at least be complemented with the principle that each individual is to be accountable for the actions and tasks associated with his/her position.

In a worker-controlled firm system, differences in pay levels will be observed within one and the same cooperative and between different firms. Intra-firm income differences produced by the application of centrally fixed coefficients are socially determined by definition, while the higher pay levels granted to certain categories of workers in exchange for special work inputs should be fixed by the workers themselves at their meetings. In this case, as the workers must have regard to the conditions prevailing in the market, it is more appropriate to say that the resulting coefficients are socially determined just in part, since the social essence of the decisions made by the government on the one hand and by the partners on the other is attenuated – though not entirely nullified – by external market pressures.

Are there grounds for assuming that socially determined distribution coefficients will help reduce inequality?

In point of fact, supply and demand do not obey the same rationale. Whereas demand for labour fluctuates in accordance with the conditions prevailing in markets and with corporate requirements (firms hire fresh workers according to need), supply is not solely determined by market factors, varies over considerably longer time spans and is therefore much less volatile. Accordingly, the prices of the production factors are not

---

[54] The two alternative distribution models discussed by Panico (2015, pp. 96–7) and other authors differ from each other because they respectively emphasise material constraints versus historical and conventional factors. Distribution patterns are held to be mainly market-determined in capitalistic systems and socially determined in a democratic firm system.

determined by the law of supply and demand, as are those of commodities. In a system of cooperative firms, Krugman wrote (2009, p. 7),
'institutions, norms, and the political environment matter a lot more for
the distribution of income' and 'impersonal market forces matter less'
than economic manuals might lead you to believe (see also, inter alia,
Fleetwood 2006; DiQuattro 2011, pp. 533–7).

Let us assume that the distribution coefficients of a cooperative system
are determined by the social choices made by parliament irrespective of
the conditions prevailing in markets. A priori, there is no evidence to
back up the assumption that a socially determined distribution pattern,
once put in place, would level out demand and supply for any category of
workers. But what would happen in a cooperative system in the event of
disequilibrium in a single labour market?

When supply for a given job description exceeds demand, firms will be
able to recruit personnel with the most suitable qualifications and the
long-term unemployed will have no way out but to switch to different
jobs. Time series analysis of labour market trends has shown that young
people in search of a first job tend to shun those qualifications for which
supply systematically exceeds demand and that even in times of excess
labour demand firms have difficulty finding workers with the requisite
qualifications. In the long run, however, the market develops its natural
response, in terms of inducing the unemployed to choose those job
descriptions for which employment prospects are greatest.

In point of fact, due to the combined effects of the educational system
and the practice of recruitment by means of competitive examinations
such spontaneous market responses will not entirely cancel the socially
determined nature of distribution. By its very nature, this recruitment
system is a tool that balances out labour supply and demand. And the role
played by the educational system in determining the professional choices
of the young is well known and need not be entered upon here. In many
respects, the educational system and recruitment by competitive examination are designed to attain the same goal.[55] In other words, if the public
hand regulates labour supply in such a way as to determine the desired
adjustments to demand, the pay rates of the factors can be fixed at levels
that social conscience will perceive as fair.[56] And the social conscience of

---

[55]   The idea that distribution may be socially determined is at the basis of the
movement for participatory economics promoted by Albert (see Albert 2003).

[56]   Departing from this approach, Miller (see 1984, chs 6 and 7) maintains
that in a self-managed firm system distribution is determined by the market, but
that suitable corrective actions by the State might raise its level of social
acceptability well beyond that prevailing in capitalist systems.

individuals working in a system where capitalists have no say tends to develop in the direction of egalitarianism.

All this said, it is fair to admit that the above objection is hardly strong enough to reverse the conclusion that distribution will be more egalitarian in a system of cooperatives than it is under capitalism.

Before we conclude our analysis of distribution, it is worth mentioning the weighty objection that workers expected to take all the risks associated with production may not be fully satisfied with incomes fluctuating in accordance with the changing fortunes of their firms (see, for instance, Ben-Ner 1987 and 1988, pp. 295–6). To refute this objection, it is possible to argue that the best way to organise a democratic firm is to fix the pay rates of the partners at levels enabling the firm to report a surplus, to allocate the undivided surplus to a reserve and to use the relevant funds to offset falls in revenues possibly caused by downturns in business.

A closing and fairly obvious observation is that even in situations where distribution coefficients are socially determined, the State would nonetheless be called upon to play a part, for example by using taxation, fiscal incentives and subsidy policies to correct glaring inequalities (just as happens in capitalist systems).[57]

Concluding, we cannot subscribe to the widely shared assumption that even in a system of worker-controlled firms the law of markets would necessarily perpetuate those appalling inequalities which to date, more than ever, afflict humanity (see Derrida 1993, p. 110).[58]

7 INTERNAL CONTROL AND FIRM SIZE IN A DEMOCRATIC FIRM SYSTEM

One of the reasons why the 'one man one vote' principle is a major plus point of a worker-managed firm system is its potential for reducing systematic interfirm control. The cross-holding structure of group companies is, indeed, both anti-democratic and extremely unfair because it enables holders of relatively small stakes to control large business sectors and creates the assumption for the holding company to appropriate the

---

[57]   Whereas an interesting book by Dunn (2005) contrasts markets as the domain of egoism with democracy as the domain of equality, our attempt, in this book, has been to show that economic democracy would tend to reduce the sharp inequalities that are typically observed in capitalist systems.

[58]   The top executives in major US corporations sometimes draw paychecks in hundreds of millions of dollars, 300–400 times the pay of their employees.

profits of any of its subsidiaries by simply passing a majority resolution to this effect.

To a large extent, the dark shadow cast over world politics by the business world is one of the effects of the proliferation of multinational corporations, and the growing political power of firms is the main driving force behind the advancement of post-democracy. An additional advantage of an all-cooperatives system is hence the potential of lesser external firm control to sweep away multinational corporations from the business scene.[59]

At this point, it is worth raising the question whether less systematic interfirm control is likely to scale up the size of cooperatives above the present-day average size of capitalistic business enterprises.

Vanek laid considerable emphasis on the tendency of cooperatives to keep the size of their firms to scale with those of their production units (see Vanek 1970, p. 273). Upon reaching the dimensional optimum of its production unit, a capitalistic company feels encouraged to implement plant enlargements and upgrades on the assumption that this will generate comparable rises in profits; and this is how monopolies arise. In contrast, a cooperative will consider plant upgrades only in connection with the entry of new members and leave per capita incomes roughly unaltered. It is this that accounts for the differences in scale between capitalistic companies and cooperative firms.[60]

In the opinion of Gordon (1976), the main driving force behind the growing industrial concentration levels typical of capitalistic economies is not the prospect of securing economies of scale, but the process he terms 'qualitative efficiency': the aim of the ruling class to keep in check the working class and exercise full control over production. Indeed, capital concentration makes for tighter capitalistic control over production and leaves workers less and less scope for opposing employer decisions. It is the typical response of the ruling class to the struggle of labour for fairer income distribution patterns. This opinion is another explanation for the differences in scale between capitalistic companies and cooperative firms.

The benefits of the lower industrial concentration levels observed in cooperative systems include a downward trend in advertising expenditure (see Steinherr 1975) and an appreciable drop in transport costs: if nine firms operate in a given industrial sector in place of a single monopolist

---

[59]   Hence the comment of Crouch (2003) that this insight would have induced first-generation revolutionaries to campaign for the abolition of capitalism.

[60]   Authors attaching major importance to this characteristic of cooperative firms include Barreto (2011).

– Vanek computed (2006, p. 18) – the distance to be covered in supplying consumers assumed to be evenly distributed in space will decline by one third of the previous total.

Hence, the smaller average size of cooperatives versus capitalistic firms results in a number of advantages for a labour-managed firm system. And in Vanek's view this is a very important strong point of such a system and, arguably, one whose scope is far from confined to the domain of economic theory (Vanek 1993, p. 90).

8 REDUCED BANKRUPTCY RISKS IN DEMOCRATIC FIRMS

As mentioned before, minimal insolvency risks are a major strong point of a system of cooperative firms. Companies face insolvency when their costs exceed revenues. Hence, the absence of the largest cost item – wages and salaries – would greatly help confine risks of insolvency in a democratic firm system.

An additional argument is relevant in this connection: if the pay rates of a firm fall below the average level for the system, the partners will tend to leave. However, considering the aversion to the entry of outsiders postulated by the theoretical model of cooperatives, finding better-paying jobs will be all but easy. Hence, on occasion the benefits stemming from minimal insolvency risks in an all-cooperatives system may be offset by the need to put up with lower incomes.

On closer analysis, the downward trend in insolvencies is the result of a major difference between capital- and employee-managed firms: in the former, workers take precedence over capital providers since they cash their wages and salaries on a monthly basis; in the latter, the members participate in the 'residual' and, although this may be paid out in monthly instalments as well, it is determined after the whole of the firm's costs, including capital charges, have been duly settled.

In other words, it is possible to argue that the lower bankruptcy risks faced by worker-run firms are the result of the fact that those holding job relations in these firms would cease being privileged creditors entitled to be satisfied before other creditors in the event of bankruptcy proceedings. Since they are partners, these workers carry the risk and limited liability for a company failure on their shoulders.

Our arguments in support of low bankruptcy frequency – we must add – are only relevant to the theoretical cooperative model in which workers earn variable incomes. In actual fact, in most existing cooperatives the members are paid fixed wages and salaries.

In a system where incomes may be zeroed workers must evidently enjoy some measure of protection, but this goal calls for state intervention into the economy.[61]

The remote bankruptcy risks of cooperatives are interrelated with more remote risks of dismissal. A cooperative may respond to declining demand by reducing the working hours of its workers instead of laying off part of its workforce. On the one hand, it is this that explains why cooperative firms rarely face bankruptcy even in situations of excess headcount and/or drops in income; on the other, it is possible to argue that the low destaffing levels typical of cooperatives can be traced to the lower insolvency risks run by such firms. Hence, one advantage flowing from the reduced insolvency risks run by employee-managed firms is to make jobs in cooperatives safer and last longer. (These points are discussed at length in Smith & Rothbaum 2013, pp. 4–7.)

9 CONCLUSION

In Musgrave's approach (see Musgrave 1986, p. 453), a commodity is classed as a merit good (as opposed to a demerit good) if its production is concordantly rated as beneficial both by its direct users and by the community at large. Accordingly, each newly founded democratic firm can be categorised as a merit good if it generates benefits for its workers, strips capitalists of their power through the enforcement of the 'one man one vote' principle, helps cool down inflation, positively influences the personalities of its members and produces any of the additional advantages discussed in this chapter.

The categorisation of the democratic firm as a merit good explains why a wait-and-see policy would be a mistake. In a 'free competition' context, cooperatives might fail to assert themselves in their own right and lose out to capital-managed businesses because entrepreneurs planning to set up new firms or reorganise existing ones have little incentive to opt for the cooperative form. Inasmuch as this is true and if democratic firms are actually merit goods, the task of furthering their growth cannot be left to private initiative.

Deploring the narrow scope of a great many policy decisions, Rawls remarked that efficiency considerations are but one, and often a relatively

---

[61] The argument that bankruptcies are an exception among employee-managed firms (also for reasons other than those highlighted in this paper) is supported by empirical evidence (see Ben-Ner 1988; Stauber 1989; and Dow 2003, pp. 226–8).

minor basis of decision, and spoke out against the tendency of society to 'acquiesce without thinking in the moral and political conception implicit in the *status quo* or leave things to be settled by how contending social and economic forces happen to work themselves out' (Rawls 1971, p. 229). He expressed the hope that specialists in economic policy would at long last broaden their horizons. These are convincing opinions.

Concluding, as soon as cooperatives are categorised as merit goods, it follows quite naturally that any government, whatever its political-economic orientation, should make it its task to further the growth of a democratic firm system by enforcing tax or credit benefits for this purpose. On this point, though, Dow (2003, p. 75) has objected that nothing can prevent sceptics from arguing that the sheer level of social spending that would be required to fund the growth of the cooperative movement is barely commensurate with the benefits that can be expected from such a policy.[62]

My analysis of the plus points of cooperation should now be completed by an overview of the criticisms that cooperatives have traditionally come in for, but as these criticisms are dealt with elsewhere, the reader is referred to my previous work in which I addressed this subject (see, for example, Jossa 2014a, chs 3–5).

---

[62] Jacobsson et al. (2007, p. 762) have argued that the concept of merit good, though well established within economic science, is devoid of a sound theoretical basis.

5. Marx, Marxism and the cooperative movement

1 INTRODUCTION

On several occasions Marx declared himself strongly in favour of cooperative firms, maintaining that their generalised introduction would result in a new production mode. At different times in his life he even seems to have been confident that cooperatives would eventually supplant capitalistic firms altogether. As for Lenin, in a 1923 paper entirely devoted to the analysis of cooperation he went so far as to equate it with socialism at large. More precisely, in this article he described cooperation as an important organisational step in the transition to socialism and spelt out the idea that 'cooperation is socialism' (Lenin 1923). Notwithstanding this, ever since the time of the Paris Commune the cooperative movement has received little attention from Marxists.

From my perspective, this scant attention for the cooperative movement is due at least in part to the kind of cooperative – a firm in which workers are 'their own capitalists' (Marx 1894, p. 571) – that has asserted itself in history, because this leads to endorse the view that a system of producer cooperatives is not a genuine form of socialism.

Modern economic theory has shown that the pure cooperative is Vanek's LMF (see Vanek 1971a and 1971b), which does not self-finance and whose workers can consequently not be correctly described as 'their own capitalists'. And this consideration disproves the arguments of those Marxists who maintain that cooperatives are, by their very nature, an intermediate form between capitalism and socialism.

But what is the implication of these reflections?

In the light of Marx's view of cooperation as a new production mode which supersedes capitalism, Marxists can be subsumed within two distinct groups: those maintaining that in Marxian terms socialism must be identified with a system of self-managed firms and those still equating socialism with a state-planned command economy. And concerning these two groups it is possible to argue that 'both are aware that it is very difficult to find any consistent chain of authentic evidences indicating Marx's willingness to subscribe to either system' (see Selucky 1974, p. 49).

As is known, there is general consensus that Marx's writings, especially those about the economic system of the future, contain no doctrine, but only fragments (see Balibar 1993, p. 169) and that to Marx methodology was the only thing that mattered. In support of this view, Horvat (1969, p. 90) quotes a passage from Engels (1895) stating that 'all concepts of Marx are not doctrines but methods. They do not provide complete doctrines but starting points for further research and methods for that research.' With all the caution required by such considerations, I do think it possible, I repeat, to argue that an efficient system of producer cooperatives is a socialist order which may supersede capitalism in full harmony with Marxist thought.

Hence this chapter has a dual aim: firstly, to draw attention to a number of passages in which Marx explicitly extolled the cooperative movement and thereby confuted the wrong, but widely held assumption that Marx was inimical to the market and rejected cooperation as a production mode even for the transition period; secondly, to argue that the continuing neglect of Marxists both of the cooperative movement and of the passages from Marx (and Engels) that present a system of producer cooperatives as a new production mode can be traced back in part to the late emergence of an economic theory of producer cooperatives.

2 MARX'S AND ENGELS'S APPROACHES TO PRODUCER COOPERATIVES

An excerpt from Marx (1864) runs as follows:

> But there was in store a still greater victory of the political economy of labour over the political economy of property. We speak of the co-operative movement, especially of the co-operative factories raised by the unassisted efforts of a few bold 'hands'. The value of these great social experiments cannot be over-rated. By deed, instead of by argument, they have shown that production on a large scale, and in accord with the behest of modern science, may be carried on without the existence of a class of masters employing a class of hands; that to bear fruit, the means of labour need not be monopolised as a means of dominion over, and of extortion against, the labouring man himself; and that, like slave labour, like serf labour, hired labour is but a transitory and inferior form, destined to disappear before associated labour

plying its toil with a willing hand, a ready mind, and a joyous heart. (Marx 1864, p. 11)[63]

And in the third volume of *Capital* Marx argues:

> With the development of co-operatives on the workers' part, and joint-stock companies on the part of the bourgeoisie, the last pretext for confusing profit of enterprise with the wages of management was removed, and profit came to appear in practice as what it undeniably was in theory, mere surplus-value, value for which no equivalent was paid. (Marx 1894, pp. 513–14)

These passages are clear evidence of Marx's belief that a system of cooperative firms is not only feasible, but bound to assert itself in history and that it gives rise to a new production mode in which wage labour is swept away and the means of production – what economists term capital – would no longer be used to enslave workers. In such a system, workers would not only cease being exploited; they would feel free and happy to work for firms owned by them.

The system of producer cooperatives envisaged by Marx is a market system where workers become 'their own masters' (Mill 1871, p. 739) and where owners of capital are deprived of decision power concerning production activity. This system is 'in accord with the behest of modern science' and, at the same time, efficient – even more efficient than capitalism – because it entails a new production mode arising spontaneously within the older production mode and improving on it.[64]

This thesis is confirmed by other well-known passages from *Capital*, which clearly reveal how Marx looked upon a system based on producer cooperatives as a new production mode superior to that of capitalism. Immediately before the lines quoted below Marx had described joint-stock companies as a first step towards 'the abolition of capitalist private industry', though 'within the capitalist system itself' (Marx 1894, pp. 570–1), and further on we read:

> The co-operative factories run by workers themselves are, within the old form, the first examples of the emergence of a new form, even though they naturally reproduce in all cases, in their present organization, all the defects of

---

[63]   The 'Inaugural Address' of 1864 has been described as an attempt at theorising a political economy of labour (see Balibar 1993).

[64]   A great many authors have endorsed the notion that this new production mode will arise out of capitalism. Among them, let us mention C. Offe, who stresses the structural incompatibility, within capitalist society, of new subsystems or structural elements which functionally conflict with the logic of capital valorisation (see Offe 1972, ch. 3).

the existing system, and must reproduce them. But the opposition between capital and labour is abolished there, even if at first only in the form that the workers in association become their own capitalists, i.e. they use the means of production to valorise their labour. These factories show how, at a certain stage of development of the material forces of production, and of the social forms of production corresponding to them, a new mode of production develops and is formed naturally out of the old ... Capitalist joint-stock companies as much as cooperative factories should be viewed as transition forms from the capitalist mode of production to the associated one, simply that in one case the opposition is abolished in a negative way, and in the other in a positive way. (Marx 1894, pp. 571–2)

To understand why Marx emphasised the need to abolish wage labour even in a production system remaining purely mercantile in nature, we have to bear in mind that one main advantage of producer cooperatives (from the perspective of a critic of capitalism) is to realise economic democracy as an essential component of political democracy. Marx, Marxists and, generally, critics of society think of political democracy of today as merely formal, since power remains firmly in the hands of capitalists or, in other words, capital is still the economic power holding everything in its sway.

Engels's approach to producer cooperatives is illustrated by a few excerpts from his works. In 1874, he wrote: 'The tendency to literally sanctify the Commune is a sign that people are incapable of critical thinking!' (The 'Commune' mentioned in this quote, which appears in Haupt (1978, p. 56), is the 'Paris Commune' of 1871.) With an evident change of focus, however, in later years he argued that 'the Commune ordered a statistical tabulation of factories which had been closed down by the manufacturers, and the working out of plans for the carrying on of these factories by workers formerly employed in them', and that (p. 23) the Commune's decrees concerning economic affairs were mainly drafted by Proudhonians, supporters of worker management (from the introduction to Marx 1871, p. 19). Although 'competition, division of labor and private property' were positive 'economic forces', he added (p. 24), in the awareness that the Commune 'could not manage with the old state machine', the working class had to 'do away with the old repressive machinery previously used against itself' in an effort to safeguard 'its only just conquered supremacy' (p. 24). Further on in the same work (p. 27), Engels drew the conclusion that the replacement of the former state power with a new and fully democratic state is described in detail in the third section of *The Civil War*, where Marx spelt out that actually the state 'is nothing but a machine for the oppression of one class by another ... in the democratic republic no less than in the monarchy' (1871, p. 27).

Engels's introduction ends with the following concluding remarks: 'Of late, the Social-Democratic philistine has once more been filled with wholesome terror at the words: Dictatorship of the Proletariat. Well and good, gentlemen, do you want to know what this dictatorship looks like? Look at the Paris Commune. That was the Dictatorship of the Proletariat.'

The emphasis on the Commune's decision to transfer corporate management powers to the workers and the definition of the State as a machine for the oppression of one class by another are evidence that by 1891 Engels had ceased endorsing centralised planning and had come to believe that socialism, the dictatorship of the proletariat, boiled down to worker management.

3 WHY DID MARX ASSIGN A MAJOR ROLE TO COOPERATION?

The cooperative system Marx had in mind was a market system which made workers 'their own masters' (Mill 1871, p. 739) and stripped capital owners of their one-time power to make decisions in matters of production. In Marx's view, such a system was 'in accord with the behest of modern science' and even more efficient than capitalism: a new production mode which was bound to arise spontaneously within the older system and ultimately supplant it.

Quite a lot of Marxists are firmly convinced that this new mode of production will arise right within the capitalist order. Among them is Offe, who describes capitalistic society as a system characterised by escalating structural imbalances caused by the emergence of new structural elements or partial systems which clash with the logic of capital valorisation (see Offe 1972, p. 65).[65] The step forward that the creation of cooperatives marks on the road towards economic freedom – Marx clarified (Offe 1972) – is the highest degree of freedom attainable within the realm of necessity, i.e. as long as resources are scarce and man is obliged to work in order to maintain and reproduce life.

According to Marx, political democracy as connotes bourgeois society emancipates man within the political sphere, but not in the material relationships he entertains during his life on earth. In this context, he appears to be 'corrupted by the whole organization of our society' and acts as a man who has lost himself, has become a prey to alienation and

---

[65] Unlike him and Marx himself, Sweezy holds that socialism will not arise right within capitalistic society (see Sweezy 1971; see also, for the opposite view, Basso 1971, pp. 819ff.).

has been 'handed over to the rule of inhuman conditions and elements' (Marx 1844b, p. 90). This leads to the conclusion that Marx thought of the emancipation of man within his economic relationships as a means of purging political democracy of the evils associated with top-down command in enterprises and, consequently, turning political democracy into a reality.[66]

4 MARX ON COOPERATIVES AS A STARTING POINT FOR STATE PLANNING AND THE ROLE OF THE STATE

In Marxian terms, cooperative production is not an end to itself, but 'a lever for uprooting the economic foundations upon which rests the existence of classes' (Marx 1871, p. 334) and a means of organising the domestic production system in line with an all-inclusive plan. This can be inferred from Marx's comments on the experience of the Paris Commune:

> The Commune, they exclaim, intends to abolish property, the basis of civilization! Yes, gentlemen, the Commune intended to abolish that class-property which makes the labour of the many the wealth of the few. It aimed at the expropriation of the expropriators. It wanted to make individual property a truth by transforming the means of production, land and capital, now chiefly the means of enslaving and exploiting labour, into mere instruments of free and associated labour ... But this is Communism, 'impossible' Communism! Why, those members of the ruling class who are intelligent enough to perceive the impossibility of continuing the present system – and they are many – have become the obtrusive and full-mouthed apostles of co-operative production. If cooperative production is not to remain a sham and a mare; if it is to supersede the capitalist system; if the united co-operative societies are to regulate national production upon a common plan, thus taking it under their control, and putting an end to the constant anarchy and periodical convulsions which are the fatality of Capitalist production – what else, gentlemen, would it be but Communism, 'possible' Communism? (Marx 1871, p. 335)

In Marx's view, the Paris Commune 'supplied the Republic with the basis of really democratic institutions' and could therefore be looked upon as 'the political form, at last discovered, under which to work out the economical emancipation of Labour' (Marx 1871, p. 334). It brought

---

[66]   See, inter alia, Baglioni 1995, p. 89.

about 'the expropriation of expropriators'. And Engels added that 'the Paris Commune demanded that the workers should manage cooperatively the factories closed down by manufacturers' (Engels 1886, p. 389).

In this connection, Easton has rightly argued that Marx 'sees co-operatives as the economic corollary of the "really democratic institution" of the Commune' and that 'in his view of the state he sees cooperative production not as a matter of simple negation of the existing capitalist system, but rather as a dialectical transcendence that negates as it preserves' (Easton 1994, p. 162).

In his critique of Bakunin's *Statehood and Anarchy*, Marx himself provided the following explanation of his contention that the proletariat was to organise itself in such a way as to become the dominant class:

> It means that the proletariat, instead of fighting individual instances against the economically privileged classes, has gained sufficient strength and organization to use general means of coercion in its struggle against them; but it can only make use of such economic means as abolish its own character as wage labourer and hence as a class; when its victory is complete, its rule too is therefore at an end, since its class character will have [disappeared]. (See Marx 1875b, p. 519)

This passage illustrates how the proletariat may acquire the strength required to abolish wage labour, but in today's democratic societies, where workers' interests are endorsed by political parties capable of winning the consensus of the majority of the people, there are no reasons to deny that the 'general means of coercion' needed to contrast the economically privileged classes could well be a single act of parliament prohibiting wage labour altogether. When asked if private property could be abolished by peaceful means, Engels replied that 'it is to be desired that this could happen, and Communists certainly would be the last to resist it' (Engels 1847a, p. 349), but he added that such peaceful means were being opposed by the class in power and that the use of violence to deviate progress from the direction in which it was heading was likely to induce the oppressed proletariat to fight a revolution in order to acquire its freedom (Engels 1847a, pp. 349–50).

The work from which these passages have been taken, namely the *Principles of Communism*, was written at roughly the same time as Marx and Engels's *Manifesto* and Engels explicitly emphasised that differences between the two texts arose from the fact that in the *Manifesto* their shared ideas about the road towards communism had only been expounded to the extent it was thought expedient to make them public (see Engels 1847a, p. 114, as quoted in Lawler 1994).

The part democracy can play in fostering the advent of socialism is also suggested in the following excerpt from Engels (1895, pp. 515–16):

> The Communist *Manifesto* had already proclaimed the winning of universal suffrage, of democracy, as one of the first and most important tasks of the militant proletariat, and Lassalle had again taken up this point. Now that Bismarck found himself compelled to introduce this franchise as the only means of interesting the mass of the people to his plans, our workers immediately took it in earnest and sent August Bebel to the first, constituent Reichstag. And from that day on they have used the franchise in a way which has paid them a thousandfold and has served as a model to the workers of all countries.

However, according to our authors, the contention that cooperatives can assert themselves in a capitalistic system thanks to State aid is only applicable to situations in which workers have already attained political power, for neither Marx nor Engels believed that the State could be expected to help workers in their effort to 'expropriate expropriators' in a society in which the bourgeoisie wields power.

In the *Critique of the Gotha Programme* Marx rejects both Lassalle's idea of the State and his belief that workers' emancipation should be brought about by a system of state-aided producer cooperatives. Based on the Gotha programme, a means of solving social problems was to demand State aid to fund the establishment of producer cooperatives under the democratic control of the mass of the working people. Marx disagreed on this point by objecting

> that the workers' desire to establish the conditions for cooperative production on a social scale, and first of all on a national scale, in their own country, only means that they are working to transform the present conditions of production, and it has nothing in common with the foundation of co-operative societies with state aid. (Marx 1875a, pp. 93–4)

Otherwise – Marx argued – socialism would be established through State action – in stark contrast with the central idea of scientific socialism that workers will only achieve emancipation through their own efforts. If workers were to require the support of the State for their revolutionary movement, they would thereby only reveal their 'full consciousness that they neither rule nor are ripe for rule!' (Marx 1875a, p. 93).[67]

---

[67] Elsewhere we are told that the *Programme* 'shows that its socialist ideas are not even skin-deep, in that, instead of treating existing society … as the basis of the existing state … it treats the state rather as an independent entity that possesses its own intellectual, ethical and libertarian bases' (Marx 1875a, p. 94).

Accordingly, Marx concludes that 'as far as the present co-operative societies are concerned, they are of value only insofar as they are the independent creations of workers and not *protégés* either of the governments or of the bourgeoisie' (Marx 1875a, p. 94).

The foregoing reflections suggest the conclusion that from the perspective of Marx and Engels a gradual growth of the cooperative movement 'fostered by national means' could even come about by peaceful means, though only after workers have acquired a majority of the seats in parliament.[68] The egalitarian implications of such a thesis are evident.

Let me repeat that Marx's pro-cooperation attitude is to be viewed in the light of his fundamental belief that neither legal relationships nor political organisation systems can be properly understood in their own right, since they have their roots in material production relationships, i.e. in that web of relations that Hegel termed 'civil society' (see Marx 1859, p. 262). As mentioned before, a 'civil society' organised as a system of producer cooperatives is one where capital is no longer the economic power holding everything in its sway and where the wealthy are prevented from imposing their will upon the rest of the population. The commodities manufactured by democratically managed cooperatives cease to be 'in the first place an external object' unrelated to work (see Marx 1867, p. 125 and Holloway 2001, p. 66), and turn into the product of free choices made by workers in association.

In the light of the reflections developed so far, the question as to why Marxists and, generally, the left continued to give little attention to the cooperative movement still remains to be answered.[69]

---

[68] In the *Manifesto* we read that the first step in the revolution by the working class is to raise the proletariat to the position of ruling class, to win the battle of democracy (Marx & Engels 2014 [1848], p. 504). And in Engels's introduction to *The Class Struggle in France* we read: 'The irony of world history turns everything upside down. We, the "revolutionaries", the "over-throwers", we are thriving far better on legal methods than on illegal methods and overthrow' (Engels 1895, p. 522). Consequently we agree with Sowell (1985, p. 210), according to whom 'Marx and Engels had envisioned a long mass struggle for power, extending over decades, during which the proletariat would acquire the experience and clarity needed to become a politically effective force in a democratic society'.

[69] According to Bettelheim (1974, p. 489), the writings of Marx and Engels in which cooperation is assigned 'great importance' have sunk into 'oblivion' (see Bettelheim 1974, p. 489; see also, Bukharin 1982, pp. 102–104, 110–21, 142, 184).

5 LENIN AND PRODUCER COOPERATIVES

According to Lewin (1974, p. 512), Lenin's political views were not shaped by a precise theoretical principle, but tended to change in accordance with developments in the prevailing political situation. Indeed, an article that Lenin published during the very last year of his life (and which after the advent of Stalin was completely forgotten) clearly reveals that he had gained an awareness of the advantages associated with a system of cooperative firms to the point of claiming that such a system fully coincided with socialism.[70]

But six years back, on the assumption that the main aim of a socialist system was setting up a well-planned economy coordinated by a central authority for the benefit of the people at large (see Carr 1953, p. 487) or mindful of the risk that the transfer of firm management powers to workers might deprive the Bolsheviks of their long-awaited political hegemony (see Massari 1974, p. 178), he had boldly proclaimed that the Bolsheviks were suggesting 'nothing like the ridiculous transfer of the railways to the railwaymen or the tanneries to the tanners' (Lenin 1917c, p. 14),[71] but his 1923 article is evidence of a thorough change of focus.

In the 1923 article, Lenin wrote that the burgeoning role of the cooperative movement within the framework of the 'New Economic Policy' (NEP) was a clear indication that the task, at once simple and complex, that lay before them was to organise the bulk of the population into cooperatives. In essence, he wrote, what we actually need is 'to organize the population of Russia in cooperative societies on a sufficiently large-scale' (see Lenin 1923, p. 1797).

However, on reaching the conclusion that the task before them was to organise the bulk of the population into cooperatives, Lenin simultaneously realised that his views concerning the very nature of socialism had undergone radical change. Now, he argued, 'we are entitled to say that the mere growth of cooperation ... is identical with the growth of socialism',

---

[70] Pérotin (2006, pp. 296–7) reports that many cooperatives were established during period of social unrest or political change, for instance during the 1930 and 1848 revolutions, after the establishment of the Paris Commune, during the strikes proclaimed in the years 1893–4 and 1905–6, by Popular Front governments in 1936 and in the aftermaths of the two great wars.

[71] Chiarini's argument that following Lenin's advent to power in 1917 the reformist plan to establish a worker-run firm system, despite its extremist colouring, had no more room in his political creed (see Chitarin 1973, p. 62) is evidence that this author is of one mind with Lewin.

and 'at the same time, we have to admit that there has been a radical modification of our whole outlook on socialism' (Lenin 1923, p. 1802).[72]

Cooperation, he continued, 'which we formerly ridiculed as huckstering', constitutes the social regime we have to support by any means. As soon as those advocating a transition to communism seize power, 'cooperation under our conditions nearly always coincides fully with socialism' (see Lenin 1923, pp. 1797–803).

Accordingly, this article is evidence that by 1923 Lenin had come to think of cooperation not as a component of the NEP, but as the regime that better than any other could help establish a real and proper socialist order.[73] We look at cooperation, he wrote, from a perspective which has so far been underrated, i.e. 'the transition to the new system by means that are the simplest, easiest and most acceptable to the peasant' (p. 1798):

> But this again is a fundamental importance. It is one thing to draw out fantastic plans for building socialism through all sorts of workers associations, and quite another to learn to build socialism in practice in such a way that every small peasant could take part in it. That is the very stage we have now reached. (p. 1798)

As cooperation 'is adjustable to the level of the most ordinary peasant', at last we are in a position to argue that 'there are no other devices needed to advance to socialism' (p. 1799). Consequently in Lenin's later approach cooperation is described as the appropriate road, at last discovered, leading to the edification of socialism.[74] 'Owing to the special features of our political system cooperation acquires an altogether exceptional significance', so much so that it is possible to say – let us repeat this – that it 'coincides fully with socialism' (pp. 1801–802).

To conclude, by 1923 Lenin had ceased believing that central planning was the prerequisite for the attainment of communism. 'Our state

---

[72] It is worth mentioning that back in 1918 Lenin wrote (1918, p. 227): 'Until workers' control has become a fact, until the advanced workers have organised and carried out a victorious and ruthless crusade against the violators of this control, or against those who are careless in matters of control, it will be impossible to pass from the first step (from workers' control) to the second step towards socialism, i.e., to pass on to workers' regulation of production'.

[73] Lenin described the NEP as 'State capitalism' and held it to be superior to war communism (see Lenin 1921a, 1921b, pp. 200–201, 1922a and 1922b, pp. 1745–6). Cooperation is doubtless superior to the NEP and amounts to socialism proper also for this reason.

[74] Accordingly, we do not share the claim (see Hegedüs 1980, pp. 538–9) that in Lenin's theoretical approach the role of state-owned firms in realising the values of socialism by far exceeds that of cooperatives.

apparatus is so deplorable, not to say wretched that we must first think very carefully how to combat its defects' (Lenin 1923, p. 1815). As regards the transition to socialism, Lenin was greatly impressed by the experience of the Paris Commune and, more specifically, by a decree ruling that 'all factories and workshops abandoned or shut down by their owners were to be turned over to associations of workers that were to resume production' (Lenin 1957–70, vol. 17, p. 126).

6 A DIALECTICAL APPROACH TO THE ISSUE OF THE TRANSITION TO SOCIALISM

In Marxist theory, cooperatives are held to perpetuate some of the main defects of capitalism, in particular the anarchical nature of production and, generally, all the shortcomings of a market economy; but is it possible to think of cooperatives as the typical institutions of the transition to communism?

To shed light on Marx and Engels's notion of transition we have to contrast a dialectical view of the passage from one form of society to another with a 'nihilistic' stance envisaging the total destruction of the previous social order. The latter view is held by all those maintaining that the rise of the working class to power should be promptly followed by the establishment of a new social order with characteristics diametrically opposed to those that Marx and Engels criticised in capitalism: the division of society into classes, with masters exploiting the working class, and the anarchical nature of production (see Engels 1882b, p. 285). The new social order to be established forthwith after the abolition of capitalism would consequently have to be a classless society with centralised planning: the order that the Soviet Union established following the rise of Stalin to power and which finally collapsed in 1989.

This view of transition, which Lawler described as 'nihilistic', goes back to some of Marx and Engels's own writings, including the *Manifesto of the Communist Party*, where the task assigned to the proletariat following the attainment of power is 'to centralise all instruments of production in the hands of the State' (Marx & Engels 1848, p. 504).[75]

---

[75] A few passages in which Marx seems to share a 'nihilistic' view of transition can probably be traced to the fact that in his early years Marx was deeply influenced by Feuerbach, who opposed the Hegelian 'negation of the negation' concept in that he equated it with a return to teleology (see MacGregor 1984, pp. 246–7).

In *Antidühring* Engels (1878, pp. 269–70) writes: 'With the seizing of the means of production by society, production of commodities is done away with, and, simultaneously, the mastery of the product over the producer'.[76]

On closer analysis, though, Marx and Engels's idea of transition is a dialectic view in which the way capitalism is negated depends both on what is negated and on the end to be attained.[77] This means that those in power must guarantee the transfer of some traits of the older social order into the new one. In this dialectic view, private property is a step or stage in the evolution of humankind, not a form of cancer that must be eradicated to enable the healthy members of the social organism to assert themselves (Lawler 1994, p. 188).[78] Far from entailing a regression, socialism must ensure an advancement over capitalism just as it negates it; and with respect to the creation of material wealth, it must ensure levels of growth exceeding those of capitalism, rather than bring about a generalised level of poverty, however egalitarian.

The dialectic approach also necessitates thinking of the transition from the older to the newer social order as an extended period of gradual adjustment, not as a short process in which the salient characteristics of capitalist society are negated at one stroke.[79]

---

[76] A 'nihilistic' rationale also seems to underlie Gramsci's argument that every revolution 'must necessarily break up and destroy the present social system in its entirety' and that 'nothing can be anticipated' concerning the way this new society will be organised (Gramsci 1919–20, p. 155).

[77] 'You must never look to the future without an awareness of your aims; nor will you gain an awareness of your aims without a correct appreciation of the reality from which you are starting out' (Mondolfo 1952, p. 111).

[78] In Gramsci's view, conversely, the error of reformism lies 'in the fact that – to avoid destroying the process altogether – the dialectic process must "mechanically subsume" the thesis within the related antithesis and that the process is consequently "conceived of" as one of never-ending, arbitrarily pre-fixed and mechanical reiteration' (Gramsci 1948, p. 185).

[79] Marx's acknowledgement of his debt to dialectical thinking is confirmed in a letter he wrote to Kugelmann on 6 March 1868: 'Hegel's dialectic is the basic form of all dialectic, but only after being stripped of its mystic form, and it is precisely this which distinguishes my method' (Marx 1868, p. 544). Dissenting from this view, Schumpeter argued that, while Marx's Hegelianism was certainly reflected in all his writings, it was a mistake to 'make it the master key to the system', for this meant 'to make a mistake and an injustice to Marx's scientific powers'. In his opinion, Marx 'enjoyed certain formal analogies which may be found between his and Hegel's argument', but 'this is all' (see Schumpeter 1976, pp. 9–10). Also Rosenthal (1988) has argued that dialectic will nowhere help understand Marx.

The contrast between these two different views of transition first surfaces in an early work such as the *Economic and Philosophical Manuscripts* of 1844 (1844a, pp. 294–5), which describes a coarse and material form of communism aimed 'to destroy everything which is not capable of being possessed by all as private property' and to oppose 'universal private property to private property'. In Marx's view, 'this type of Communism – since it negates the personality of man in every sphere – is but the logical expression of private property, which is this negation' (p. 295). It is born of envy and greed, because 'the thought of every piece of private property as such is at least turned against wealthier private property in the form of envy and the urge to reduce things to a common level' (p. 295).[80]

As mentioned above, the *Manifesto* includes reflections and arguments in support of both a nihilistic and a dialectic view of transition. One of the latter reads as follows: 'the distinguishing feature of Communism is not the abolition of property generally, but the abolition of bourgeois property' (Marx & Engels 1848, p. 498). And Marx and Engels made it clear that workers are entitled to the results of their work and that each of them is to be allowed to appropriate what he produces. Hence they argue: 'Communism deprives no man of the power to appropriate the products of society; all that it does is to deprive him of the power to subjugate the labour of others by means of such appropriation' (p. 500).

These excerpts are in line with the idea that the overthrow of capitalism coincides with the abolition of hired labour and that in a new social order born of the ashes of the older world the importance of

---

In contrast, based on the *Grundrisse* we are inclined to endorse Rosdolsky's argument that no academic critic should as much as approach Marx's economic work without a preliminary study of his method and its relationship with Hegel's because 'if Hegel's influence on Marx's *Capital* can be seen explicitly only in a few footnotes, the *Rough Draft* must be designated as a massive reference to Hegel, in particular to his *Logic*' (Rosdolsky 1971, p. xiii). Nonetheless, Marx's dialectic is by no means Hegel's (see Croce 1899, pp. 4–9; Hyppolite 1969, pp. 300–303; and Garaudy 1969, pp. 312–14).

On the role of dialectic in Marx, see also, Lukàcs (1971), dal Pra (1972), MacGregor (1984, ch. 8) and Fine (2001).

[80] The criticisms against this course and material form of communism are those levied in an early writing by Gobetti (1929): 'the means whereby Bolsheviks intend to translate this conception into action are, in essence, political, which means they reverse the traditional Marxian dependence of politics on economics and, by negating the evolutionary essence of Marxism out of sheer violence, they end up by generating an even more degenerated and harmful version thereof'.

producer cooperatives operating within the market springs from the abolition of the very possibility to hire the wage labour that capitalistic firms use.

An even more significant point is the gradual nature of the process whereby the old society will give way to the new social order – a notion set forth in numerous passages of the *Manifesto* including the following: 'The proletariat will use its political supremacy to wrest, by degrees, all capital from the bourgeoisie, to centralise all instruments of production in the hands of the State' (p. 504).

The stepwise nature of this process is also emphasised in Marx and Engels's programme for the period immediately after the rise of the working class to power. Among others, this programme includes the following measures (p. 505):

- the abolition of property in land;
- a heavy progressive income tax;
- the abolition of all rights of inheritance;
- the confiscation of property owned by rebels and emigrants;
- the concentration of credit and transport in the hands of the State;
- the nationalisation of an increasing number of firms.

The fact that Marx and Engels did not think of transformation as the instantaneous nationalisation of all means of production and simultaneous launch of an all-comprehensive centralised plan emerges even more clearly from *Principles of Communism*. There Engels argued that once in power, workers would create 'a democratic constitution' and that 'democracy would be quite useless to the proletariat if it were not immediately used as a means of carrying through further measures' – progressive income taxes, heavy inheritance and legacy taxes and the gradual expropriation of owners of land, buildings, railways and vessels, in part due to the competition of State industry and in part directly, against payment of compensation (Engels 1847a, pp. 350–1).

As Engels had just argued that private property was to be abolished 'only gradually' (Engels 1847a, p. 350), the above passage makes it clear that this gradual process was to be fuelled both by the 'spontaneous' mechanism of competition and by compensation payments by the State – in short, without recourse to revolutionary violence.[81] Nonetheless, Marx

---

[81] Nowhere in the works of Marx or Engels are there elements in support of the argument of Marković (1969) and others that only a very short transition period will prevent the process from degenerating into repression. By contrast, given the long period of time needed to break up the market relations established

sees it as natural, even inevitable, that upon seizing power workers oppressed by capitalism will embrace the nihilistic view of transition (see Marx 1844a, pp. 204–95; Lawler 1994, p. 189).

On the subject of the nihilistic view to the transition, let us add that while Marx and Engels certainly conceived of the plan as an antidote to the anarchical nature of the capitalistic market, they were thinking of a plan for abolishing the production of commodities and so not based on the law of value; in other words, they conceived of the dialectic market-plan opposition as an example of the conflict between necessity and freedom. In their view, therefore, the opposite of the capitalist market was not the socialist plan, which remains the realm of necessity, but the plan of a communist society, because 'the realm of freedom really begins only where labour determined by necessity and external expediency ends; it lies, by its very nature, beyond the sphere of material production proper' (see Marx 1894, pp. 958–9; see also Engels 1878, pp. 266–71 and Marx & Engels 1845–46, pp. 51–2 and 81).

The arguments set forth in this paragraph should have provided sufficient evidence that a system of cooperatives is hardly objectionable in Marxian terms. Being a market economy, from a Marxian perspective it must rather be looked upon as a transitional economic system.

7 THE LOGIC BEHIND MARXIST CRITICISMS OF COOPERATIVES

As cooperatives cannot be blamed for failing to do away with the market instantly, on what grounds did Marxists resolve not to rely on them for the transition to communism?

One reason behind the scant attention of Marxists for the cooperative movement to this day is the fact that Marx himself ceased to concern himself with cooperative firms following the collapse of the Paris Commune. And this may in turn be explained with the difficulties experienced by the cooperative movement from the 1870s onwards (see Bernstein 1899, pp. 149–52). Marxism has always been held to be a form of 'scientific socialism', a movement which in lieu of simply 'preaching' the advent of communism, theorises it as an inescapable event;[82] and an

---

in a socialist economy, most Marxists have rather endorsed the view that this transition period should be fairly long (see, among others, Baran & Sweezy 1966, pp. 336–7; Sweezy 1969 and Bettelheim 1969a, ch. 3).

[82] In Kautsky's view, in scientific socialism the emergence of a socialist order is looked upon as inescapable because both class struggle and the victory

unsuccessful movement will hardly be rated a proper vehicle for the establishment of communism. The cooperative production mode – Kautsky wrote – may only arise in a sparse and incomplete manner, without ever asserting itself as the dominant form (Kautsky 1892, p. 109).[83]

In the early twentieth century a well-known Italian Marxist endorsed much the same opinion when he argued that for some time Marx showed confidence in the cooperative firms that workers in association were running as 'their own capitalists', but that later on he lost such confidence; and he ascribed this loss of confidence to the collapse of many producer cooperatives between 1860 and 1870 and to Marx's own reappraisal of the very nature of the transition stage (see Leone 1902, p. 287). Thus it is possible, though not certain, that Marx lost faith in the cooperative movement.

More convincing is the argument that the scant attention of Marxists for the cooperative movement after a given point in time was due to Kautsky's and Lassalle's turn to statism. Marxists increasingly equated socialism with the nationalisation of production means and when, following the Bolshevik Revolution, a choice was to be made between State enterprises and cooperative firms, they systematically gave priority to the former over the latter (see, for all, Preobrazhensky 1926, pp. 17, 218ff. and 238ff.).

Still another explanation of the criticisms levied by Marxists against cooperation may be suggested by the following excerpt from the *Manifesto of the Communist Party* (2014 [1848], p. 513):

> We may cite Proudhon's *Philosophie de la misére* as an example of this form. The Socialistic bourgeois want all the advantages of modern social conditions without the struggles and dangers necessarily resulting therefrom. They desire the existing state of society minus its revolutionary and disintegrating elements. They wish for a bourgeoisie without a proletariat. The bourgeoisie naturally conceives the world in which it is supreme to be the best; and

---

of the proletariat are inevitable (Kautsky 1907, p. 202). However, although Tucker argued (in the *Introduction* to his 1961 book) that this view could no longer be held following the publication of the *Economic and Philosophical Manuscripts* in Russian (1927) and German (1932), the approach to Marxism as a view of the world in which socialism is inevitable is still far prevailing (see, among others, the articles of Altvater 1968, Poulantzas 1968 and Murgescu 1969, p. 196).

[83] In the estimation of Massari (1974, p. 101), the main reason why Marx initially opposed the cooperative movement is his unwillingness to admit that it is possible to overturn the existing production relations by means of piecemeal stepwise adjustments.

bourgeois Socialism develops this comfortable conception into various more or less complete systems.

These lines may justify the doubt that Marx and Engels thought of a system of producer cooperatives as a 'conservative or bourgeois form of Socialism'. However, restricting our analysis to this passage for the moment, is it possible to argue that a system of producer cooperatives is a society with 'a bourgeoisie without a proletariat' or with a proletariat and no bourgeoisie? Or, can this passage from the *Manifesto* be read as a criticism of producer cooperatives? Clearly, so long as we think of bourgeois society as a system characterised by capitalist production relations and dominated by the owners of production means who subjugate the class of proletarians[84] and picture to themselves the world in which they are supreme as one bound to last forever, these questions will have to be answered in the negative.[85]

Nonetheless, Beatrice Webb, Rodbertus and Bernstein spelt out in bold letters that cooperation can at most be equated with a middle way between capitalism and socialism, not with socialism proper (see Potter 1893 and Bernstein 1899, pp. 154–5).[86]

In my opinion, the late formulation of an economic theory of cooperation may be one further explanation of the scant attention of Marxists for cooperative firms. Ward's analysis, which was published in 1958, is the very first economic theorisation of producer cooperatives. Thus there is every reason to believe that existing cooperatives have not been organised in line with criteria of economic efficiency and that the late emergence of an economic theory of producer cooperatives may be at least in part responsible for the scant success of the cooperative movement (see Vanek 1971a and 1971b).

Discussing the distinction between WMFs and LMFs and the factors which determine that WMFs (unlike LMFs) are doomed to fail by their very nature (see below), Vanek argued (1971b, p. 187):

---

[84] The bourgeoisie is 'the class of the big capitalists, who in all advanced countries are in almost exclusive possession of the means of subsistence' (Engels 1847b, p. 100).

[85] In a recent book Screpanti has extensively discussed his thesis that 'the basic capitalistic institution is the contract of employment' (see Screpanti 2001, p. 258). If his theory holds true, a system of producer cooperatives has nothing to do with capitalism. See also, Screpanti (2002).

[86] In recent years, several authors have argued that an economic system where capitalists are dispossessed of capital while firms continue to operate freely in the market is not a socialist system; among them, see Roemer (1986, pp. 285–6).

> In my opinion ... the arguments presented hereafter are so powerful in explaining the shortcomings of traditional or conventional forms of producer cooperatives and participatory firms that they offer an ample explanation of the comparative failures of these forms in history ever since they were first conceived of by the writers of the eighteenth and nineteenth centuries. The development of this analysis was to me personally most gratifying. It had always puzzled me how it could have been possible that a productive organization based on cooperation, harmony of interests and the brotherhood of men, so appealing and desirable on moral and philosophical grounds, could have done so poorly when subjected to a practical test. It seems to be that we now have both an explanation and a way of remedy.

But there is more to this, for the late appearance of an economic theory of cooperation also points to ideological causes behind the scant interest of Marxists in the cooperative movement.

Defining cooperatives in his own (and Marx's) time in an 1865 work and discussing the distinctions made by economists between the main sources of wealth, land, capital and labour, Walras argued that individuals tend to accumulate ever greater quantities of all three types of wealth until, in due time, they gradually become owners of land, capital and labour. Carrying his point to extremes, Walras went so far as to describe economic progress as the road towards a fuller access of individuals to all categories of wealth and, in particular, of workers to the ownership of capital (Walras 1865, p. 14).

Accordingly he ascribed to cooperatives two distinctive elements:

(a) in terms of scope, a tendency towards creating venture capital which is indivisible because owned by all the members, and
(b) in terms of the source of such resources, the fact that this venture capital is formed of wage deductions. (See Walras 1865, pp. 5–6)

Based on the above, Walras maintained that the essence of cooperation could succinctly be described as a means of enabling workers to acquire capital through saving (p. 7).

Walras's analysis sheds light on the causes of the scant concern of Marxists with cooperation. As he theorised the approach to cooperation in his own and Marx's time better than any other, his arguments may both explain Marx's description of cooperatives as firms in which workers were 'their own capitalists' and why Marxists gradually adopted the view that a system of cooperatives would result in a sort of 'producer capitalism'. And there is little doubt that, insofar as a system of cooperatives is a form of capitalism, it may not be worthwhile fighting for it.

This provides an opportunity to stress how the contribution recently made by economists to the theory of cooperation may help disprove the criticisms of Marxists. Following the appearance of Ward's 1958 article, economists drew a distinction between two different types of cooperatives, WMFs and LMFs. The former, which are widespread in the Western world, self-finance and consequently do not strictly separate labour income from capital income; their members earn mixed incomes (from capital and work) in place of pure incomes from work. By contrast, LMFs are cooperatives which fund themselves with loan capital and consequently draw a clear-cut distinction between incomes from work and incomes from capital or property. And Vanek and others have produced in-depth analyses of the reasons – in the first place the need to avert underinvestment – as to why cooperatives should be LMFs.

For the purposes of this book the above distinction is decisive. If we describe the LMF as the 'ideal type' of producer cooperative, we are also in a position to show that cooperatives are truly socialist firms. There are three 'factors of production': land, capital and labour. Excluding land, which gradually lost importance following the Industrial Revolution, a firm setting out to operate in the market may choose between two organisational options: management by the owners of capital (or their representatives) or management by the workers themselves (or their representatives). In the former case it is a capitalistic firm, in the latter case it is a real and proper socialist firm.

Thus the producer cooperatives theorised by economists are not only non-capitalistic firms, but socialist firms proper, since compared to their capitalistic counterparts they effectively reverse the capital–labour relationship.[87] And this clearly entails that in genuine Marxian terms a system of cooperative firms would afford a major advancement over capitalism within a market economy.

In the light of this clarification, the excerpts in which Marx enthusiastically anticipates the advent of a system of cooperatives will promptly appear in the right perspective.

8　CONCLUSIONS

As late as 1886, Engels wrote (p. 389): 'My proposal envisages the introduction of cooperatives into existing production ... just as the Paris Commune demanded that the workers should manage cooperatively the

---

[87]　This subject is addressed in greater detail in Jossa and Cuomo 1997, pp. 144–6.

factories closed down by the manufacturers'; and he added that neither
Marx nor he himself had 'ever doubted that, in the course of the
transition to a wholly communist economy, widespread use would have
to be made of cooperative management as an intermediate stage'. Like
others quoted above, these passages lead us to endorse the conclusion of
Brachet, one of the earliest writers to have focused attention on Marx's
opinions on self-management: 'those holding socialism to be a system
where workers self-manage the production and distribution apparatuses
are perfectly in tune with Marxian thought on this point' (see Brachet
1975, p. 303; see also, among others, Damjanovic 1962; Bourdet 1974,
p. 49ff.; Selucky 1974; Pelikan 1977, p. 143ff.; Schweickart 1992; Lawler
1998; for a different opinion, see, inter alia, Ollman 1998, pp. 113–18).

At this point it is worth asking ourselves if we have adequately
accounted for the scant enthusiasm of Marxists for the cooperative
movement. As mentioned above, in our opinion an important reason for
this neglect is that existing cooperatives fit into the self-financing type
(WMFs) in which workers are 'their own capitalists' because this
corroborates the approaches of Beatrice Webb, Rodbertus and Bernstein,
according to whom cooperatives are, by their very nature, an intermediate
form between the capitalistic and socialistic firm and do not consequently
deserve being stoutly upheld by Marxists. Yet recent economic theoris-
ations on producer cooperatives have cut these criticisms at the root. As
Vanek has argued more cogently than others, the moment when cooperatives are prevented from self-financing (i.e. provided they are
organised as LMFs), the description of producer cooperatives as firms
run by workers as 'their own capitalists' will no longer apply. And as the
LMF reverses the capitalistic relationship between capital and labour, it
can doubtless be rated a genuine socialist enterprise in which workers
cease acting as their own capitalists.

Concluding, we wish to mention that this chapter is not intended to
provide evidence that Marx consistently and continually thought of a
system of cooperative firms as the best way out of capitalism. Such a
purpose, which would need the support of a historical analysis of Marx's
thought, lies outside the scope of this chapter, whose concern is neither
with the history of thought nor with the historical evolution of the
socialist movement. Rather, what we set out to show was that following
Vanek's contribution a system of producer cooperatives is fully consistent
with Marxist thought and can no longer be viewed as a disguised form of
capitalism.

6. Recent criticisms of the labour theory of value: the democratic firm and Marxism

1 INTRODUCTORY NOTES ON THE LABOUR THEORY OF VALUE

Recent research findings in the area of democratic firm management have a distinct bearing on Marxism since they once again call into question Marx's labour theory of value. In the light of the fact that earlier criticisms of this theory were not rated as fully convincing by quite a lot of Marxists, this new objection acquires major relevance. From my perspective, it is so compelling as to be one of the two reasons justifying a new reading of Marxist theory. The second, as the reader knows, is my firm belief that the social order to rise from the ashes of capitalism will be a system of democratically managed firms, rather than a centrally planned system.

Considering that the true focus point of this chapter is a new criticism of the labour theory of value implied in the democratic firm management studies, it is worth starting with a few introductory notes on Marx's labour theory of value.[88]

In Marx's theoretical approach, work is looked upon as a constituent element of every commodity. On the one hand, work is objectified in capital goods; on the other, when it is conceived of as subjectivity, or living labour, it is objectified in the production process.

These reflections are at the basis of Marx's well-known demonstration of the labour theory of value. In Marx's words (Marx 1857–58, p. 256): 'In the exchange between capital and labour, the first act is an exchange

---

[88]   Hobsbawm 2011 (p. 212) reports that an 1844 article written by Wickstead 'with sympathy and courtesy' and that the emotional diatribes of a Foxwell or a Flint created, among socialists, the mistaken feeling that Marx's value theory was somewhat irrelevant to the economic justification of socialism. This remark has a distinct bearing on the line of reasoning that will be developed further on in this book.

which falls entirely within ordinary circulation; the second is a process qualitatively different from exchange, and only by misuse could it have been called any sort of exchange at all'. 'It stands directly opposite exchange', he explained, because it is 'an essentially different category'. To understand the difference between these two acts it is necessary to draw the distinction between labour and labour power (which Marx himself rated as his principal contribution to a proper understanding of capitalism (see Marx & Engels 1972, vol. 5, pp. 52 and 132, and Engels 1891b, p. 18).[89] In Marx's approach, in the first act of the exchange between capital and labour capitalists purchase a commodity, labour power, whereas labour, the *physical act of working*, is no commodity, has no value (value being a specific attribute of commodities only) and can therefore neither be sold nor bought. Marx's conclusion is that the phrase 'price of labour' is as irrational as we would rate a phrase such as 'a yellow logarithm' (see Marx 1894, p. 931).

The labour–labour power distinction is used by Marx to rectify a logical error he perceives within classical political economy. For this purpose, he starts out from the following reflection:

> If the exchange-value of a product equals the labour time contained in the product, then the exchange-value of a working day is equal to the product it yields. In other words, wages must be equal to the product of labour. In fact the opposite is true. *Ergo*, this objection amounts to the problem: how does production on the basis of the exchange-value solely determined by labour time lead to the result that the exchange-value of labour is less than the exchange-value of the product? (Marx 1859, pp. 43–4)

It is to answer this query that Marx draws the distinction between labour and labour power. The value of labour power is calculated by determining the amount of work required to produce a worker's means of subsistence; and, considering that a fraction of a working day would be more than enough to produce such means of subsistence, it is necessary to conclude that throughout the remaining part of the working day the wage earner works for the benefit of his employer and thereby generates the surplus value which constitutes the profit accruing to the latter.[90]

---

[89] A great many Marxists and Marx commentators share Marx's view concerning this point (see, inter alia, Grossman 1940, p. 95, Dobb 1970, p. 14 and Hodgson 1982, pp. 235–6).

[90] Marx's explanation of the origin of profits appeared to Dobb 'so simple that it might seem surprising that so much ink has been spilled to disprove it and to propound alternative explanations' (Dobb 1954, p. 246).

In capitalism, the function of wages is to camouflage labour exploit-ation, viz., to conceal the circumstance that a portion of the wage earner's daytime is taken up by the capitalist. In pre-capitalistic societies, exploit-ation was glaringly evident, whereas in capitalistic societies it is masked by a contract of employment.

These reflections lead to two conclusions. Firstly, it is the value of labour power that constitutes the price, or value, of the work done, while notions such as the 'value' or 'price' of work are actually meaningless. Secondly, the work input required to produce commodities is paid for only in part and its unpaid portion translates into surplus labour.[91]

To explain the deviation of prices from values in capitalistic systems, Marx proceeds to his transformation of values into prices, which is rated as one of his major achievements. To understand how Marx addresses the transformation issue, we will start from the assumption that all prices are set by reference to the number of hours required to produce the relevant commodities. When this is the case, the profit rates earned by different firms will differ from firm to firm and capitalists will strive to scale them up until they level out everywhere within the context concerned. Accord-ing to Marx, however, during this process there will be no changes either in the aggregate value produced (since the aggregate hours worked will remain unaltered), nor in the sum total of the resulting surplus value. What will change is the way the resulting value will be distributed among the capitalists involved, since these will appropriate the surplus value no longer rateably to the part of the investment capital used to remunerate the workers, but in proportion to the aggregate capital each of them has invested (see Sweezy 1942, pp. 128–35). In other words, in Marx's approach the two above-mentioned equalities, aggregate prices = aggre-gate values and total profits = total surplus value, will be unaffected by the conversion of values into prices.

At this point, it is worth clarifying why Marx distinguished between exploitation in a capitalistic society and exploitation in pre-capitalistic systems. In Book I of *Capital* Marx argued that a capitalist setting out to extract surplus value from a commodity 'must be so lucky as to find, within the sphere of circulation, in the market, a commodity whose use value possesses the peculiar property of being a source of value', i.e. a commodity 'whose actual consumption is itself an embodiment of labour, and, consequently, a creation of value'. This commodity, he concluded, is

---

[91] Rubin (1928, pp. 102–103) and Dunayevskaya (1988, p. 100) have called attention to the fact that in earlier years (at least up to 1859) Marx did not draw any distinction between value and exchange value (see Kliman 1998).

labour power, whose use value exceeds its exchange value (Marx 1867, p. 270). This statement and the conclusion Marx draws from it are clear evidence that a capitalistic society exploits workers even when prices are made to equal values. Conversely, in the earlier drafts of what was to become *Capital* he maintained that usurer's and mercantile capital did earn surplus value even without subjecting labour to capital because prices used to be set at levels well above the corresponding values (for an in-depth analysis of this point, see Skillman 2013).

Coming to the criticism which has customarily been levelled against the labour theory of value, it was first raised in the 1870s, when the newly forged marginalist theory of value was set against the classical value theories of Smith, Ricardo and Marx and was so well received by the scientific community as to be looked upon as the mainstream price theory, until the appearance of Sraffa's work in 1960.

The appearance of Sraffa's *Production of Commodities by Means of Commodities* marked a major turning point, in terms that Sraffa rehabilitated the classical theory of value as a theory of production costs, rather than labour value, and thereby induced even Marxists to 'revert to the classics' – specifically Ricardo, rather than Marx. Consequently, a great many post-Sraffa theorists describe themselves as Marxists although they deny the potential of the labour theory of value to offer a satisfactory explanation of the mechanisms governing the working of capitalism (see Wright 1995, p. 11).[92]

2 EQUILIBRIUM PRICES IN CAPITALISM VERSUS A SYSTEM OF PRODUCER COOPERATIVES: THE EPISTEMOLOGICAL VALUE OF A CONTRIBUTION BY DRÈZE

Let us consider the case of a Vanek-type LMF cooperative, a firm which uses no wage labour and funds all its investments with loan capital. Further on, we will show that such a firm literally upturns the typical capital–labour relation of capitalistic economies because its partners take out loans, pay capital providers a fixed income (interest) and appropriate the firm's output and earnings. Hence, the question is: considering that

---

[92] Theorists who rate themselves as Marxists and endorse the validity of Marx's labour theory of value, though they think that, far from explaining how prices are formed, it sheds light on the mechanisms governing production activities and on capitalism, include Fine et al. (2010).

prices in long-equilibrium contexts are identical in capital and worker-managed firm systems (see Drèze 1976, 1989 and 1993), are there grounds for claiming that the labour theory of value can explain how prices are formed in a system of producer cooperatives?

As the partners of a cooperative cannot be categorised as a labour force proper, in a system formed of enterprises of this kind the distinction between labour and labour power is not applicable: work becomes a physical act, as is in the nature of things, there is no market where labour power could be sold in commodity fashion and Marx's labour theory of value is stripped of its very underpinning.[93] Although the workers of self-management using loan capital would not appropriate the whole income generated by their firms, it would be impossible to rate labour power as a commodity which is bought at its exchange value and can be used to generate surplus value because its purchase price is below its exchange value.[94]

In Marx's approach, hired labour (or commoditised labour as distinct from work as a physical act) 'is the essential condition for the real transformation of value advanced in the form of money into capital, into a value producing surplus value' (Marx 1885, p. 33).[95] Consequently, since hired labour, or labour power, is unknown in a self-managed firm system it is neither possible to speak of value, nor of surplus value, and the labour theory of value is stripped of its very foundations.[96]

The implication emerging from cooperation theory is that, due to its failure to offer a convincing explanation of the way prices are formed in a democratic firm system, the labour theory of value is ultimately unable

---

[93] Howard and King (1975, p. 167) hold that the labour theory of value is undermined by the difficulty to distinguish between labour and labour power. From my perspective, this non-distinction scathes its tenability as a price theory.

[94] The reversal of the capital–labour relation which is triggered upon the establishment of a system of cooperative firms cancels the nexus which in capitalism reveals the concealment of the abstract in the concrete, i.e. a nexus which determines that the abstract wealth that is created by the relationship between non-equals ends up by being dissimulated in the free confrontation and exchanges between equally free and individual entities (see Fanelli 1997, p. xxix).

[95] In contrast, Virno holds (2008, p. 108) that the notion of labour power 'is crucial to Marx's critical approach to political economy'.

[96] Skillman (2013) has shown that in preparatory drafts of *Capital* surplus value and exploitation are not necessarily associated with the existence of wage labour, the subjugation of work to capital.

to explain the mechanisms governing price formation *in a capitalistic economy as well.*[97]

Today, some Marxists call into question Sraffa's critique of the transformation issue[98] either because they flatly deny the relevance of the transformation issue or because (unlike Sraffa) they think that values can be converted into prices without calling into question the aggregate prices = aggregate value or total profits = total surplus value equalities postulated by Marx (see Lipietz 1982; Sinha 1982; Wolff et al. 1982, 1984 and 1998; Carchedi 1984; Moseley 1982 and 1993; McGlone & Kliman 1996; and Kliman 1998).[99]

Even within the framework of the 'New Approach' to the labour theory of value the extraction of living labour in the form of surplus value is traced to the appropriation of labour power, the despicable practice that

---

[97] 'Analytical Marxists' flatly deny the tenability of the labour theory of value as a theory of prices (see, inter alia, Tarrit 2006, pp. 598–9).

[98] This argument was first set forth by Southworth 1972.

[99] Within the framework of the new approaches to the transformation problem Sraffa is criticised (a) for starting out from individual magnitudes instead of Marx's aggregate magnitudes (Moseley 1982, pp. 286–8) and (b) for failing to distinguish between labour and labour power within the neo-Ricardian model and the resulting impossibility to claim that the essence of value is work or that surplus value is generated by surplus labour (Bellofiore 1993, pp. 75–6).

In the opinion of some, the starting point for these new approaches was a mistake made by some Marx critics. In particular, according to Bellofiore these critics were wrong because the capital accounts to which the mean profit rate was applied when converting values into production prices were still expressed in terms of labour value. This entailed the use of two antithetical calculation methods. When a commodity is looked upon as a product, the method for determining its production price is the one described above (the traditional procedure used in older interpretative approaches); conversely, when the same commodity is looked upon as a capital good or means of subsistence, the amount used is once again expressed at its labour value (see Bellofiore 1993, pp. 64–5). Other theorists find fault with the transformation method of the 1960s and 1970s because the value of the constant capital which is the basis of the value of a commodity should be expressed in terms of its exchange value. According to them, this is because 'due to the redistribution of abstract labour through exchange, some commodities embody more labour than they would otherwise', some less than the labour embodied in them contained on the conditions under which they were produced (see McGlone & Kliman 1996, p. 32). Yet, all the representatives of the 'new approach' are agreed that the main error of those authors was to have to split the capitalistic economy into two spheres, price and value – a procedure departing from Marx's method (see, inter alia, McGlone & Kliman 1996 and Ramos-Martinez & Rodriguez-Herrera 1996).

the establishment of a market economy with self-managed firms is expected to sweep away.

Present-day advocates of the labour theory of value object to Sraffa's use of a moneyless price system. When the labour theory of value is applied to a moneyless system, they argue, it is stripped of its Marxian essence and there is no option but to revert to Ricardo's labour theory of value.[100] This objection is equally applicable to a monetary economy regardless of the role that money is ascribed: within a system of producer cooperatives, a system in which the capital–labour relation specific to capitalism has been literally upturned, capitalists cannot be said to 'suck' living labour.

3 THE NOTION OF ABSTRACT LABOUR

There is an additional criticism of the labour theory of value as a price theory which is implied in the findings of economic theorists of producer cooperatives. Quite a lot of Marxists equate abstract labour with wage labour (see, for instance, Eldret & Hanlon 1981 and De Vroey 1982).[101] One of them, Kozo Uno, argues that only in capitalism does abstract labour turn into value-generating labour (see Ishibashi 1995, p. 48) and in

---

[100] Moseley (1998) maintains that a revised transformation method with a distinct focus on money would validate the labour theory of value. In Marx's approach values and prices appear as two different sets of exchange relations and in the neo-Ricardian approach to the transformation problem total price and total value are just the sum totals of the individual magnitudes. In contrast, Moseley argues that Marx's method is characterised by the fact that the sum total is to be determined beforehand and independently of the individual magnitudes. According to Wolff et al. (1998, p. 46), considering that values in capitalism are not exchanged in their own right, but as generated by capital, they do not reflect the labour time which is embodied in the monetary equivalents for which they are exchanged. Moreover, they argue, the constant capital component of the products is not commensurate with the labour embodied in the means of production (as would be the case if the circumstances under which they were produced were deemed to be relevant), but with the labour time, in the form of money, expended by capitalists (for parallels and differences between Moseley's approach and that of Wolff et al., see Wolff et al. 1998, p. 52).

[101] 'The free laborer in capitalist production', Dunlap writes (1979, p. 321), 'appears as qualitatively undifferentiated labour-power completely substitutional for any other instance of labor-power. The free laborer is the economic analogue of the isolated, solipsistic ego of the Cartesians which resulted in an entire tradition of philosophical idealism.'

his overall approach his disciple, the Marxist scholar Sekine, also holds
abstract labour to fall in with hired work (see Sekine 1995a and 1995b).
Similarly, in Tom Bottomore's dictionary of Marxist thought we read that
'the abstraction which renders embodied labour abstract labour is a social
abstraction, a real social process quite specific to capitalism' (Mohun
1991, p. 2). Other theorists argue that in *Grundrisse* abstract labour is
deduced not only from exchange, but also from production. As the living
labour of a hired worker is abstract labour 'in the making', in Marx's
approach the basis of abstract labour appears to be the subjugation of
labour to capital and abstraction and the exploitation of labour are
coextensive categories (Fineschi 2005, pp. 245 and 147 and 2006,
pp. 99–103; see also, Marcuse 1954, p. 348; Carandini 1971, p. 59 and
1973, pp. 81–2; De Angelis 1995; Bellofiore & Finelli 1998; Bonefeld
2010 and 2011; and Carchedi 2011). And this is an additional reason
explaining why the labour theory of value, which presupposes abstract
labour (in other words, where 'commodities, the cells of the system, are
values because they embody abstract labour' – see Miconi 1981, p. 163)
is erroneous in a system of worker-run firms without hired labour.[102]

The abstract labour notion is one of the most controversial points of
Marxian theory (in Sweezy's words, 'it is not an easy concept to
comprehend' – see Sweezy 1942, p. 35).[103] It is well known that Sweezy
looked upon 'abstract labour' as 'labor in general', i.e. as a kind of work
common to all human production activities. And Sweezy's idea of
abstract labour as nothing but a mental construct has recently been
reproposed by Kicillof and Starosta (2007 and 2011). Dissenting from
Sweezy on this point, Colletti has argued that abstract labour should not
be understood as an abstract mental construct, but rather as 'an abstraction which materialises in exchange relations day after day' (Colletti
1968, p. lii). Indeed, before any of the commodities manufactured by
workers can be exchanged in the market, they have to be graded and
matched in terms of value, but as exchanges are made irrespective of the
real use values of such commodities, we also abstract from the degree of
specificity the work that went into their making. The point on which
Colletti and Sweezy are of one mind, however, is that the phrase 'abstract
labour' denotes both work in general and hired labour.

---

[102] Colletti has made it clear that Marx's labour theory of value differs
greatly from Ricardo's value theory because it is founded on the notion of
abstract labour (see, inter alia, Colletti 1979, pp. 69–76).

[103] Rovatti (1973, p. 118) holds that 'abstract labour' is a category specific to
capitalistic production and must be identified because it is the starting point for a
correct understanding of the myriad facets of capitalism.

Even Colletti's approach, though, comes in for some criticism. At first, he links abstract labour to exchange and describes it as common to every mercantile society; subsequently, he argues that 'the process whereby work is abstracted from the individual worker and made independent of man as such reaches its high point in the modern hired worker' (Colletti 1968, footnote on p. liv) and, consequently, ends up by suggesting that labour is abstract especially, if not only, in capitalism. Further on, he points to a link between labour, alienation and expropriated human subjectivity (pp. liii–lviii); and as the establishment of a system of democratic firms produces the effect of greatly abating alienation (as will be shown in greater detail further on), it is necessary to conclude that abstract labour is only, or mainly, associated with capitalism as such, not only with exchange.

Marxists critical of Ricardian Marxism include the representatives of the circulationist conception, who argue that value can only become reality through the exchange of products against money and, obviously, that abstract labour occurs in every market economy (see, for instance, Mavroudeas 2004 and Kicillof & Starosta 2007). In contrast, the representatives of a movement known as the 'class struggle' approach maintain that abstract labour falls in with wage labour (see, for instance, De Angelis 1995, p. 108; Saad-Filho 1996 and 1997; Arthur 2001; and Wennerlind 2002, p. 4).

The real meaning of Marx's 'abstract labour' notion, however, became clear upon the publication of Marx's 1861–83 manuscripts in MEGA2. As pointed out by Arthur (2009, p. 150), there Marx initially specified that the phrase 'formal subsumption of the work process' was to be interpreted as the control of capital over work and the workman, but further on he added that, whenever work is thus subsumed, it is reduced to a certain amount of abstract labour (see Marx 1861–63, vol. 30, pp. 71 and 93).

From this, it follows that Marx's labour theory of value is untenable since no such extension is possible in a system of worker-run firms.[104] In a few words, the issue can be summed up as follows: since long-term equilibrium prices in capitalism and a self-management system are seen to be the same, Marx's labour theory of value could only be rated as tenable if it held in a market economy where firms are funded by the

---

[104] Until some time ago, most of the Italian 'philosophical Marxists' flatly refused to admit that the labour theory of value was no correct price theory (see Badaloni 1972; Cassano 1973; and Curi 1975). Consequently, they never as much as addressed the issue which is the focus of this book, i.e. which parts of Marxism will stand after the labour theory of value has been refuted.

workers and employ neither labour power nor abstract labour.[105] It is widely held that Marx started out from Ricardo's labour theory and further developed it by extending it to the notion of surplus value which he had previously deduced from the concept of value. Subsequently, he used the notion of surplus value to explain how capitalists appropriated unpaid labour (Vygodsky 1967, p. 16).

4 THE THEORY OF VALUE AND THE EXPLOITATION ISSUE

The question to be answered at this point is whether the demonstration that the labour theory of value is no viable price theory will automatically rule out exploitation in capitalistic societies. Back in 1899, this question was answered in the negative by Bernstein (1899, pp. 75–84), and more recently Duménil and Levy (2001) have argued at length that despite its classification as an inappropriate price theory the labour theory of value is in many respects the precondition for a correct understanding of the world in which we live. 'In Chapters 13–15 of Book I of Capital', Lazonick writes (1978, p. 3), 'Marx shows that the appropriation of surplus value and the real subjection of labour are two sides of the same relation'.[106] Samuelson, too, is prepared to admit that the labour theory of value is not a correct price theory, but he holds it to be a valuable tool for a correct understanding of exploitation (see Samuelson 1967, p. 620).[107]

---

[105] In the *Supplementary Considerations* included in the preface to the Italian edition of Book I of *Capital*, Engels claimed that the labour theory of value was applicable to any market economy, and especially to a simple mercantile system (even more than to capitalism). Engels rated Marx's law of value as a correct, though somewhat approximate reflection of the conditions prevailing between the time when products became marketable commodities (i.e. the rise of an early exchange economy) and the fifteenth century (see Engels 1894b, pp. 38 and 39).

Unlike Engels, Levine holds that in a pre-capitalistic society 'it does not make sense to speak of value, and of exchange governed by the law of labour value' (Levine 1998, p. 6).

[106] According to Gintis and Bowles (1981, p. 2), although 'in its economic form the labour theory of value is merely a particularly cumbersome theory of the relations between the technical conditions of production and the structure of wages, prices and profits', it must be upheld because it shows that neither labour nor labour power can be reduced to mere mercantile relations.

[107] Chiodi has argued that Marx used the labour theory of value as a means of measuring the social product and that his ultimate aim was to provide

If we back this view, before answering the question raised at the beginning of this section we have to examine the exploitation theory of Garegnani, an author who rejects the labour theory of value, but thinks it possible to develop a theory of exploitation which is consistent with Marx's thought.

According to Garegnani, the assumed link between labour value and exploitation was theorised by 'utopian' socialists based on Ricardo's value theory. Insofar as it is true – they argued – that the value of a product reflects the labour time embodied therein workers have the title to the *whole* output of their work and profits and rents are the proceeds of worker exploitation. However, as Garegnani, like Marx himself, rejects both ethical readings of the notion of exploitation and any approach to it from the perspective of the doctrine of natural law, the true import of his notion of labour exploitation remains vague. However, given that Garegnani, like Marx, strongly opposed both ethical readings of exploitation and the idea that exploitation is part of the natural order, it is not clear what he actually means by exploitation.

As argued by this renowned Italian economist (and by Marx himself), exploitation was practised in pre-capitalistic societies and was even more ruthless in the feudal age than it is in present-day capitalistic societies, but the argument that exploitation exists must be backed by two distinct forms of evidence. On the one hand, it must be possible to provide evidence that in our modern industrial societies workers are not allowed to appropriate the *whole* social product. This demonstration is fairly easy to provide and does not require the support of *any* specific theoretical approach. But it is not enough, in itself, to justify the characterisation of a social system as exploitative in nature. Nor does Garegnani think that any other theory confining itself to explain why profit and rents exist can be equal to this task. What is needed, Garegnani argues, is incontestable evidence that these forms of revenue *arise solely* from 'the bare fact that the prevailing organisation of the economy prevents workers from taking possession of the entire social product' (see Garegnani 1981, pp. 87–8; see also, Garegnani & Petri 1982, pp. 807–12).[108]

---

evidence that the working class is exploited in all capitalistic systems (see Chiodi 2008, p. 190).

In the estimation of Wennerlind (2002, p. 3) the theory of value 'is neither an alternative economic theory of exchange, nor just a theory of economic exploitation, but a theory of the social constitution of value'.

[108] Well-known analyses of exploitation which are not examined in this book are owed to Hodgson (1982) and Roemer (1982 and 1988, ch. 9), two authors who dismiss the labour theory of value as untenable.

Is this explanation satisfactory?

As said, in the estimation of Garegnani a theory explaining why capitalists earn profits is not enough to demonstrate that there is exploitation (so much so that he goes so far as to argue that if the marginalist theory were tenable, neither surplus nor exploitation would exist). He holds that conclusive evidence of exploitation can only come from a theory of profit which not only offers a correct explanation of the reason why profits are generated, but is also capable of proving that they are entirely unjustified. From his perspective, such a theory does exist and is the theory of profits as surplus value which propounds that profits arise because wages are kept below the net social output and are hence inadmissible.

The question now is what kind of 'justification' Garegnani requires. Considering his comments on 'utopian' socialism and marginalism, it is unlikely that he is thinking of an 'ethical' justification.[109]

5 EXPLOITATION THEORY AND THE SOCIALIST REVOLUTION

Hence, Garegnani seems to suggest that the question as to whether exploitation exists can only be answered in the affirmative if one provides the demonstration that the appropriation of profits by capital *serves no useful function*. To what extent can he be said to have actually offered this demonstration?

Before we try to answer this question it is worth drawing the customary handbook distinction between profit and interest. Today, competent marginalists are prepared to accept the conclusion (reached at the end of the well-known debate between the two Cambridge schools of thought) that the interest rate is to be understood as the cost of capital, rather than a measure of capital shortage (as traditionally propounded by theorists).[110]

---

[109] In Freeman & Carchedi (1996, p. 1) we read that back in 1844 Marx himself spelt out in bold letters that economics and ethics were inextricably intertwined. On this point, see also, Thomas (1984), Gilbert (1984) and Backhouse (1985, p. 122).

[110] In the opinion of some, the contention that interest payments lack any ethical justification need not be backed by this finding, however relevant, because even if capital is deemed to be productive, the claim that *owners* of capital deserve the accrual of interest on it is and remains unwarranted (see DiQuattro 1981, p. 122). In point of fact, DiQuattro's thesis should be supported

As for profit, there is general agreement, among economic theorists, that in *capitalistic societies* their functions are anything but negligible. Among other things, they are a reward for risk bearing, they further capital accumulation (in part because profits tend to rise in direct proportion to the accumulation rate) and are a powerful stimulus to entrepreneurship, technological innovation and, generally, free enterprise. From the perspective of neoclassical theorists, profit is the 'soul of capitalism' and any actions in its defence will help safeguard capitalism at large.

The view of profit as the soul of capitalism is shared by several non-neoclassical theorists and by authors such as Robinson and Eatwell, who argue that 'the function of profit is to further accumulation' (see Robinson & Eatwell 1973, p. 263).[111] Marx himself described profit as 'the driving force in capitalist production' (see Marx 1894, pp. 312–13).

At first sight, the finding that profit does perform positive functions in capitalism would seem to strip Garegnani's theory of exploitation of its very underpinning;[112] on closer analysis, however, its validity is confirmed by an analysis of a system of cooperative firms.

Let us consider two 'twin' enterprises, a capitalistic company and an LMF cooperative run by its workers. Based on the demonstration provided by Dréze as mentioned above, but with slight adjustments posed by the risk factor, in long-term equilibrium situations these two types of firm will have comparable business and earning potentials, but the profits earned (not interest as well) will accrue to capital owners in the former and to the workers in the latter. This finding is evidence that the appropriation of profits by one or the other class is made possible by the economic order that is in place, and that profits are not necessarily the prerogative of capitalists.[113]

At this point, we will set out from the idea that the only viable aspect of the labour theory of value is the statement that labour is the sole

---

by the demonstration that saving entails no sacrifice and is therefore not commendable. To show that saving is unrelated to the interest rate it is possible to refer to Keynes, but this is not what DiQuattro does.

[111] There is general agreement that a positive profit rate is the precondition for the existence of capitalism (see, for instance, Morishima 1973, p. 17 and Blundell-Wignall 1976, p. 278).

[112] Some theorists find fault with Garegnani's theory of exploitation because it departs from Marx in presenting exploitation as unrelated to production processes (see, for example, Sinha 1982, pp. 272–4).

[113] Croce went so far as to argue that Marx was to be given major credit for focusing attention on the social essence of profit, which economic theorists in his day held to be a miraculous offshoot of capital (Croce 1899, pp. 152–3).

'source' of value.[114] Far from being a simple definition, this argument entails the major implication that the income generated should entirely and solely fall to the share of workers (an idea which was shared by Ricardian socialists, but which Marx himself dismissed as 'utopian' – see Marx 1847, pp. 67–8; Engels 1884, p. 13; and Walras 1987, vol. 5, p. 46). The Ricardians were wrong when they maintained that this criterion was applicable in their own day because the proposal to assign the total revenue from production to workers is, at best, a hopeful prospect for the future.[115]

Engels himself made it clear that the definition of capitalist appropriation of the value produced as *unjust* has, admittedly, 'nothing to do with economics', but was probably correct 'from the point of view of world history' (Engels 1884, p. 13). 'If mass moral consciousness declares an economic fact to be unjust', he explained, this means that 'other economic facts have made their appearance due to which the former has become unbearable and untenable'.[116] In this connection, Gintis and Bowles have argued (1981, p. 4) that 'the labour theory of value, by focusing on the contingent nature of surplus-value, bids us analyse those technical, political, and cultural mechanisms within the site of capitalistic production that allow such a surplus to arise and be reproduced'.

This is why I share Engels's view that a *labour theory of value* should propound that (a) all value is solely and entirely generated by labour and that no theoretical approach explains why profit should necessarily accrue to capital owners,[117] that (b) all the income generated must be

---

[114]   The phrase 'labour theory of value' can either designate a method for the determination of the prices at which commodities are to be exchanged or a procedure to investigate into the origin of their values. In an interesting analysis of this point, Screpanti defines the claim that labour is the sole source of value as the 'value substance axiom' (see Screpanti 2003, p. 157).

[115]   As pointed out by Perri (1998, pp. 213–14), Marx rated as 'just' whatever actions that do not stand in the way of the advancement of society.

[116]   In the opinion of Joan Robinson (1942, p. 20), the theory of value, looked upon as a theory of relative prices, is not the core of Marx's system and, consequently, 'no point of substance in Marx's argument' can be said to descend from the labour theory of value. In other words, this means that the consistency of Marx's overall theoretical approach is by no means undermined by the invalidation of the labour theory of value. This conclusion is all the more true if we assume that the categorisation of the partial appropriation of value by capitalists as an unjust action is – paraphrasing Engels – correct from the point of view of world history.

[117]   According to Robinson, to claim that capital is productive or that its existence is the precondition for making labour productive is a matter of no great

assigned to labour in full keeping with Locke's teaching that any commodities produced are the property of those who produce them,[118] and (c) that we *must work towards* the establishment of a social order in which the whole social product will be assigned to the workers.[119]

Hence, the idea that labour is the only source of value and that the assignment of profit to capitalists, rather than workers, is unjustified implies the conclusion that a social order in which the balance between revenues and costs of production is not entirely assigned to the workers is to be rated as a system founded on exploitation. Put differently, the capitalism-exploitation equation, far from being true *by definition*, requires the support of a demonstration (which indeed is offered by Garegnani).

It is worth emphasising that the approach to exploitation adopted in this chapter departs from that of Wright (1985) because the latter has reference to the distinction between a quantitative and qualitative aspect of the labour theory drawn in Sweezy (1942), and to the definition of exploitation suggested in Roemer (1982). In Wright's approach, a class is said to exploit another when, with everything constant, its consumption would increase in the absence of the other, i.e. when it appropriates a portion of the surplus which is generated by the work of another class (see Mattick 2002, pp. 29–30). In other words, in Wright's estimation revenue is the joint output of all the so-called 'production factors' and it is this that leads him to argue that 'there is complete symmetry in the structure of exploitation in a system in which capital hires wage

---

importance; what really matters is 'to say that *owning* capital is not a productive activity' (1942, p. 16). In point of fact, this claim is only admissible if it is proved that saving requires no sacrifice.

The idea that value is solely and entirely created by labour is unscathed by a criticism which Adam Smith levelled against Epicurus: you tend to 'indulge a propensity which is natural to all men, but which philosophers in particular are apt to cultivate with a peculiar fondness, as the great means of displaying their ingenuity, the propensity to account for all appearances from as few principles as possible' (Smith 1790, p. 567).

[118]   In Marx's own words, 'Property, then, originally means – in its Asiatic, Slavonic, ancient classical, Germanic form – the relation of the working, producing or self-reproducing subject to the conditions of his production or reproduction as his own' (Marx 1857–58, vol. 2, pp. 122–3).

[119]   'Value is the abstract labour unit (its subsistence) and money (its form) and is consequently connoted both by an immanent or intrinsic magnitude (socially necessary labour) and by an extrinsic magnitude (exchange value or price)' (see Ramos-Martinez & Rodriguez-Herrera 1996, p. 51).

labourers and in a (hypothetical) system in which workers rent capital' (1985, p. 10) and 'thereby exploit capitalists'.

The view of labour as the sole source of value and the associated claim (laid in by Ricardian socialists) that the revenue generated should entirely fall to the share of the working class are often rejected because of their supposed 'ethical' implications and consequential conflict with Marx's 'scientific' criticism of capitalism.[120] Buchanan, in particular, has laid stress on Marx's belief that legal considerations were of no avail in explaining social phenomena (see Buchanan 1982, ch. 4, p. 52). Nonetheless, the conviction that value judgements have no place in scientific speculation[121] is not at odds with the argument that the call for allowing workers to keep for themselves the whole revenue they generate is no ethical consideration so long as it is not used as a pretext to categorise capitalism as unjust (for failing to allow them to do so) or to claim that the whole income generated should fall to the share of workers *even at the capitalistic stage* of an economy (an utterly inconsistent proposition). The scientific status of this claim will at once become apparent if, paraphrasing Engels, it is construed as suggesting that the ultimate goal of historical evolution is sweeping away capitalism and vesting title in all revenue in workers. Although this is doubtless a Hegelian view of history as an idea materialising in the world, it is, at the same time, a Marxian proposition because it conceives of historical development as the stepwise solution of existing contradictions.[122]

In my opinion, Garegnani's theory of exploitation has elements of truth because it affords a correct perspective on the socialist revolution. As it cannot be denied that no one theorist has come up with a viable economic theory explaining why profit should fall to the share of capitalists, socialists are called upon to initiate a revolution capable of

---

[120] Hodges has categorised Marx's notion of 'value' as a subjective value judgement which is out of place in a scientific discipline such as political economy (see Hodges 1965 and 1970). Morris, rather, has appropriately argued that acknowledging the value of a thing or human being is tantamount to describing a man as strong or virtuous and that Marx took over his notion of value from the scientific analyses of earlier classical economists (see Morris 1966). Others still think that value (unlike use value) is the characteristic that commodities have in common and thanks to which they become comparable (Duffield 1970).

[121] Authors who do not see any antithesis between value judgements and science include, among others, Bush (2009).

[122] For my part, I reject the view of authors such as Hess, Grün and others who categorise the advent of socialism as an act of justice, rather than a necessary historical development (see Berlin 1963, p. 149, footnote).

solving the contradictions inherent in a social order in which capital owners are deemed to have title to cash all profits and transferring the relevant title to workers – as would be the case in a system of cooperative firms.[123]

According to Isaac Deutscher, the labour theory of value is important because 'the notion of value as created by human work contains the seed of revolution' (1970, p. 214);[124] and it is common knowledge that the rise of marginalism is often traced to the fact that a great many post-Marx theorists look upon classical economic theory as dangerous because it is based on the labour theory of value.[125]

Looked, then, upon as an attempt to restore momentum to the idea of revolution as a process leading to worker control of firms and put an end to the unjustified appropriation of profit by capital owners, the claim that labour is the sole source of value has all but negligible implications.[126]

Consequently, there are grounds for arguing that when the labour theory of value is read as an approach which contains 'the seed of revolution', rather than a theory of prices, its importance and cognitive potential are magnified.

As has been rightly argued, as soon as we categorise the labour theory of value as logically untenable, we have to cope with the formidable task of rethinking Marx's economic system in the light of sound logical foundations but without scathing its theoretical vigour and critical potential (see Mayer 1994, p. 2).[127]

---

[123] As Murray puts it (2002, pp. 250–2), one need not be a Marxist to claim that work is the only source of value and that all enterprises should be converted into worker-owned cooperatives. Ricardian socialists did so no less than Marx himself.

[124] See, also, Lippi (1976, p. 151).

[125] Antonio Labriola wrote (1895, p. 50, note 2) that certain critics, including Wieser, 'propose to abandon Ricardo's theory of value because it paves the way for the establishment of socialism'.

[126] 'The essential discovery of Marxism', Sartre wrote (1960, p. 225), is that the real foundation of the organisation of social relations is 'labour as a historical reality and as the utilisation of particular tools in an already determined social and material situation'.

[127] Van Parijs suggests that Marx found fault with capitalism 'not so much because it entailed the exploitation and oppression of workers, but because of its inability, from a certain stage onwards, to bring about an appreciable development of the productive forces' (1993, p. 234). In actual fact, this claim is untenable, in terms that a careful analysis of Marx's writings will show that the idea of capitalism as founded on exploitation is much more central to his thought than the view of capitalism as an obstacle to development.

A reader feeling that this line of reasoning may surreptitiously smuggle ethical considerations into the debate is hereby referred to the claim of some analytical Marxists that a measure of morality will not scathe the scientific fabric of Marxism when the overall mode of speculation is consistent with the canons of scientific research and that the combination of normative thought with Marxist theory does not undermine the scientific standing of Marxism (see Mayer 1994, p. 21).[128]

From Benedetto Croce (1899, pp. 57–9) we learn that the use of the labour theory of value as a theory of prices was first called into question by Sombart (on grounds that Marx's law of value was a category of thought, rather than an empirical fact – see Sombart 1894, pp. 555–94) and that comparable criticisms were later raised against it by Labriola. Specifically, the latter argued (1902, p. 191) that it 'does not represent an empirical fact drawn from vulgar induction, nor a simple logic expression, as some have chronicled it. It is rather the typical premise without which all the rest of the work is unthinkable'. To endorse, or simply explain, Labriola's remark, Croce added that Marx's approach to value was something which, with respect to capitalistic society, performs 'the function of a term of comparison, of a standard, of a type' (Croce 1899, p. 59) and that this interpretation had induced quite a lot of scholars to describe the equation of value with labour as 'an ideal of social ethics, a moral ideal' (p. 60).

6 CAPITALISM AS A SYSTEM FOUNDED ON UNEQUAL EXCHANGES

In this chapter, then, I lay the claim that even theorists who reject the labour theory of value as a pricing theory can share the view that

---

The importance that Marxists attach to the issue of exploitation is emphasised by Balibar (who forcefully rejects the description of Marxism as an economic discipline proper): 'due to the ideological struggle that has been incessantly raging within the Marxist community ever since its very beginning', he writes (see Balibar 1974, pp. 111–12), 'all theoretical attempts, whether conscious or not, to refound political economy (after the double rupture caused by the appearance of Marx's work) have been undermined by the misinterpretation of the notion of surplus value'.

[128] DiQuattro's argument is that, even where the labour theory of value is shown to be utterly untenable, nothing would stand in the way of claiming that all the revenue produced should fall to the share of the working class for ethical reasons if this claim is founded on a clear-cut distinction between theoretical analysis and moral justification (see DiQuattro 1981, p. 123).

exchanges in capitalism are neither symmetrical nor fair. As mainstream price theory (which even Marxists rejecting the labour theory must accept) categorises landowners' rents and interest payments to capital owners as production costs, the issue of exploitation, or asymmetrical exchange, in capitalism must necessarily be associated with profits. In other words, the problem is why capital owners should have title to appropriate profits in addition to the revenue from interest payments to which mainstream theorists think they are lawfully entitled. Since mainstream theory teaches that each of the three factors of production, labour, capital and land, earns an income in exchange for the contribution it makes to production, it is hard to understand – let this be repeated – why capital owners should be entitled to cash profits in addition to the income which is legitimately generated by their capital resources. In line with a theory which goes back to Knight, this title is associated with the fact that it is capitalists that take on all the risks associated with production. In fact, this claim stands on shaky legs since workers are far from safe from these risks. Considering that the usual response of employers to declining revenues and a looming crisis is destaffing, it is fair to argue that workers take the relevant risks well ahead of others. Admittedly, when crises escalate to levels which make losses inevitable, it is capital owners that have to pay off a firm's debts, but this is fully consistent with the principle that each factor of production is liable in proportion to its function. Labour pays for its diminished work input with loss of wages and jobs; capital resources which cease generating surplus are used to cover losses and pay off debts.

The claim that profits are the reward to which capitalists are entitled for organising production processes is not only unwarranted, but even contradicted by practical experience, in terms that more often than not a firm's business is organised by a manager, rather than capital owners.

Consequently, it is difficult to grasp the rationale behind the fact that it is capital owners that appropriate profits. From the perspective of Engels, this was the effect of the institutions that were in place and had nothing to do with political economy. Institutions as established by the capitalistic legal system, he argued, create a playing field in which profits inevitably fall to the share of capitalists.

In Marx's opinion, the appropriation of profits by capitalists is the direct effect of unfair exchanges between capitalists and workers, viz., of labour contracts which are entered into between parties who are not on an equal footing. 'Capital', Marx wrote (1857–58, vol. 1, p. 233), 'is not a simple relation, but a process, in whose various moments it is always capital'. And capital, by its very nature, remains such as long as there is hired labour for it to purchase. Exchanges between labour and capital fall into two stages. Initially, capital purchases labour power at its exchange value; at the second stage, the use value of labour power is employed by capital within the framework of a production process intended to produce exchange value in excess of the price paid in connection with its purchase. From Marx's perspective, this is the situation of inequality from which profits flow. 'If it is said that capital is exchange value which produces profit' or, if nothing else, is set on producing a profit, 'then capital is already presupposed in its explanation, for profit is a specific relation of capital to itself' (Marx 1857–58, vol. 1, p. 233).

This point requires a few explanatory notes. While it is true that from the perspective of a purchaser, the use value of a commodity always exceeds its exchange value, no commodity, excepting labour power, enables its buyer to earn a profit by selling it at a price above the production cost and, hence, appropriating the resulting surplus.

This means that Marx's surplus theory is founded on the wrong assumption that when a commodity is sold, any amounts above the sum of the wages paid to produce it turn into surplus value. Surplus value does not include rents and interest, both of which are classified as production costs, while profit is the portion of the revenue produced that capitalists appropriate without any justification.

Therefore, whereas the rent and interest theories that are part of mainstream economics can be categorised as correct, a Marxist can be expected to object to its theories of profit.

7   VALUE THEORY AND CLASS THEORY

The question to be raised at this point is whether Marx's theory of classes will survive the rejection of the labour theory and simultaneous retention of the exploitation theory.

Turning to Marx's own approach, at the end of Book III of *Capital* (1894, pp. 1025–6) Marx asked himself 'What makes a class?' and provided the following answer: at first sight, what makes a class is 'the identity of revenues and revenue sources', as would indeed seem to be suggested by Ricardo's theoretical work on the subject of the relations between workers, capitalists and landowners. However, Marx added, 'the same would hold true for the infinite fragmentation of interests and positions into which the division of social labour splits not only workers but also capitalists and land-owners', for example doctors and government officials. Concerning this point, Mattick argues (2002, pp. 31–2): 'It is to illuminate not the existence of conflicting social interests, which are indeed legion, but the question of fundamental social transformation that this analysis abstracts from the myriad occupational groupings and income levels in order to focus attention on the distinction between the producers and appropriators of surplus-value.'

According to Marx, therefore, there are only two classes. This is why he wrote the following (Marx 1867, p. 874):

> In themselves, money and commodities are no more capital than the means of production and subsistence are. They need to be transformed into capital. The confrontation of, and the contact between, two very different kinds of commodity owners; on the one hand, the owners of money, means of production, means of subsistence, who are eager to valorize the sum of values they have appropriated by buying the labour-power of others; on the other hand, free workers, the sellers of their own labour-power, and therefore the sellers of labour ... With the polarization of the commodity market into these two classes, the fundamental conditions of capitalistic production are present.[129]

8 CONCLUSION

In this chapter, I have discussed new arguments which go to strengthen the idea that Marx's labour theory, while admittedly untenable as a price theory, offers conclusive evidence that capitalism is a social system which entails exploitation as a matter of course. The moment we admit that work is the sole source of value, the idea that capitalism breeds exploitation is no longer tautological, but implied in the labour theory of value.

---

[129] For an in-depth analysis of this point, see Dahrendorf (1957, pp. 19ff.).

7. Further reflections on the links between Marxism and producer cooperatives

1 INTRODUCTION

As said in the Introduction, those who rate Marx's 'history-as-totality' conception as the true core of his theory of society attach major importance to the concept of 'mode of production'. In Marxian theory, production, distribution, exchange and consumption are different links of a single chain, i.e. different facets of one unit. Commenting on this point in a youthful work on historical evolution, Lukàcs (1968b, p. 34) remarked that Marx, much like the German philosophers and chiefly Hegel, conceived of world history as a unitary process and an everlasting revolutionary avenue towards liberation, and that the uniqueness of his approach lay in the way he consistently prioritised a comprehensive global approach. In the light of these ideas the point to be analysed in this chapter is whether the introduction of an all-cooperatives system may be considered a Marxist proposal.

2 MARX'S AND LENIN'S DEFINITIONS OF SOCIALISM AND COMMUNISM

Like Lenin, a great many Marxists think of socialism and communism as different social systems. A significant passage from *Capital* runs as follows:

> Let us picture to ourselves, by way of change, a community of free individuals carrying on their work with the means of production in common, in which the labour-power of all the different individuals is consciously applied as the combined labour-power of the community ... Labour-time would, in that case, play a double part. Its apportionment in accordance with a definite social plan maintains the proper proportion between the different kinds of work to be done and the various wants of the community. On the other hand, it also serves as a measure of the portion of the common labour

borne by each individual, and of his share in the part of the total product destined for individual consumption. The social relations of the individual producers, with regard both to their labour and to its products, are in this case perfectly simple and intelligible, and that with regard not only to production but also to distribution. (See Marx 1867, pp. 110–11)

The distribution model proposed in this excerpt, a system which apportions the social product among the workers rateably to their respective work inputs, is basically the one he fleshed out for his first collective society model in the *Critique of the Gotha Programme*,[130] i.e. back in 1875. There, Marx argued that the proceeds of the aggregate work output of a community working collectively with jointly owned work tools and implements constitutes the total social product that should be distributed after the deduction of the following items:

- a portion needed to replace used-up capital goods or accumulate fresh capital resources;
- a reserve fund to cover expenses necessitated in connection with accidents or natural calamities;
- a portion to fund overheads, i.e. expense items not strictly associated with production proper;
- a portion allocated for the provision of public goods and services, it being understood that such portion was to exceed that usually earmarked for such purpose in capitalistic systems and was to be stepped up continuously according to need;
- a provision for those unable to work (Marx 1875a, p. 959).

The remainder, Marx argued, was to be apportioned among the population rateably to the work inputs contributed by each individual (p. 960).

---

[130] The apportionment criterion which rules that each worker is paid in proportion to his individual work input recalls, with some deviations, the capitalistic distribution principle which rules that the factors are to be remunerated in proportion to their respective marginal productivity levels (three distribution criteria are discussed in Albert & Hahnel 1991, pp. 8–9 and Hahnel 2004). These criteria have in common the principle that the marginal productivity indexed remuneration is commensurate with productivity; they differ from each other because Marx's concept of productivity was not identical with the notion of *marginal* productivity.

It is a matter for debate whether Marx thought that work in a socialist system was to be remunerated by reference to quantity or quality, i.e. in proportion to the number of hours worked or the value of the work accomplished, though theorists tend to prioritise the latter hypothesis (see Roemer 2008, p. 15).

By way of addition, Marx conceded that the distribution criterion proposed by the society he was picturing to himself was, admittedly, still 'stigmatized by a bourgeois limitation' (p. 961), but concluded that 'these defects are inevitable in the first phase of communist society' because 'after the enslaving subordination of the individual to the division of labor', that is to say at the last stage of socialism, society will be able to 'inscribe on its banners: from each according to his ability, to each according to his needs!' (pp. 961–2).

This stage fits within the utopian vision of communism to which Marx held on throughout his life. Indeed, the idea that society is called upon to abolish the division of labour was first expressed in *The German Ideology*, which dates from 1845–46 and includes the following, highly significant passage (p. 24):

> In communist society, where nobody has one exclusive sphere of activity but each can become accomplished in any branch he wishes, society regulates the general production and thus makes it possible for me to do one thing today and another tomorrow, to hunt in the morning, fish in the afternoon, rear cattle in the evening, criticise after dinner, just as I have a mind, without ever becoming hunter, fisherman, herdsman or critic.

Incidentally, this passage is in part debatable since it is difficult to understand how the idea that production is to be regulated by society can be reconciled with the claim that individuals should at all times be free to decide what they wish to do.

Be that as it may, the excerpts just quoted are evidence that the differences between the distribution criteria envisaged by Marx for these stages are such as to justify the customary distinction that theorists draw between socialism as the first and communism as the second.[131]

Like Lenin, orthodox Marxists hold that capitalism tends to gravitate towards a 'state capitalistic' stage and that 'socialism is merely state-capitalist monopoly which is made to serve the interests of the whole people and has to that extent ceased to be capitalist monopoly' (Lenin 1917d, p. 340). Accordingly, they think that to establish socialism it is

---

[131] Unlike myself in this book, in a monograph on the transition from capitalism to communism Di Marco mentions the two successive steps of the transition process only in passing (see Di Marco 2005, pp. 118–19). Concerning the distinction between socialism and communism, Pagano (2006) argued that in Marx's approach these two models of society were totally and irredeemably different from each other: the two social models that Marx sets against capitalism, he wrote (p. 106), are so thoroughly different that they simply cannot be reconciled.

only necessary to replace the State of capitalists and landowners with a different model of state organisation willing to dismantle all privileges and make full democracy a reality. In other words, since large-size capital-owned concerns are socialised entities (in terms that their output is jointly manufactured by a plurality of workers) and the State apparatus of a state-monopolistic system has already taken over the power to regulate production which it would wield under socialism, what remains to be done, in Lenin's view, is enforcing decrees that will 'transform reactionary-bureaucratic regulation into revolutionary-democratic regulation' (Lenin 1917d, p. 319).[132] In this connection, though, it is worth bearing in mind that in Lenin's approach this transformation results in the 'withering away of the state'. In Lenin's own words, 'the state only exists where there are class antagonisms and a class struggle' (Lenin 1917b, p. 61) and 'revolution alone can "abolish" the bourgeois state. The state in general, i.e. the most complete democracy, can only "wither away"' (p. 74).

These passages clearly show that Lenin divided the transition to socialism into two main steps: firstly the nationalisation of large-size monopolistic concerns, particularly banks, and secondly, a reform of the State apparatus in the direction of democracy and bottom-up control.

In point of fact, Lenin specified that the nationalisation of banks and large-size monopolistic concerns would neither 'directly, i.e., in itself, affect property relations in any way' (1917b, p. 327), nor 'deprive any owner of a single kopek' (p. 314) because his plan was amalgamating all banks into a single megabank, joining all the manufacturers active in each industry into large district-based or nation-wide associations and, consequently, creating the assumptions for the effective control and regulation of economic activity.

Concerning the issue of nationalising banks he argued that 'even if commercial secrecy, etc., were abolished' there were no means of exercising 'effective control of any kind over the individual banks and their operations' because it was 'impossible to keep track of the extremely complex, involved and wily tricks that are used in drawing up balance sheets, founding fictitious enterprises and subsidiaries, enlisting the services of figureheads, and so on, and so forth. Only the amalgamation of all banks into one', he argued, 'which in itself would imply no change whatever in respect of ownership. and which, we repeat, would

---

[132] 'In point of fact', Lenin added 'the whole question of control boils down to who controls whom, i.e., which class is in control and which is being controlled' (Lenin 1917d, p. 325). And this conclusion is an excellent resumé of the roadmap to socialism as envisaged by Lenin.

not deprive any owner of a single kopek, would make it possible to exercise real control' (p. 314).

Hence, it follows that the goal that Lenin wanted to achieve by seizing power was not the expropriation of capitalists, but the acquisition of all such power as was needed to exercise control over the State apparatus by democratic means and thereby to accelerate the 'withering way of the state'.[133]

Lenin's numerous followers include Panzieri, who argued that the capitalistic production model is progressively being extended to society as a whole at every step forward in the advancement of capitalism (see Panzieri 1994, p. 68). On closer analysis, this statement can even be construed as a corollary of the popular Marxist belief that a long drawn-out stage of competition-based capitalism will be followed by a stage during which monopolies and oligopolies will seize hold of society and gradually turn capitalism into 'planned capitalism' (see Turchetto 2001, pp. 290–1).

As mentioned above, in due time Lenin did develop a different view of the transitional period and eventually he came to embrace the idea that the truly socialist enterprise was the cooperative (see Lenin 1923; Boffa 1976, p. 240; Jossa 2008, sect. 13.3; and Cortesi 2010, pp. 533–49).

3 THE TRADITIONAL MARXIST VIEW OF THE CAPITALISTIC STATE

As mentioned above, to accept the type of transition advocated in this book one has to reject 'the view of the State as the enemy and the master to which the working class has been holding on to this day not without reason' (see Tronti 1978, p. 24), that is to say the description of the State as the spokesman for a single class that has been called into question in this book. Whereas in the *Critique of Hegel's Philosophy of Right* and again in *The Eighteenth Brumaire of Louis Bonaparte*, which respectively date from 1843 and 1851, Marx argued that a state bureaucracy could seize hold of the authority to make decisions and exercise it independently of the class in power, in later years, with a thorough change of focus, he bluntly proclaimed that the capitalistic state apparatus was firmly in the hands of a single class. This means he had embraced an idea

---

[133] Not only the reflections just reported, but, more generally, the whole of Lenin's approach are more akin to the ideas of Engels than Marx (see for instance, Rockmore 2005, pp. 167–8). For a critique of Lenin's views, see, for instance, Westra (2002).

which Offe advanced in a well-known study no later than 1977, which is still widely held by the Marxist community and which only few Marxists speaking against the tide dare to categorise as partly unwarranted.[134]

From Offe's perspective, a state can be categorised as a class-based power structure when its institutional mechanisms provide scope for its apparatus to perform a selectivity function designed to further given events to the detriment of others. The underlying assumption here is that the bourgeoisie uses the State apparatus in an effort to advance interests which it would otherwise be unable to attain. Consequently, the primary criterion against which the class character of a State is to be measured is the extent to which the goal selection process performed by its apparatus is designed to identify and further the 'overall interests of capital' *in defiance* of individual aggregations of capitalists or lobbying groups (Offe 1977, p. 133). An additional, no less far-reaching selectivity function is designed to protect capital from anti-capitalistic attacks. In other words, selectivity comes in two forms: it is positive when it generates events designed to help capital avoid erroneous moves; it is negative and repressive when it produces 'non-events' designed to protect capital from its enemies.

A similar line of reasoning underlies Balibar's claim that 'State power cannot be shared' (1976, p. 43) and that 'to develop the analysis of the State from the proletarian standpoint of the class struggle is ... tantamount to criticising resurgent bourgeois legal representation' and representing the State as the 'sphere and the organization of public interests and of public power, as against the private interests of individuals or groups of individuals and their private power' (p. 44). On closer analysis, this criticism boils down to arguing that

> bourgeois legal ideology thus performs a clever conjuring trick: it ceaselessly explains, convincing itself and especially convincing the masses (it is only the experience of their own struggles which teaches them the contrary) that the law is its own source, or, what comes to the same thing, that the opposition

---

[134] In Bobbio's opinion, for instance, the reason why the workers' movement has no theory of the State is that Marx failed to flesh out such a theory (see Bobbio 1976 and, for a discussion of Bobbio's argument, Vv.Aa. 1976). Unlike Bobbio, Tronti (1977, p. 67) holds that Marx's theoretical edifice, though, admittedly not a theory of the State proper, was 'developed in writings other than *Capital* and the *Grundrisse* and is therefore not part of his critique of political economy'.

between democracy (in general) and dictatorship (in general) is an absolute opposition. (Balibar 1976, p. 45)[135]

As far as I can see, both Offe and Balibar fail to consider the fact that even the representatives of the working class may come to power, in which case the implementation of the pro-worker political agenda would doubtless be slowed down by the legal system in place, by cultural drawbacks and by the resistance that the business world would certainly put up, but the workers' representatives would nonetheless secure a measure of political elbow room, gradually amend the legal system and reshape the prevailing cultural sentiment. Whereas the capitalistic State is not necessarily bourgeoisie-oriented, all the economic business that is run therein is and remains the exclusive domain of one class and continues to have a pervasive impact on politics even when power is wielded by working-class representatives. Rather than an agent of the bourgeoisie, a capitalistic State ruled by the representatives of the working class must be looked upon as an agent of the latter whose action is conditioned and, hence, refrained by the power of capital. In other words, although the action of the State will doubtless be constrained by the strong resistance that the bourgeois are able to put up thanks to their sway over the economy, there are chances that the interests of the workers might nonetheless be promoted and that power might ultimately be vested in those employed. In the words of Lelio Basso (1969, p. 43): 'when performing his function as a mediator between opposed interests, far from confining itself to obeying the dictates of the ruling bloc, the State should take heed of the demands and put to advantage the energies of all power groups, including those of workers and other non-capitalistic classes'. Although there is some truth in Tronti's argument that 'an accurate review of the history of capitalistic society clearly shows that there is no such thing as one class which has always had the overhand or a single class which has always been in subjection' (see Tronti 1977, p. 53),[136] it remains that the needs of groups which are not allied with

---

[135] In the opinion of Braudel, 'capitalism can only triumph when it is identified with the State, when it *is* the State' (see Braudel 1977, p. 64).

[136] With respect to Tronti's occasionally obscure analysis of the 'autonomy of the political', Bobbio rightly objected that 'political power is never autonomous or fully self-sufficient; inasmuch as it "is needed", i.e. "functional" to something, it is in a condition of dependence' (see Bobbio 1977, p. 38). The move of a government vesting corporate powers in the workers under the pressure of a revolutionary movement can barely be categorised as fully autonomous since it can be assumed to have been conditioned by outside factors: the economic cycle, the relative weights of the two opposed classes (also an

capital will feature on the State agenda only insofar as the relevant strategies will ultimately play into the hands of the ruling class as well (see Agnoli 1975, p. 22).

Wright Mills and other conflict theorists speak of a power elite, i.e. of power blocs which are not controlled by democratic institutions and prevent rival groups from seizing power. Casting this thesis into even more radical terms, Offe argued that the position of a ruling bloc is invariably attained by those who are able to solve problems which affect society at large (see Offe 1977, pp. 36–7).

The 'rival' anti-capitalistic groups Offe had in mind were certainly those advocating a Soviet-type centrally planned system, but if, conversely, it is assumed that these groups speak out for parliamentary democracy, for instance the establishment of democratic firm management, it is difficult to believe that the elite will actually prevent them from achieving their aim. Democratic firm management would bring a solution to major problems affecting society at large (for instance the unemployment issue – see Jossa 2008), and as it is even able to tackle inadequacies of the democratic system, a society which proclaims itself democratic can barely be expected to withhold power permanently from a movement which advocates full-fledged democracy.

It is worth specifying that the thesis opposed in this book is not the idea underlying the so-called 'theories of influence', i.e. approaches which acknowledge a more or less far-reaching influence of individual capitalists on government action, but not the influence of capitalism as a class. Although I am strongly impressed by Offe's lucid analysis of a dual type of selectiveness which characterises government action because of class influences on the state apparatus and although I do agree with him that certain selection mechanisms play into the hands of the class which is in control of the economy of a capitalistic state, I do not believe that he has provided conclusive evidence that the capitalistic state is always a 'class state'.[137]

The Austro-Marxists Karl Renner, Otto Bauer, Max Adler and Rudolf Hilferding were the first leftist thinkers to challenge the view of the State as consistently concerned with promoting the interests of the bourgeoisie. Renner suggested that the State's increasing concern with the interests of the proletariat was digging a gulf between the State apparatus and the

---

'economic factor') and the willingness of the workers themselves to face the risks entailed in the takeover.

[137] The line of reasoning adopted in this section closely recalls the arguments developed by Kelsen in a 1924 paper written to refute the thesis advanced by Bauer and Bauer's answers (as reported in Marramao 1977, pp. 69–77).

business community; Bauer laid stress on the fact that State power was actually wielded by the classes; Adler held that the 'dictatorship of the proletariat' could be exercised within the framework of political democracy and Hilferding emphasised the need to rethink Marxist political theories, specifically to proceed from anarchism to statism by abandoning the base-superstructure distinction and acknowledging the far-reaching influence of the organised forces of the proletariat on the superstructure. As for Kelsen, he argued the case for treading in the steps of Lassalle instead of Marx, i.e. acknowledging that nothing would prevent a State from framing a democratic political agenda designed to meet the needs of the proletariat (see Marramao 1980).[138]

4 THE PARLIAMENTARY ROAD TO SOCIALISM

On several occasions, Marx and Engels made it clear that the revolution they had in mind could come about *by democratic means* and be enforced by a parliament. In *The Principles of Communism*, Engels emphasised that, once in power, the working class would enforce a democratic constitution, for 'democracy would be quite useless to the proletariat if it were not immediately used as a means of carrying through further measures' (Engels 1847a, p. 350). And many years later Engels also wrote (1891a, p. 226):

> One can conceive that the old society may develop peacefully into the new one in countries where the representatives of the people concentrate all power in their hands, where, if one has the support of the majority of the people, one can do as one sees fit in a constitutional way: in democratic republics such as France and the USA, in monarchies such as Britain.

Moreover, in Engels's introduction to *The Class Struggles in France* we read: 'The irony of world history turns everything upside down. We, the "revolutionaries", the "overthrowers", we are thriving far better on legal methods than on illegal methods and overthrow' (Engels 1895, p. 552).

---

[138] Authors who reject the description of the capitalistic state as the power structure of one class include Nicos Poulantzas, who dismissed it as 'oversimplified' and 'vulgarised' (1968, p. 326 and the whole of section IV), and Lelio Basso, who laid stress on the function of the State as a mediator and 'clearing house of contradictory energies' (see Basso 1969, pp. 165–6).

In a number of works published in the last years of his life, Engels concerned himself with specific events in the economic and political lives of individual nations and expatiated on changes in political climate recorded over the years. As is known, the collapse of Bismarck's regime marked the eclipse of policies aimed at the outright suppression of socialist parties. Reviewing similar trends in other European nations, Engels remarked that on realising the changing scene, the socialist parties of the day found that legal methods served the interests of the working class much more effectively than the violent methods associated with insurrections could have done:

> The attempt must be made to get along with the legal methods of struggle for the time being. Not only we are doing this, it is being done by all workers' parties in all countries where the workers have a certain measure of legal freedom of action, and this for the simple reason that it is the most productive method for them. (Engels 1890, p. 78)

In a polemical 1890–91 paper written in stark opposition to Brentano, Engels argued that the power of factory legislation and trade unions to improve the conditions of the working class (which was Brentano's contention) had been underscored by Marx and himself in a wealth of writings ranging from *The Condition of the Working Class in England* and *The Misery of Philosophy*, through *Capital* down to later ones. However, he also added that this statement was to be taken with caution, since the positive effects of trade union action were confined to periods of thriving business and were bound to become erratic in times of stagnation and crisis (Engels 1890–91, pp. 97–8).

A pregnant analysis of this subject is found in the introduction to *The Class Struggles in France* written by Engels in 1895. The teachings of earlier revolutions, especially those in France in 1789 and 1830, he admitted, had exerted a strong influence on both of them, but later developments, he added, proved those approaches wrong and, moreover, the conditions under which the proletariat was expected to carry on its struggle had meanwhile undergone radical change. Each of those earlier revolutions had resulted in replacing one ruling class with another, but the ruling groups coming to power were all found to be small minorities compared to the mass of those ruled. Moreover, upon seizing power, each such minority group remodelled the state apparatus in accordance with its own needs and the majority of the governed did nothing but support that minority or, at any rate, show themselves acquiescent. In Engels's words, 'if we disregard the concrete content in each case, the common form of all these revolutions was that they were minority revolutions' (Engels

1895, p. 510), and after each such minority revolution – he continued – the feelings of the masses always, and often presently so, changed from enthusiasm to utter disappointment and even despair.[139]

From these reflections Engels drew the conviction that the times were not ripe for a socialist revolution; in fact, as a result of post-1844 developments and the introduction of universal suffrage in Germany in 1866, he had come to believe that a revolution was to be enacted by parliamentary means, through a real and proper majority resolution. From Engels's perspective, therefore, universal suffrage had laid the foundations for a new method of proletarian struggle, and from then on 'the bourgeoisie and the government came to be much more afraid of the legal than of the illegal action of the workers' party, of the results of elections than of those of rebellion' (1895, p. 516).

However, Engels's confidence in a final victory was far from eroded by the prospect of a parliamentary road to socialism. The electoral successes of the proletariat and its new allies, he argued, were steady and irresistible and, though tranquil, as unavoidable as a natural process. For workers to win out in the end, they must 'simply refuse to let themselves be lured into street fighting' (p. 523).[140]

---

[139] As mentioned by Lenin (1917b, p. 78), however, in an 1895 letter complaining of the difficulties he had come up against in publishing his introduction to *The Class Struggles in France*, Engels wrote: '[Liebknecht] has played me a nick trick. He has taken from my *Introduction* to Marx's articles on France in 1848–50 everything that could serve his purpose in support of *peaceful and antiviolent tactics at any price*, which he has chosen to preach for some time now, particularly at this juncture, when coercive laws are being drawn up in Berlin. But I preach those tactics only for the Germany of today and even then *with many reservations*.' The passages just quoted are clear evidence that Lenin was wrong when he wrote that 'this view of violent revolution lies at the root of the entire theory of Marx and Engels' (Lenin 1917b, p. 79). Conversely, Lenin himself held on to the idea that the revolution was to be carried through by violent means (see Cortesi 1970).

[140] In Hobsbawm 2011 (p. 75) we read that 'what was to give rise to particular controversy was his [Engels's] insistence on the new possibilities implicit in universal suffrage, and his abandonment of the old insurrectionary perspectives – both clearly formulated in one of his last writings, the *aggiornamento* of Marx's *Class Struggles in France* (1895) ... Yet in fact, in spite of some ambiguity in Engels's last writings, he certainly cannot be read as approving or implying the legalistic and electoralistic illusions of later German and other social democrats'.

In his preface to the English edition of Book I of *Capital*, Engels mentioned Marx's firm belief that England was 'the only country where the inevitable social revolution might be effected by peaceful and legal means'.

Marx, too, repeatedly declared himself in favour of a peaceful transition to communism. With reference to his description of universal suffrage as one of the primary goals that the proletariat was to pursue, a commentator has argued that he equated the takeover of the proletariat with a successful battle for democracy even in such an early work as the *Manifesto of the Communist Party* (Avineri 1968); and in *Capital*, Marx attached major importance to factory legislation and, generally, the role of assemblies returned in elections by universal suffrage, besides dwelling extensively (in hundreds of pages) on the fact that in parliaments the interests of the working class had often taken precedence over those of employers (see Sidoti 1987, p. 280).

5 SOCIALISM AS A FORESEEABLE DEVELOPMENT

The claim that an escalating capital–labour confrontation paves the way for reversing the capitalistic capital–labour relation can hardly be called into question.

Technological evolution is currently moving in the opposite direction to Fordism. As a result, at this stage the argument that the advent of economic democracy is being expedited by the degradation of human labour caused by Fordism and Taylorism is unwarranted. Does this validate the opposite assumption that the higher educational and expertise levels required by modern technology are expediting the transition to democratic firm management and, hence, restoring momentum to labour management theory? According to Laibman (2006, pp. 315–16), there is a stage, in the evolution of production processes, at which efficiency and productivity gains become strictly dependent on autonomy, creativity, critical discernment as well as modes of behaviour supported by sound criteria. From this, he argues, it follows that when this threshold is reached and people interiorise the idea that quality and productivity are inextricably interconnected, the high road to socialism will be followed as a matter of course.

This idea is widely shared. By general agreement (see, for instance, Ben-Ner 1987 and 1988, pp. 295–6), the living standard of workers is a major determinant of both the advantages granted to labour-managed firms and the difficulties they come up with. There is evidence that workers become less averse to risk and develop greater entrepreneurial skills accordingly as their income levels increase. This is why I agree with Zamagni that 'as human and social capital acquire a greater strategic role than physical and financial capital, the overriding importance of democratic governance modes becomes more and more evident also on a strictly economic plane' (Zamagni 2006, p. 60). Indeed, the greater a worker's educational level and qualifications, the less he will be prepared to work at the behest of another and the more he will tend to acquire the abilities necessary to run a firm by himself. Also, according to Bowles and Gintis (1996b, p. 82), higher-income workers find it more convenient to work for a firm which they run directly. Very often – they argue – workers in self-managed firms have the feeling that their incomes may be at risk and that they may prove unable to finance a decent standard of living for their families, but this feeling recedes in proportion to increases in income.

The abolition of hired labour in a labour-managed system gives rise to a more democratic system in which workers are no longer alienated because they cease being under coercion from employers; and according to Hayek (1960) coercion is a social evil which turns a useful thinking individual into a tool for the achievement of another's ends. Accordingly, anyone thinking, like Marx, that mankind will gradually gain more and more freedom (even though via the most tortuous of paths) can hardly doubt that democratic firm management is bound to become a reality at some point in time. As I stated in the introduction, in the words of Lukàcs (1968a, p. 34), 'Marx, much like German philosophers and chiefly Hegel, conceived of world history as a unitary process and the high road towards liberation'. Consequently, Tosel's conclusion that communism brings liberalism to completion deserves to be heartily endorsed (Tosel 2005, p. 329).

In short, it is reasonable to assume that labour management is bound to make headway in history as manual labour loses importance and workers acquire greater educational and professional qualifications (see, e.g. Mandel 1973, p. 349).[141]

---

[141]   In this connection, Bobbio wrote (1995, p. 39): 'As predicted by Toqueville with some concern in the nineteenth century, the call for ever fuller equality is and remains irresistible notwithstanding the aversion and strenuous resistance it arouses at any turn of history. Indeed, it is one of the main driving forces behind historical development.'

6 STATE INTERVENTION IN A SYSTEM OF PRODUCER COOPERATIVES

In conclusion, it is worth raising the question if and how the State should intervene in the economy of a worker-controlled firm system.

Besides predicting the 'withering away' of the State upon the establishment of communism and the dictatorship of the proletariat, Lenin wrote (1917b, p. 94):

> To confine Marxism to the theory of the class struggle means curtailing Marxism, distorting it, reducing it to something acceptable to the bourgeoisie. Only he is a Marxist who extends the recognition of the class struggle to the recognition of the dictatorship of the proletariat. That is what constitutes the most profound distinction between the Marxist and the ordinary petty (as well as big) bourgeois.

From my perspective, considering the State's duty to ensure the public peace and redress market failures, the only function it is expected to perform in line with the logic governing a 'dictatorship of the proletariat' is the enforcement of a ban on the establishment of medium to large-size enterprises.

Some authors have recently argued that markets are incompatible with government in any form. Moreover, in an analysis of industrial countries Barro has shown that the redistributive State policies required for each piecemeal extension of democracy, though designed to further such a basic component of democracy as equality, are actually at odds with efficiency (Barro 1996).

Arrow and Barro argue that any State action requiring tax increases stands in the way of the achievement of a Pareto optimum. In an attempt to back up the theoretical approaches of liberalist academics with experiential data, Barro (1996) mentions an awkward link between slow growth and political freedom that should induce governments to reduce State intervention: in a political freedom index (ranging between 0 and 1) of some 100 countries which had provided their 1960–90 data, it was observed that countries with an index value above 0.5 were those where growth was slowest.

As these objections are well argued, they can help us pinpoint some of the plus points of a system of producer cooperatives.

A major finding of economic science is the potential of a perfect-competition system to generate a Pareto optimum within the utilitarian tradition of well-being. On closer analysis, however, a Pareto optimum maximises well-being only with respect to a specific initial distribution of economic resources and within a system to which the 'survival assumption' is found to apply. As a result, if we take as a starting point a Pareto-optimal situation, a new situation with a better initial income distribution will improve the well-being of a community. Indeed, this is the reason why governments attempt to improve income distribution.

These reflections suggest a weighty argument in support of a co-operative system. As argued by Mill, production activities are usually contrasted with income distribution because the former are said to obey mechanical rules, while the latter is thought to be socially determined. Inasmuch as this is true, fairer income distribution patterns can be put in place in two alternative ways: (a) by enforcing tax bracket adjustments and, hence, both hampering the free working of markets and preventing the achievement of Pareto optimums; and (b) by enforcing legislation designed to pave the way for equal access opportunities to the more lucrative professions. Hence, it is possible to argue that a democratic firm system stripping capital of its power and control rights can bring about a fairer income allocation structure even in the absence of actions designed to modify the taxation system or interfere with the working of markets. Options available to governments include policies with a negligible impact on market mechanisms, for example a reform of the educational system, a well-organised system of competitive examinations to govern recruitment or the enforcement of a well-orchestrated succession tax regime. In overall terms, governments can be expected to shape goal-specific strategies ensuring the implementation of State intervention policies capable of improving income distribution without encroaching upon the free working of market mechanisms.[142]

In point of fact, government action is not only aimed at shaping more equitable income distribution patterns, but also at scaling down risks of 'market failure'. Especially in a globalised world, unwanted economic crises are sure to be sparked off by the workings of the invisible hand as long as there are markets, but despite the obvious implication that

---

[142] The persuasion that the legal 'superstructure' of the bourgeois state was a historical necessity induced Marx to argue that no alternative formal criterion for the control of the economy was likely to outperform it even at the early stages of a communist system (see Zolo 1974, p. 47). In this connection, Galgano della Volpe wrote: 'As long as a state – albeit a democratic one such as a socialist state – does exist, and as long as there is a social order organised in accordance with the criterion of the distinction between governors and governed, there is no way of deflecting from the basic principle that a limit is to be placed on the power that the state should be allowed to wield over the citizens' (della Volpe 1964, p. 47).

downturns in the economy will continue to be a risk even in markets where capitalists have been ousted from power, there are reasons to assume that such undesirable turns of events would be less frequent than they are in capitalistic systems. Indeed, in a system freed from the control of capitalists the State will find it easier to intervene in the economy for the purpose of fending off crises. The multitude may act as one or as many, and it may become a political agent either by developing unity of will or through the workings of the invisible hand. But such unity of will as is expressed through political majority resolutions is much less forcefully counteracted by the action of markets (the invisible hand) if the markets concerned cease being conditioned by the requirements of capital.

To shed light on additional facets of this problem, a comparative analysis of such antipodal systems as a pure capitalistic market economy and one where the State strives to correct malfunctions is likely to suggest the prima facie conclusion that problems can be readily handled if 'market failures' are exceptional occurrences and State action can hence be confined to a minimum. In point of fact, it is widely held that market failures are the rule and that massive intervention by a State bureaucracy may generate even grimmer inefficiencies than those self-generated by the market. This poses a need to establish if, and to what extent, a system of producer cooperatives would actually be in a position to outperform capitalistic markets in terms of averting, or at least remedying, the typical failures of a system driven by the private profit motive only. Experience has taught that many issues likely to degenerate into classical market or State failures (dismissals, excess or ineffectual work input control, environment-averse actions, etc.) can be effectively tackled by communities. As these, contrary to the State or markets, have crucial information about the needs and abilities of their members (see Bowles & Gintis 2002, pp. 425–6), near-community organisations such as producer cooperatives might take the place of the State or supplement its action in a wide range of situations and reduce the need for public intervention.

In overall terms, a democratic firm system where capitalists have been stripped of power is able to tackle most of the causes of market failure even in the absence of State intervention. Inasmuch as this is true, the State would be called upon to intervene in the economy even in a democratic firm system, but its intervention would be less pervasive than it tends to – and must – be at the present day.

Concluding, a considerable advantage of a cooperative firm system is its potential to further the smooth working of markets thanks to a lesser need for State action.

8. Some critics of labour management

1 INTRODUCTION

A well-known Italian cooperation theorist once sounded a weighty note of caution: 'It is always dangerous, if not fatal, to indulge in false ideas. Setting up producer cooperatives is not a simple undertaking and workers poised to run them on their own will come up against serious obstacles' (see Rabbeno 1889, p. 609). This necessitates clarifying what these obstacles are.

Ever since the publication of Ward's theory of price determination in cooperatives back in 1958, the efficiency of worker-run enterprises has been called into question by numerous authors. One objection, the risk of a 'perverse', i.e. dangerously downward sloping supply curve, was first raised by Ward himself (see Ward 1958, 1967, pp. 190–91 and 197–8; Vanek 1970, ch. 3) and was initially perceived as crucial. In due time, however, the arguments and criticisms advanced by other theorists helped bring the issue into its true perspective (see Domar 1996; Horvat 1967, 1975; Meade 1972, pp. 409–10; Berman 1977; Steinherr & Thisse 1979a, 1979b; Sertel 1982; Brewer & Browning 1982; Miyazaki & Neary 1983; Hansmann 1996, pp. 84–5; Jossa & Cuomo 1997, ch. 9; Dow 1998; and Jossa 1999, 2002, ch. 2, 2005b, chs 4–6).

According to Dow (1998, p. 992), the slope of the LMF's supply curve is 'perverse, but the true reason for this is not worker control as such, but lack of opportunity costs with respect to the external labour option'. Anyone holding Dow's view should bear in mind that analyses conducted by Miyazaki and Neary (1983) as well as Craig and Pencavel (1995) in later years showed it to be empirically negligible. Indeed, it was argued that the assumption of a declining supply curve was to be backed up by the demonstration that its slope is, as a rule, steeper than that of the demand curve and that the result is instability – a conclusion which is barely realistic.[143]

---

[143] Craig and Pencavel's survey of the US plywood industry (1995), which is probably the most exhaustive analysis of the behaviour of the supply curves of cooperative firms, showed that they were certainly less sensitive to price

Obstacles to an appreciable increase in the number of democratic firms include the need to lodge the collateral required to back up loans, the resulting underinvestment issue, lack of portfolio diversification opportunities, as well as monitoring and control issues. As will be argued in greater detail below, some of these obstacles can be averted if co-operatives are organised in accordance with the LMF model.

The first of the problems mentioned above has been analysed at length by a wealth of theorists (see, inter alia, Furubotn & Pejovich 1970b and 1973; Furubotn 1976 and 1980; Vanek 1971a and 1971b; Jossa & Casavola 1993; and Jossa 2005b, ch. 8). The gist of their argument is that underinvestment is caused by the principle that investment resolutions require a favourable vote cast by a majority of the partners. Since exiting partners forfeit the right to the labour incomes generated by the co-operative, it is argued, those about to exit for seniority or other reasons are likely to vote against many of these resolutions. In point of fact, most of the surveys addressing this issue have found that underinvestment is frequent in WMFs, but the exception is LMFs. In particular, it is worth emphasising that a simple move such as the allotment of bonds in the value of the amounts the partners would have cashed if the profits had been distributed would be enough to take Furubotn and Pejovich's limited time horizon problem from the ground, in terms that exiting partners would be able to retain – and even freely trade – the bonds received upon the adoption of the firm's financing resolutions. In a cooperative organised in keeping with the LMF model just described, the partners are jointly liable for the firm's debts as long as they stay with the firm and have claims on it in respect of the amounts they made available to it in helping finance its investments, whereas upon their exit they cease being liable towards outside creditors while retaining their claims.[144]

An additional advantage of the cooperative model just described is its potential to help avert the risk that the partners should 'swallow up the firm', i.e. dismantle it by selling its capital goods and apportion the proceeds of the sale among themselves – a risk assumed to be faced by publicly owned cooperative enterprises of the type existing in Yugoslavia during the self-management experiment (see, inter alia, Vanek 1972,

---

variations than those of capitalistic enterprises, but hardly ever showed the 'perverse' slope which is ascribed to them.

[144] There is wide agreement that the Furubotn-Pejovich underinvestment effect would be inconsequential if the partners were entitled to freely trade their interests in worker-controlled enterprises (see, inter alia, Zanotti 2016, p. 115).

pp. 220–1). Indeed, if the partners have authorised borrowing arrangements, such a move would expose them to the risk of defaulting on their obligations.

These reflections shed light on the reasons why this model would even help solve the portfolio diversification issue, which is and remains one of the weak points of democratic firm management. Whereas the shareholders of capitalistic enterprises are free to diversify their investment as they like, the partners of cooperative firms are bound to the single firm for which they work. The organisation model recommended in this book would enable bondholding partners to diversify their investment portfolios by selling their bonds to third parties and purchasing bonds of other firms. This solution is not applicable to the WMF, which self-finances its investments without issuing any bonds and whose partners have no means of diversifying the incomes they earn on their interests in the firm.

One more point to be considered is that self-management socialism, i.e. a producer cooperative system, is to be established by democratic means following a favourable majority vote of the electorate – a result which might be achieved as soon as most would-be economic operators feel that they have secured sufficient means to face the risks incidental to the direct management of enterprises.

Lesser layoff risks are an additional advantage offered by cooperatives. Compared to the employees of capitalistic enterprises, in the event of a downturn in business the workers of a cooperative run lesser layoff risks for two main reasons: (a) destaffing resolutions, where any, have to be adopted democratically and (b) the partners of the firm will barely be prepared to dismiss their fellow partners. And as the system recommended in this book of cooperative firms envisages the right of LMFs to take on a limited number of wage or salary earners, risk-averse individuals might ask to be hired based on conventional contracts of employment.

The plant-monitoring issue is an additional objection raised by Alchian and Demsetz in a well-known article dating 1972. If the cooperative is a WMF, they argued, the partners will hardly deem it worthwhile incurring the maintenance costs required to keep the capital goods of their firms in good order and repair. This objection can be countered by arguing that no such problem would arise if firms were organised as LMFs, since the partners' right to retain the bonds received on the adoption of self-financing resolutions would make them eager to keep the firm going even after their exit.

The capital goods maintenance issue is inextricably intertwined with the control problem. In Jensen and Meckling's own words (1979, p. 487):

'It seems to us unlikely that outside investors would voluntarily entrust their funds to a labor-managed enterprise in which the workers maintained complete control and the investors were allowed to hope that the worker-managers would behave in such a way as to leave something for them'. This passage sheds light on an additional weak point of worker-run firms: whereas in capitalistic enterprises the shareholders remain in control, an external provider of funds to a cooperative has no control over the firm they finance because they do not hold any position in it. Is this a good reason for prioritising WMFs over LMFs? This question might be answered in the affirmative only if LMFs, departing from the optimal model recommended above, should abstain from self-financing their investments. As things stand, given the partners' right to take away their bonds, even those about to leave the LMF will deem it reasonable to keep the firm going.

With reference to decision making, Jensen and Meckling (1979, pp. 488–9) argued that no theorists had been able to come up with a satisfactory solution to this problem in cooperative firms:

> No one has specified a well-defined set of procedures for solving the decision-making problem within the firm when the preferences of the workers are not all identical. It is usually simply assumed that the workers will have a common set of preferences and that no conflicts will arise in translating these into operational policies at the firm level.

From my perspective, to clear the field of this objection it is worth bearing in mind that the appointment of managers with full power to run all the operations will help medium to large-size cooperatives to head towards a satisfactory performance.

In a well-known book (1996), Hansmann argued that collective decision-making costs were by far the main problem cooperatives were called upon to tackle, but although he did discuss the matter at some length, his analysis just covered cooperatives existing and operating in the Western world in his day, so that his firm sample did not include any employee-managed enterprises organised in keeping with the model fleshed out by modern economists. These reflections prompt the conclusion that right upon the appointment of managers allowed full freedom of action the problem pointed out by Hansmann will become negligible as a matter of course.

2 FURTHER REFLECTIONS ON THE APPOINTMENT OF MANAGERS

The second prerequisite for the efficient operation of employee-managed firms is having them run by one or more managers.[145] John Stuart Mill (1871, p. 745) held that

> individual management, by the one person principally interested, has great advantages over every description of collective management ... Unity of authority makes many things possible which could not or would not be undertaken subject to the chance of divided councils or changes in the management. A private capitalist, exempt from the control of a body, if he is a person of capacity, is considerably more likely than almost any association to run judicious risks, and originate costly improvements.

This opinion of Mill's is fully in sync with Hansmann's argument that the main obstacle to the growth of the cooperative movement is the considerable collective decision-making costs faced by these firms (see Hansmann 1996).

Such a simple measure as the appointment and full empowerment of managers would literally sweep away these obstacles. On this point, Dahl argued that the question as to whether workers are less qualified to run their cooperative (in terms of choosing able managers) than the shareholders of investor-owned enterprises could be answered by claiming that they were even more qualified (see Dahl 1989, p. 331).

According to Bernstein (1899, p. 158), however, the greater or lesser ability of workers to choose really able managers was a fairly inconsequential issue compared to the sheer incompatibility of economic democracy with the discipline required to run the operations of any business enterprise – the cause he perceived to be behind the failure of most self-managed factories. In his own words,

---

[145] The appointment of one or more managers can hence be looked upon as an alliance of sorts between the working class and the 'competence pole'. According to Bidet (2005, p. 291), 'politics from beneath' is not only the result of the union of its components, but also a 'politics of alliance' with the competence pole and a constant practice within what is termed the 'workers' movement'. This means that the 'left', far from being a structural element, will only rise to power on condition that those at the bottom, rising to a hegemonic position within the competence pole, manage to sever the links between its components and the owners.

given the tasks which the management of a factory entails, where daily and hourly prosaic decisions liable to cause friction have to be made, it is simply impossible that the manager should be the employee of those he manages and that he should be dependent for his position on their favour and bad temper.

Marshall himself once warned that the practice of allowing employees to sit on the board and argue with the managers over the tiniest of management details was surely a shortcut to the destruction of an enterprise (see Marshall 1889, p. 243).[146]

Bernstein's cogent objection resounds in Einaudi's argument that 'able proactive managers are likely to walk out as soon as a workers' council walks in'.[147] On closer analysis, though, due to the problems inherent in the collective management mode cooperatives have no option but to appoint managers and grant them full powers. Incidentally speaking, experience has taught that this objection is barely decisive since those cooperatives that have vested full powers in their managers are seen to operate at satisfactory efficiency levels.[148]

As reported by John Reed (1920, pp. 72–3), on the outbreak of the March revolution in Russia the owners and managers of a great many

---

[146] According to Marshall, one of the points over which contrast was likely to prove divisive was the scale of the remuneration packages to be granted to the managers (Marshall 1889, p. 244).

[147] The gist of Bernstein's objection underlies Williamson's argument that vesting the monitoring function in a single individual is at odds with the essence of cooperation, in which the notion of hierarchy has no place (1975, p. 53).

[148] Putterman (1984, p. 172) mentions the well-known paper in which Alchian and Demsetz argued that whenever the authority vested in the manager includes the right to hire and dismiss its workers the appointment of such a manager proves detrimental to economic democracy. And Cugno and Ferrero (1992, pp. 140ff.) and Sacconi (1992, p. 179), when using the term 'capitalist' to describe the person in charge of the monitoring function, implicitly endorse the view that the appointment of a monitor will turn a cooperative into an altogether different firm.

Unlike them, I firmly hold that the appointment of a manager will barely scathe the democratic essence of a cooperative both because the powers that really count remain firmly in the hands of the workers and because the true strong points of democratic firms lie elsewhere and have nothing to do with the running of its day-to-day business by the workers (in addition to the reflections developed below, see, for instance, Jossa 2004). In this connection, let me mention that the Spanish Mondragon complex has developed a number of institutions and practices which tend to make participation as meaningful as possible and, hence, to avert the risk of reducing the involvement of the workers in the affairs of the individual firms of the group, all of which are run by managers (see Campbell 2011).

industrial concerns either quit or were driven out by the workers. The result was serious management problems which came to an end when a workman rose to his feet during a factory committee meeting and said:

> Comrades, why do we worry? The question of technical experts is not a difficult one. Remember the boss wasn't a technical expert; the boss didn't know about engineering or chemistry or bookkeeping. All he did was to own. When he wanted technical help, he hired men to do it for him. Well, now we are the boss. Let's hire engineers, bookkeepers, and so forth – to work for us![149]

The relevance of this anecdote with respect to the purpose of this chapter lies in the suggestion that the type of firm which is likely to prove most efficient and to which reference should be made is the medium to large-size cooperative.[150] In smaller cooperatives, which can barely afford to appoint professional managers, decisions will usually be made jointly by all the partners – though one of them will generally act as leader.

3 DIFFICULTIES AT THE START-UP STAGE

The scant concern of economic theorists with economic democracy can be traced to a variety of reasons other than the assumed shortcomings of cooperatives discussed above. While most of these must necessarily fall outside the scope of this book, one of them, the obstacles cooperatives come up against at the formation stage, is worth discussing here.[151]

---

[149] Theorists who attach great importance to the direct involvement of the workers in the firm's operations hold that the headcount of a self-managed firm should not exceed a certain limit thought to be compatible with the participation of all the partners in the firm's management. Bernstein (1980) estimated this headcount at a number of partners within the range of 250–300 at the most.

In the opinion of Trower, freedom of choice is not the only point which is at stake. As soon as we acknowledge that a form of managerial control is needed in industry, we have to admit that at this stage of society collective bargaining is of no avail when it comes to democratising such control (see Trower 1973, p. 141).

[150] One major implication is the need to analyse the behaviour of this type of cooperative by reference to 'managerial' enterprise models, rather than the traditional 'closed box' model (see Cuomo 2003, pp. 109–18).

[151] The obstacles impeding the establishment of new cooperatives have been analysed in depth in a number of historical outlines of the evolution of the cooperative movement. In particular, more than one theorist has laid special stress on the inability of the would-be founders of a new cooperative to raise the

It is widely held that the efficient working of a system of democratic firms is much more conditional on the rise of new firms than that of capitalistic systems in comparable circumstances (see, inter alia, Meade 1972, pp. 420–1 and 1979, p. 787 and Jensen & Meckling 1979, pp. 478–9), but that the achievement of this goal is often impeded by greater fundraising difficulties cooperators tend to face compared to the founders of investor-owned enterprises. A capitalistic firm is set up when a person of means resolves to hire wage and salary earners in the awareness that he is in a position to lodge the collateral needed to obtain credit. The same is not applicable to the founders of a democratic firm. Rather than setting up a cooperative and sharing decision powers and earnings with others, a person with organisational skills and sizeable financial resources will prefer to establish an entrepreneurial firm in which he will retain all powers, be sole proprietor and appropriate the whole of the firm's surplus (see, inter alia, Dow 2003, p. 17 and Gunn 2006, p. 346). Theorists addressing this point have emphasised that a person resolving to invest resources in a cooperative will not be entitled to the whole revenues of the firm for two reasons: (a) due to the need to apportion the earnings of his initiative among all the partners; and (b) because he will not be entitled to any share of the revenues that the firm will continue to earn thanks to his initiative even after his exit. In the opinion of Ben-Ner, a new firm will be organised in line with the cooperative model only if its founders are (a) able to conceive a well-organised action plan; (b) prepared to accept risks of losses; (c) in a position to raise funds; and (d) capable of funding the required start-up expenses. These are the areas, he concluded, in which workers are at a disadvantage compared to capital owners (see Ben-Ner 1987, pp. 289–90). This is why two cooperation specialists of considerable standing wrote: 'A high net worth individual poised to raise the capital resources for a possibly lucrative enterprise is likely to opt for a limited company or a partnership, according as he deems fit, but will hardly ever choose the cooperative form' (Riguzzi & Porcari 1925, p. 5). In a recent study (Pérotin 2006, p. 296), the comparative paucity of worker-run firms even in countries where structural problems have been solved is traced to difficulties at the start-up stage, rather than to the closure of existing cooperatives.[152]

---

requisite starting capital (see, inter alia, Cole 1953a, vol. 1, chs 14 and 24 and vol. 2, especially chs 5 and 9; Putterman 1982, pp. 150–1; Zangheri et al. 1987; and Gunn 2006, p. 35).

[152] A saying by Olson (1965) has it that the difficulties faced in setting up a collective organisation and the effort and expenditure required to organise its

The reflections developed so far prompt the conclusion that only persons without financial means of their own and without specific entrepreneurial skills will find it convenient to set up a cooperative firm.[153] For that matter, historical experience has taught that the main obstacle standing in the way of the further development of the cooperative movement is the obstacles faced by cooperators when they come to raising the funds necessary at the start-up stage. Few people indeed will be prepared to provide funds to non-propertied people.

Difficulties at the start-up stage are hence one of the reasons behind the scant success of these firms that Vanek has repeatedly emphasised (see, for instance, Vanek 1970, p. 318).[154]

Once established, however, cooperatives tend to prove viable enough. According to Ben-Ner (1988, p. 296), running a going concern is easier than managing a start-up because of lesser capitalisation requirements and reduced overheads. These reflections suggest that the economic democracy model to be upheld and promoted by all means is a mixed system, rather than one entirely consisting of cooperatives. Private individuals should be allowed to create and own comparatively small-size firms (with a headcount of a dozen workers at the most)[155] and the cooperative form should be restricted to enterprises over a given threshold size and/or firms eligible for State aid.

More than any other author, Vanek has chosen as his favourite focus the difficulties faced by cooperatives at the start-up stage and the effects

---

operations often exceed the benefits that the promoters are likely to draw from it (see also Jossa 2006b).

[153]   Some authors trace the difficulties of cooperatives mainly to the fact that their directors are usually wealthy philanthropists or artisans lacking the practical expertise required to keep enterprises of this type going (see Briganti 1982, vol. 1, p. 58, as cited by Magliulo).

[154]   In contrast, a survey conducted by Poletti back in 1905 found that cooperatives proliferated between 1891 and 1904, but, so to say, lived through all the stages of their lifetime from birth to death in quick succession (p. 16) because of insufficient capitalisation levels impeding their efficient operation right from the start. In contrast, most commentators today concordantly emphasise that producer cooperatives tend to be rather long-lived (see, inter alia, Sapelli 2006, pp. 20 and 51). No fewer than 16 of the cooperatives operating in France today were set up before World War I (see Pérotin 2006, p. 296).

[155]   'The cooperative form', Sylos Labini wrote (2006, p. 34), 'is not suited to small-size enterprises' (see also, Sylos Labini 2004, p. 105).

of these obstacles. In a chapter of his 1970 monograph on the subject he suggested neutralising the adverse impact of these obstacles by promoting the creation of state-owned industrial sheds to be made available to cooperatives. Although Vanek's proposal is certainly worth discussing at greater length, in my estimation the ideal solution (mentioned above) is a mixed system in which small-size cooperatives would compete with small-size entrepreneurial enterprises and medium–large size ones capable of generating 'merit goods' for the community would be assigned tax benefits and credit facilities. Let me specify that only cooperatives generating 'external economies', i.e. benefits for society at large, will be eligible for such subsidies. Moreover, it is worth noting that this subsidisation policy is not a 'statist' measure, but an incentive to competition and, as such, is endorsed by economists of every political faith.

4   FURTHER REFLECTIONS ON THE FUNDRAISING ISSUE

As mentioned above, cooperatives have difficulty financing their capital investments (for a detailed analysis of this issue, see Cuomo 2004 and Jossa 2005b, ch. 9). It has also been mentioned that a person owning the resources required to venture into business will hardly opt for the creation of a cooperative and will usually prefer to set up a capitalistic enterprise in which he will exercise all decision powers and appropriate the whole of the profits earned.

In even more general terms, the main obstacle to the spontaneous rise of a system of worker-run enterprises in a capitalistic context is the so-called 'collateral dilemma' (see Vanek 1970, p. 318), that is to say the difficulty that propertyless workers come up against when it comes to lodging the collateral that providers of funds require to back up the repayment of loans.[156]

---

[156]   As argued by Drèze (1993, p. 254), the fundraising problem 'is central to understanding why labour management does not spread in capitalist economies'. In a monograph on this point, Gui (1993) reached the conclusion that the relatively small number of cooperatives in today's economic systems was to be traced to two main obstacles: the inability to attract capital and able managers and the fact that the success of a democratic firm depends (even more than that of an investor-owned company) on its ability to reach a satisfactory level of 'social performance' (see also, inter alia, Mygind 1997 and Vaughan-Whitehead 1999, p. 42). Unlike Gui, Hansmann holds that one of the principal findings of

The socialist thinkers who have addressed this problem roughly fall into two groups. At one end of the spectrum are Owen and Fourier, who called for the action of wealthy philanthropists; at the other end are Saint Simon, Blanc and Proudhon, who suggested the establishment of a national bank.

To decide if this objection is actually as weighty as current economists hold it to be it is necessary to provide a few preliminary clarifications. It is widely held that the partners of a democratic firm tend to venture into particularly risk-intensive investment projects, because thanks to their status as partners remunerated out of the residual they will cash the payoffs in case of success and, in the opposite case, they can leave the firm at any time without meeting the obligations towards its creditors (see Drèze 1976; Schlicht & Von Weizsäcker 1977; Gui 1982 and 1985; Eswaran & Kotwal 1989; Putterman et al. 1998, pp. 886–97).[157]

Actually, no such tendency is observed in practice. Since the primary concern of the partners is to protect and stabilise their incomes, they will tend to be less risk-prone (see Drèze 1976, 1989 and 1993) and will probably prioritise less risky projects than those typically launched by the managers of investor-owned enterprises. The latter make investment decisions in the exclusive interests of the owners, without regard to the interests of the workforce, which means that particularly risk-intensive projects may be launched irrespective of possible layoff risks. At the other end of the spectrum are worker-run enterprises, whose managers are appointed by the partners and will therefore screen possible projects and types of investment with due consideration to the expected cash flow and to their foreseeable impact on the stability of the firm's workforce. Sapelli has rightly emphasised that 'safeguarding existing jobs and creating fresh employment opportunities are functions which should not be regarded as external constraints, but (along with the principle of collective enterprise) as the main preconditions for the growth of the cooperative movement' (Sapelli 1982, p. 70). Hence, it is possible to conclude that due to these reasons cooperative firms will tend to prioritise moderately risk-intensive investment projects.

---

his research on firm ownership and management is that 'the capital intensity of an industry and the degree of risk inherent in the industry both play a much smaller role than is commonly believed in determining whether firms in that industry are investor-owned' (see Hansmann 1996, p. 4).

[157] Two well-known papers in which the assumed risk-proneness of cooperatives is associated with the limited liability principle are Jensen and Meckling (1976) and Stiglitz and Weiss (1981).

An additional reflection which ultimately leads to the same conclusion is the already mentioned different positions of capitalistic investors and cooperators with respect to the diversification issue, i.e. the fact that the former can diversify their investment portfolios at will, while the latter cannot work for more than one firm at a time. The acute perception of the risks inherent in their investments is one more reason which is likely to induce the partners of a cooperative to consider only investment projects with tolerable risk profiles.[158]

Coming back to the investment financing issue, is it true that co-operatives come up against particularly severe fundraising difficulties? As mentioned above, the cooperatives that the State should further through the enforcement of suitable state aid programmes are those within the medium to large-size bracket. Compared to financers of a limited company, those about to provide funds to an existing democratic firm[159] are doubtless at an all but negligible disadvantage because they do not have the option of purchasing shares rather than bonds (in the opinion of most theorists, cooperatives should not be authorised to issue shares). However, insofar as it is true that democratic firms are less risk-prone than investor-owned enterprises in launching new investment projects, this means that providers of funds to cooperatives will take fewer risks.

The lower risk profiles faced by financers of LMFs compared to financers of limited companies can also be traced to a different reason: whereas in limited companies the wage and salary claims of the workforce are accorded priority treatment over those of capital providers, in cooperatives the claims of the firm's creditors take precedence over those of the partners. In capitalistic enterprises employees receive their wages and salaries on a monthly basis over the whole span of the production cycle, loans are repaid at longer intervals and equity holders appropriate the residual; at the other end of the spectrum are co-operatives, in which the partners' claims are at the bottom of the list of priorities. Providers of funds who are paid out of the residual can be looked upon, as it were, as insuring contractual financers against some of the risks they may run. As this entails that a loan made to a cooperative is safer than one made to a limited company, it is a weighty argument

---

[158] In a study addressing this issue, Meade suggested that this was the main reason why law firms and enterprises operating in labour-intensive industries tend to choose the cooperative form (see Meade 1972, pp. 426–7).

[159] The idea that the efficiency levels of socialist enterprises should be set against those of limited companies, rather than investor-owned enterprises in general, was first suggested by Lange (1936–37, pp. 108–10), Meade (1972) and Bardhan and Roemer (1993, pp. 106–107).

which refutes the claim that cooperatives come up against unsurmount-able fundraising difficulties.[160]

In addition to this, considering that LMFs are free to self-finance their investments,[161] to provide further assurance to potential providers of funds they might consider the possibility of drafting offering prospec-tuses in such a way as to include a clause providing that the interest accruing on the partners' bonds will be payable only after the obligations towards outside creditors have been fully met. In other words, democratic firms should issue two distinct categories of bonds: (a) bonds to be offered in subscription to the partners after the adoption of a resolution to such effect by the managers or a majority of the partners, and (b) bonds with preferred rights to be offered to the general public, including the partners and/or potential external investors (see Cuomo 2003).

Provided the process is structured in line with the organisational model discussed above, i.e. if the public hand grants tax and other facilities to medium–large enterprises which are turned into cooperatives (though not to all cooperatives at the start-up stage), the argument that the greatest obstacle standing in the way of the growth of the cooperative movement is the fundraising problem is shown to be unwarranted.

5 JENSEN AND MECKLING'S CRITICISMS OF COOPERATIVES

In a 1979 paper, which due to its perceived importance was even reprinted in 1996 (Prychitko & Vanek 1996), Jensen and Meckling argued that 'the economics literature dealing with the so-called labor-managed firm has generated a special kind of labor-managed firm (or more accurately, a kind of economy) for which there is no real world counterpart' and which can be termed the 'pure rental firm'.

What is special about this type of firm, they explained (p. 477), is that

> all claims on the firms themselves are held by employees, but there is no market for these claims; that is, employees have claims on current net

---

[160] According to Bonin and Putterman (1987, pp. 63–4), potential providers of funds would feel even safer if they were allowed to examine the accounting records and annual accounts of the borrower cooperatives.

[161] Such a solution goes to disprove Baglioni's claim that due to the conflicting interests of the partners and outside providers of funds the establish-ment of LMFs is a difficult undertaking both in theory and in practice (see Baglioni 1995, p. 93).

revenues which they cannot sell to anyone else because eligibility for claims is conditional on employment, and the right to become an employee is not legally for sale.

Although it is clear that Jensen and Meckling were thinking of the worker-run enterprise they ascribed to Vanek (1970) and Meade (1972), i.e. Vanek's LMF, further on they enunciated a principle which is clearly at odds with the analysis of the ownership rights in the LMF conducted above. Specifically, they remarked that 'what is unique about the pure-rental economy is that firms are forbidden to hold claims or rights in durable productive resources like those held by individuals' (p. 477), and went on to argue that the assignment of all rights to the workers instead of the firm could be explained bearing in mind the basic idea underlying the producer cooperative literature, i.e. the principle that workers retain all claims on their firms as long as they retain their status as partners. To all appearances, the reason behind this mistake is that Jensen and Meckling did not consider what happens in worker-run firms which are about to default. Be that as it may, it remains that the equation of the pure rental firm with a Vanek-type LMF is proved wrong by the reflections that the two authors develop in the rest of their paper, in particular on page 479, where we are told that the pure rental firm hires its capital goods[162] (which is definitely not the case in Vanek-type LMFs).

There can be little doubt that only a gross misinterpretation of Vanek and Meade's model could lead Jensen and Meckling to equate this firm model with the pure rental firm and their mistake can only be explained by assuming that from the detail that these firms use borrowed financial resources the two authors failed to deduce that these resources can be used to purchase the capital goods of which the partners subsequently become the rightful owners (not lessees). Accordingly, the statement that 'what is unique about the pure-rental economy is that firms are forbidden to hold claims or rights in durable productive resources like those held by individuals' would only make sense if these firms should actually rent physical capital goods – an idea which is barely realistic. Jensen and Meckling's misinterpretation explains their conclusion that the pure rental firm is 'a special kind of labor-managed firm ... for which there is no real world counterpart'.

The equation of the pure rental firm with the labour-managed firm is clearly unwarranted. The producer cooperative model upheld in this

---

[162] The pure rental firm, Jensen and Meckling wrote on p. 479, is 'one in which all capital goods are rented'.

chapter is Vanek's LMF, i.e. an enterprise which rents investment resources, not physical capital goods, and whose organisational characteristics have been shown to refute most of the objections raised against cooperatives by its critics.

6 JOHN STUART MILL'S *ON LIBERTY* AND DEMOCRATIC FIRM MANAGEMENT

The main focus points of this much celebrated chapter are (a) Mill's argument that in his day 'fighting for freedom' (which in ancient times meant opposing tyrannical individuals) had come to mean taking a stand against the tyranny of the majority, and (b) the idea that the only admissible check on individual freedom is the ban on causing harm to others. The only part of our conduct for which we are answerable to society, he argues, is the part which concerns others (Mill 1859, p. 19). 'Wherever there is an ascendant class a large portion of the morality of the country emanates from its class interests', but the views of that majority must not be allowed to curtail the freedom of single individuals. 'There are also many positive acts for the benefit of others' which people 'may rightfully be compelled to perform', Mill goes on to argue,

> but the rule is making people answerable for doing evil to others; making them answerable for not preventing evil is the exception. Under different circumstances restrictions to the liberty of others are only justified when it comes to preventing adverse repercussions of the action of one man on his fellow-beings. Whenever this is not the case, freedom should be unrestricted.

From the fact that 'to individuality should belong the part of life in which it is chiefly the individual that is interested' Mill deduces that society should have jurisdiction only on that part of a person's conduct which 'affects prejudicially the interests of others' because each individual is

> the person most interested in his own well-being ... In the conduct of human beings towards one another it is necessary that general rules should for the most part be observed, in order that people may know what they have to expect: but in each person's own concerns his individual spontaneity is entitled to free exercise. (Mill 1859, p. 92)

If we think poorly of a person, we have a right to warn others against him, but so long as the person concerned does not harm others we have no right to punish him. What are called duties to ourselves are not socially obligatory, unless circumstances render them at the same time duties to others.

From Mill's perspective, neither *freedom of thought* nor the freedom to express and circulate our opinions should be curtailed (so long as we do not attempt to deprive others of theirs), even though this belongs to that part of the conduct of an individual which concerns other people, and freedom of speech is inextricably intertwined with freedom of thought. 'The only freedom which deserves the name is that of pursuing our own good in our own way' (p. 22).

At this point the reader will probably ask himself what bearing this conception of freedom has on the planned establishment of economic democracy. On closer analysis, Mill's well-known and widely shared conception of freedom implies what is probably the severest criticism of democratic firm management.

The effort we put in our work and the way we see to our duties are major components of individual liberty. A hired worker enters into a contract with his employer and is only answerable to the latter for the way he discharges his duties. More often than not, instead of doing his utmost he will confine himself to just that level of effort that will avoid displeasing his employer. What would the situation be in a worker-run firm? There are reasons to assume that those working alongside him would closely watch him at work and thereby deprive him of his individual freedom. Considering the awareness of the partners that their prospective income levels are strictly conditional on the effort their fellow partners put in their work, it is to be assumed that the control of the collective over the work done by each worker may become as oppressive as to deprive everybody of their liberty (in stark contrast with the thesis advanced in Alchian & Demsetz 1972). In other words, the consolidation of democracy afforded by democratic economy may ultimately prove detrimental to freedom within the firm.

9. The labour-managed firm and socialism

1 INTRODUCTION

The argument that Marx's approach and especially his writings on the economic system of the future offer fragmentary suggestions in place of a full-fledged theoretical edifice is anything but new (and is actually consistent with his own claim that methodology only is what really matters). As early as 1899, Bernstein wrote that Marx and Engels's writings could be used to demonstrate everything and Kautsky warned that it was impossible to make absolute reliance on every one of Marx's words because his sayings were often mutually contradictory (Kautsky 1960, p. 437).[163]

With reference to the social order of the transitional period, as I have already said, Marxists fall into two divisions: those who assume that the correct Marxian view of a socialist economy is one which equates socialism with self-management, and those who identify socialism with a centrally planned command economy.[164] And although Yugoslav and other self-management theorists have gone so far as to maintain that a system of labour-managed firms (or producer cooperatives) has its roots in Marx's works, in point of fact there is little textual evidence in support of either stance.

The aim of this chapter is to offer additional evidence in support of the assumption that the establishment of a system of cooperative firms amounts to a real and proper revolution because it gives rise to a new production mode capable of reversing the existing relation between capital and labour.

There can be little doubt that a social order where democratically managed firms operate within a centrally planned system is closest to

---

[163] An attentive Marx commentator such as Rubel went so far as to argue that terms such as 'Marxian' or 'Marxist' lacked any sound basis (see Rubel 1974, pp. 20–1).

[164] Zolo (1974) contends that the dirigiste model founded on centralisation was of Engels's, rather than Marx's making.

Marx's thought, but here we will attempt to press the view that a system of self-managed firms would be consistent with Marx's theoretical approach even though it should fail to adopt central planning.

This means we are hardly prepared to subscribe to Tolstoy's view that the sole reward for work done is the satisfaction we draw from simply doing it. Working for one's own account is so much more rewarding that the abolition of hired labour can appropriately be rated as a veritable revolution.[165]

2 A SYSTEM OF PRODUCER COOPERATIVES AS A NEW PRODUCTION MODE

A great many market socialism models have been theorised over the past years (see, inter alia, Stauber 1987; Roemer 1993 and 1994; Yunker 1992 and 1995; Schweickart 1993 and 2002; and Burczak 2006).[166] Among them, the system with firms run by workers themselves – the one with which we are concerned in this book – is both the simplest to prefigure and the most widely discussed.[167] The question is: is such a system a new production mode?

Among the first theorists to positively reply to this question was Fawcett (1863, p. 105), who described cooperation as 'a modified form of socialism'. In the estimation of many, on the contrary, the transfer of firm control from capitalists to workers would hardly amount to a revolution proper. According to Sweezy, for instance, to assume that a free market system with state-owned production means and firms run by non-capitalists makes up a socialist order is to mistake legal relations for production relations, because a system of firms run by workers seeking to maximise profits by manufacturing goods and placing them on the

---

[165] The reason why we insist on equating the transition to a worker-controlled firm system with a real and proper revolution, I repeat, is that Marxists have always refused to concoct 'recipes for a hypothetical future', i.e. to offer a comprehensive outline of the social order they expect to take the place of capitalism. Although Kautsky and many later Marxist theorists were strongly critical of the system that had emerged from the Russian revolution, they did not make it clear how those rejecting the Soviet central planning model were to picture to themselves a socialist order (for the silence of Kautsky on this point, see Geary 1974, pp. 93–4).

[166] As argued by Hobsbawm (1994, p. 437), the official designation for the Russian communist model of society coined by Soviet ideologists, 'Real Social-ism', implied that better models of socialism could exist.

[167] For Marx's ideas on worker control of firms, see Jossa 2005a.

market is a very near proxy for capitalistic production relations (see Sweezy 1968).

Mészàros argued that

> capital is a metabolic system, a socio-economic metabolic system of control. You can overthrow the capitalist, but the factory system remains, the division of labour remains, nothing has changed in the metabolic function of society. The only way to evade the control of capital is to do away with it. (Mészàros 1995, p. 981)[168]

Both these comments are off the mark. In Marx's dialectical or relational approach, capital ceases to exist upon the suppression of hired labour; in other words, the moment when the capital–labour relation is reversed (Ollman 2003, p. 26). And since capital entails of necessity the existence of the capitalist, the abolition of hired labour will result in the abolition of capitalism as a matter of course. The Italian philosopher Emanuele Severino reminds us that 'a change of medium necessitates a concomitant change in direction' (see Severino 2012, p. 98).

Vanek's distinction between two different types of cooperatives, the LMF and the WMF (see Vanek 1971a and 1971b), may help clarify this point. As I have already argued, it is the so-called LMF cooperative that reverses the existing capital–labour relation. Indeed, I repeat, whereas in capitalistic systems it is the owners of capital that hire workers (either directly or through managers in their service), pay them a fixed income and appropriate the surplus, in LMF-type cooperatives, which finance their investments with loan capital, it is the workers running their own firms that borrow capital, pay it a fixed income (interest) and appropriate the surplus themselves.

Some authors have taught that 'acts of choice' and freedom to act are no less important for the well-being of individuals – including the workers of a firm – than the availability of material property. In support

---

[168]   For comparable views, see, inter alia, Turati 1897; Mondolfo 1923, p. 93; Labriola 1970, pp. 271–2; Quarter 1992; Westra 2002; McMurtry 2004; Gunn 2006, p. 345; and Sylos Labini 2006, who claims that democratic firm management models have little in common with Marxism. Among Marxist authors who are agreed that this new mode of production will be a direct offshoot of capitalism, Offe points to a structural mismatch, within capitalistic society, between new subsystems and structural elements which are functionally at odds with the logic of capital valorisation (see Offe 1972, ch. 3).

of these contentions let us add that, as the nature of a business enterprise is most clearly revealed by its corporate object, the capitalistic enterprise and the worker-controlled firm are different in nature since the former is bent on maximising profit, while the latter – as taught by producer cooperative theory – has the mission of maximising the satisfaction of the majority of the workers making the decisions in it.

Thus, worker control of firms gives rise to a new mode of production despite the retention of markets. In the estimation of Zamagni (2008, p. 97), 'by its very nature, economic calculation is compatible with a variety of different kinds of individual behaviour and institutional mechanisms'.

In Marx's approach fetishism is defined as the process which reifies interpersonal relationships until they resemble relations between things; and the sway of capital over labour in the capitalistic production process is said to generate a form of fetishistic dominion. In other words, according to Marx fetishism is generated both by the fact that exchanges are made in markets and by the fact that capitalism, which decrees the control of things (capital goods) over man, reverses the 'natural' man–thing relation. 'Yet it is obvious', Marx wrote (1857–58, p. 210), 'that this process of inversion is merely an historical necessity ... a necessity for the development of the productive forces from a definite historical point of departure' and, consequently, there is no absolute need inherent in the production process itself. 'The worker's propertylessness', he argued, 'and the ownership of living labour by objectified labour, or the appropriation of alien labour by capital – both merely expressions of the same relation from opposite poles – are fundamental conditions of the bourgeois mode of production, in no way accidents irrelevant to it'. Hence, Lukàcs wrote

> only when man seizes full control of work, or, put differently, when work turns from a 'tool for life' into the 'primary life need', only when man is relieved from the constriction stemming from his self-reproduction, then, and only then, will the social path towards human activity as an end to itself be opened up. (Lukàcs 1922, p. 40)

A well-known saying by Marx runs that those who control production simultaneously control men's lives since they own the tools enabling them to pursue whatever aims they may have in mind (see, inter alia, Pellicani 1976, p. 62 and Bahro 1977, p. 23); and this argument goes to reinforce the idea that revolution is to be understood as the handover of production means from capitalists to workers and the concomitant disempowerment of capital.

The potential of a system of producer cooperatives for sparking off a socialist revolution is also called into question by those, including Pannekoek and Lukàcs, who distinguish between revolutionaries and revisionists based on whether they advocate the overthrow of the State or rate the State as a neutral institution. From our perspective, instead, the idea that revolution comes down to changing the existing production mode necessitates the conclusion that a system of producer cooperatives reversing the capital–labour relation does amount to a revolution even though the State is not altogether overthrown.

3   THE TRANSITION IN PRODUCER COOPERATIVE THEORY

At this point we will try to establish how those believing that a system of producer cooperatives would help supersede capitalism figure to themselves the process leading up to socialism, i.e. the transition.

Three distinct high roads to the establishment of a system of producer cooperatives have been theorised so far. One is endorsed by those who think of cooperatives as merit goods, i.e. as producing positive externalities. The greater benefits the community may draw from self-managed, rather than capitalistic firms are numerous (see Jossa 2012a, chs 5 and 6). Consequently, if the cooperative firm is a 'merit good', the first measures to be enforced in order to further the rise of a new mode of production are tax and credit facilities commensurate with the benefits the community draws from these firms.

The second 'high road' is identifying businesses that capitalists prove unable to run efficiently and changing them into democratic firms. This method is applicable both on a case-to-case basis and via a general strike.[169] A process of this kind was about to materialise in Italy in the so-called 'red biennium' (1919–20), when the labour unrest instigated by Gramsci's *Ordine Nuovo* movement made it so difficult for capitalists to run their firms that Giovanni Agnelli declared himself prepared to hand over the management of Fiat to the workers. The idea of a general strike as the preferred springboard for the transition to socialism is a true

---

[169]   In 1909, Robert Michels remarked that producer cooperatives are often set up at the end of a prolonged strike as tangible proof that workers are able to run production activities independently of capitalists (see Michels 1909, p. 195).

leitmotif in the thought of Rosa Luxemburg, the most democratic of all Marxists (see Negt 1979).

Several countries have a record of capitalistic firms which instead of being wound up were changed into cooperatives at various points in time. In more recent years, numerous firms on the brink of bankruptcy were occupied by the workers and run as producer cooperatives in the aftermath of the economic crisis in Argentina. Most of the approximately 200 cooperatives operating in Argentina in 2005 were firms that had been set up following the crisis. In Italy, a great many firms in serious difficulty were taken over by their workforces in 1970–71 and about 100 of these were turned into cooperatives between 1974 and 1978. Most of the cooperatives that were set up in the manufacturing industry in those days were originally defaulting capitalistic companies (see, inter alia, Zevi 1982). Vanek (1977, p. 46) has written that the default of an existing business enterprise offers, quite naturally, an excellent opportunity for setting up a self-managed firm. Some scholars have gone so far as to argue that rescuing a defaulting business is one of the main functions of cooperative firms (Roelants 2000, p. 67).

An elementary truth to be emphasised here is that – contrary to a widely held opinion – firms that do not report any profits are not destroying resources. Provided work is looked upon as a value instead of a burden, in situations of Keynesian unemployment it is firms that fail to produce value added that waste resources. And a firm that does not report any profits may nevertheless produce considerable amounts of value added.[170]

Our second road from capitalism to socialism is endorsed, among others, by Tronti in a Marxist analysis of the evolution of capitalism. He argues (1962, p. 20):

> At the highest level of capitalistic development the social relation becomes a moment of the Relation of production, the whole of society becomes an articulation of production; in other words, the whole of society exists as a function of the factory and the factory extends its exclusive domination over the whole of society. As a result, the State machinery itself tends to be ever more markedly identified with the figure of the collective capitalist. It is ever more thoroughly appropriated by the capitalistic mode of production and hence becomes a function of the capitalistic society.

---

[170] In the opinion of some, the reason why workers tend to take over enterprises in temporary distress is that sometimes enterprises have difficulty obtaining new credit due to asymmetrical information on capital markets (see De Bonis et al. 1994, p. 30).

From this, he draws the conclusion that it is a historical necessity to fight bourgeois society within the social relation of production, i.e. to challenge it from within the capitalistic production system (see p. 24). In other words, from Tronti's perspective there is a need to break the State within society, to dissolve society within the production process and to reverse the production relation within the factory and the social relationships existing there. In short, 'the goal is to destroy the bourgeois State machine right within the capitalistic factory' (p. 30).[171]

This policy goes to refute the reflections on class action developed by Olson (1965) and Buchanan (1979) in connection with the free-riding issue. Both these authors start out from the classification of revolution as a public good and the assumption that the proletariat are well aware of this. All the same – they argue – as revolution is a costly undertaking which exposes the revolutionaries to a violent backlash from the bourgeoisie, it is exactly its quality as a public good that will prevent it from being carried through. Each proletarian will shirk involvement on the assumption that the benefits flowing from the efforts of his fellow citizens, where successful, would be reaped by all. In the words of Buchanan (1979, p. 63):

> Even if revolution is in the best interest of the proletariat and even if every member of the proletariat realizes that this is so, so far as its members act rationally, this class will not achieve concerted revolutionary action. This shocking conclusion rests on the premise that concerted revolutionary action is for the proletariat a public good in the technical sense. Concerted revolutionary action is a public good for the proletariat as a group. Yet each proletarian, whether he seeks to maximise his own interests or those of his class, will refrain from revolutionary action.

In the opinion of Vahabi (2010), this line of reasoning entails that – contrary to Marxist theory – the masses fail to make history because their rationality induces them to opt for political inaction.

---

[171]   The road to worker power we are discussing can be purposely pursued by proclaiming a general strike with the aim of handing over to workers the management of all – or at least the most important – firms. In our estimation, the aim of a general strike should not necessarily be disintegrating the State machinery, as recommended by Tronti. The democratic form of socialism endorsed in this book requires the maintenance of State power. This is why we do not share the opinion of Benjamin that a general strike can be defined as 'non-violent violence' because its aim is not to found a new State, but to abolish the existing one; in other words, because its purpose is to give rise to a new system where work is neither 'imposed' by law nor by the need to survive (Benjamin 1995, p. 21).

Is this line of reasoning convincing? The degree to which Olson and Buchanan are off track will at once become apparent if we consider that the benefits associated with actions intended to help workers run firms on their own will be reaped by the workers themselves, in terms of turning them from hired workers into their own masters.

More specifically, Olson's and Buchanan's criticism is not applicable to the hypothesis of strikes proclaimed to press for the transfer of firms to workers for the following reason: although every action geared towards worker control of a firm certainly marks a stride forward in the direction of socialism and, as such, in the interests of the working class at large, it primarily benefits the workers of the firm concerned, since it is these that will stop being hired workers and become their own masters. And while it is impossible to rule out the free-riding hypothesis altogether, we have difficulty believing that many workers will be prepared to face the hatred of their fellow workers for refusing to participate in a strike for the acquisition of democratic worker control that the others deem to be in their best interests.

The third high road to the new order is a parliamentary act converting the stocks of existing companies into bonds of equal value (based on suitable regulations intended to solve the difficulties associated with such a transaction) and, at the same time, outlawing hired labour to the extent that will be deemed expedient. Such an act would automatically dis-empower capitalists and, by the same token, change existing capitalistic businesses into self-managed firms. The prerequisite for the passing of such an act is obviously a parliamentary majority of representatives of the workers or, at any rate, members of parliament favourable to such a solution.[172]

It is well known that the third of these scenarios was rejected by Lenin on the grounds that universal suffrage is far from capable of 'revealing the will of the majority of the working people' or 'securing its real-ization' (Lenin 1917b, p. 70), and nothing is there to suggest that he would not have opposed the first as well. In contrast, Lenin's claim that the State is purely and exclusively the 'lobbying group of the bourgeois class' is questionable. This point begs the question of which – if any – of these transition scenarios is preferable.

---

[172] In this connection, Panzieri (quoted in Gattei 2007, p. 163) comments that as soon as the working class takes cognisance of its status as variable capital and forcefully rejects such a role, its demands will become ever more pressing and will be more markedly focused on the acquisition of worker power than on the labour issues typically featuring in trade union platforms (Panzieri 1976, pp. 30 and 38).

On the assumption that safety should arise from piecemeal social changes and improvements in the living conditions of individuals (see, inter alia, Sapelli 2006, p. 4), we express a preference for the first two of the three policies outlined above.[173] The quote below is clear evidence that this was also the option of Rosa Luxemburg:

> The conquest of power will not be effected with one blow. It will be a progression. We shall progressively occupy all the positions of the capitalist state and defend them tooth and nail ... It is a question of fighting step by step, hand-to-hand, in every province, in every city, in every village, in every municipality, in order to take and transfer all the power of the state bit by bit from the bourgeoisie to the workers. (Luxemburg 1919, p. 629)

In 1982, Hayek argued that no real breakthrough in politics would ever be achieved through mass propaganda. The problem, he wrote (see Hayek 1983, p. 192), was persuading intellectuals that the positive externalities of a democratic firm system entailed a significant edge over capitalism and inducing them to press this idea both on political parties and on the electorate as a whole; and he concluded, the hoped-for political change might be enforced through a parliamentary vote and would amount to a fully democratic revolution.

The crux of the matter is that being at the orders of a majority is barely more reassuring than obeying the commands of one or a few individuals. As argued by Popper, 'we are democrats not because the majority is always right, but because democratic traditions are the least evil ones which we know' (cited by Zanone 2002, p. 131).

An additional point probably needs to be discussed in greater depth here. In the mind of many, there is no sense in racking one's brains over the issue of the transition to a new order. Provided it is found that cooperatives are more efficient than capitalistic companies they will eventually prevail as a matter of course; in the opposite case, the transition will never come about. For my part, I reject this idea because I firmly believe that a transition might come about even if the efficiency levels of cooperatives were found to fall short of those ensured by capitalistic companies. I think that the transition is desirable if the benefits it offers to the community are such as to vouchsafe superior social conditions. The transition I am thinking of is, indeed, not a

---

[173]   The sixth chapter of Archer's 1995 book is entirely devoted to demonstrating that there is at least one feasible road to the acquisition of a democratic socialist order.

spontaneous process, but one which is purposely pursued by a nation through the enforcement of suitable policies.

The scenarios just sketched are obviously at odds with Lenin's claim that the ultimate objective of the transition was the establishment of the dictatorship of the proletariat. After their first serious defeat, the overthrown exploiters who had neither anticipated nor as much as accepted the idea of such a reversal of fortunes would 'throw themselves with tenfold energy, with furious passion and hatred grown a hundred fold, into the battle for the recovery of their "lost paradise"' (Lenin 1918, p. 166).

4 CAN THE CAPITAL–LABOUR CONFLICT BE RESOLVED?

One of Marx's major contributions to the understanding of the social order in which we live is the insight that class struggle is the key problem of capitalistic economies. And as this idea was first stated in early writings not yet supported by a sound grounding in political economy, it is probable that Marx did not take it over from the writers on whom he drew for his later studies. The class issue features in such an early work as the *Critique of Hegel's Philosophy of Right* (written in 1843 and issued in 1844) and continued to take centre stage in Marx's later theoretical approach as well.

Accordingly, it is safe to assume that in Marx's approach the precondition for superseding capitalism was solving the dialectical contradiction inherent in the conflict between a class yielding all power and a class expected to obey passively.[174] To look upon the opposition between plan and market as the key problem, Bettelheim wrote, is a gross mistake which diverts the attention towards minor issues and, hence, away from the real crux of the issue: the existence of a class, the 'bourgeoisie', whose prime aim is to prevent workers from attaining power. This is why an occasional acceleration or stalemate in market relations at one stage or other is, in itself, not enough to make us assume that the world is either

---

[174] In quotes from Marcuse reported in Vacca (1969a, p. 333 and 1969b, p. 253), the key contradiction of capitalism is described as 'an oppressive relation opposing man to nature and subject to object, which is perceived at the root of our civilisation and which generates oppressive social relations', and industrial societies are said to be 'the outgrowth of a historical design aimed to establish control of man over man'.

progressing towards socialism or moving away from it (see Bettelheim 1969b and, among others, Poulantzas 1973 and Marek 1982, p. 751).

In short, in the minds of most Marxists the main contradiction of capitalism to be resolved during the transition to socialism is not the plan–market opposition, but the conflict between capital and labour.

In Marx's opinion, both Ricardo, who defined capital as that part of the wealth of a country which is employed in production, and other economists who described capital as the bulk of capital goods, were the victims of an 'illusion'. Dismissing this illusion as an 'absurdity', though one inherent in the very nature of the capitalistic production process, Marx categorised it as 'a very convenient method of demonstrating the eternal character of the capitalist mode of production, or of showing that *capital* is a *permanent natural element* of human production in general' (Marx 1863–66, p. 28). Yet, there is good ground for assuming that the illusion that Marx had in mind will in due time be disproved and that workers will eventually start running business firms on their own.

5   IS THE CAPITAL–LABOUR CONTRADICTION SYSTEMATICALLY ESCALATING?

If the new mode of production to rise from the ashes of capitalism is a system of democratic firms, at this point it is worth establishing if there are forces willing to further it.[175]

In Marx's own words,

> capitalist production has itself brought it about that the work of supervision is readily available and quite independent of the ownership of capital. It has therefore become superfluous for this work of supervision to be performed by the capitalist. A musical conductor need in no way be the owner of the instruments in his orchestra, nor does it form part of his function as a conductor that he should have any part in paying the 'wages' of other musicians. Cooperative factories provide the proof that the capitalist has become just as superfluous as a functionary in production as he himself, from his superior vantage-point, finds the large landlord. (Marx 1894, p. 511)

---

[175]   This problem was posited by Struve in this way (1899, p. 128): assuming there are two mutually antagonistic phenomena, A and B, is it more likely that the weaker social group will progressively become weaker and weaker or that the antagonism between the two groups will be further exacerbated? His conclusion was that progress within society was made more often through persuasion than through the attempt to abolish exacerbated antagonisms at one stroke by means of a revolution.

This single passage is sufficient evidence that Marx did envisage the disempowerment of capitalists even within a market economy. The claim that an escalating capital–labour confrontation paves the way for the reversal of the capitalistic capital–labour relation can hardly be called into question. Bourgeois individualism inevitably breeds a tendency towards proletarian collectivism.

The widening contrast between capital and labour – let this be re-emphasised – is the offshoot of a contradiction between productive forces which change in time. On the one hand, the working class is acquiring ever greater entrepreneurial skills; on the other, production relations are still controlled by capitalists, because it is they that run enterprises.[176] The degree to which the working class will train itself in the entrepreneurial skills needed to acquire hegemony within society is strictly conditional on its 'cultural' level and, specifically, on whether its members have been able to hone their overall educational backgrounds and their qualifications in areas such as technological applications and business administration (see, inter alia, Chitarin 1973, p. 33).

Provided this is true, I cannot endorse Foucault's argument that the social extraction of an individual may account for his choice of one system of thought in preference to another, but that the existence of the group concerned is not the precondition for the rise of the relevant system of thought. In my estimation it is apparent that capitalists are stout supporters of capitalism while well-informed workers tend to embrace socialism, but it is no less true that the propensity of workers for democratic firm management arises from teachings they tend to draw from culture and experience.

Woltmann lays special emphasis on the need to work towards other people's happiness and the achievement of social justice. From his perspective, this is not only a duty we owe to society, but, as it were, the 'anvil' on which individuals can 'forge' their happiness as best they can compatibly with their talents. The establishment of socialism, he concludes, is an act of social responsibility (see Woltmann 1898, pp. 49 and 314).

---

[176] Anyone believing that the transition to socialism is heralded by declining frictions between opposed classes should give their best attention to the younger Marx's saying (see Rapone 2011, pp. 169–70) that the precondition for class conflict to become an element of progress is that the two opposed actors develop an awareness of their respective roles, as well as the determination to follow them through – and this happens during the phase termed industrial capitalism and not in the decadent phase termed financial capitalism.

From my perspective, the reflections developed lead up to this conclusion. From the undeniable need to keep apart socialism from communism it follows that democratic firm management, which solves the capital–labour conflict during its present escalation process, will breed socialism.

6 ON THE END OF CAPITALISM

The Italian philosopher Emanuele Severino has recently argued that processes currently under way point to the impending death of capitalism. In the present age of brisk technological growth, he argues, capitalism is on the wane because the need to obey the imperatives of technology is obliging business enterprises to deflect from profit maximisation as their one-time overriding goal. According to Severino (2012, p. 94),

> within a logic which postulates goals and means (and has been prevailing over the entire course of human history), there is little doubt (though the consequence is less dominant than the starting assumption) that whenever an action – in this case the capitalistic mode of operation – is made to deflect from its original goal and to pursue a different one, this same logic determines that the action itself will turn into something different in content, rhythm, intensity, relevance and configuration.

On page 23 in the same book, Severino clarifies that techno-scientific considerations and needs are ever more taking precedence over those typifying capitalistic policies. As a result, he argues, it is not the inherent contradictions of capitalism highlighted by Marxists that are hastening this decline, but the gradual marginalisation of the pure capitalistic system by the techno-economic system. In his estimation, every human action is characterised by the goal it is designed to achieve. The goal is the master, and no one can serve two masters. It is the goal that makes an action what it is, and an action that is assigned a different goal changes into a different action. 'The individual's subjective aim is one thing and the objective aim of the apparatus is another; and whenever the objective aim takes precedence over the subjective aim, it is technology that gains the upper hand to the detriment of capitalism' (Severino 2012, pp. 48–9). 'When technology is turned from a tool into a goal the result is a reversal of roles, in terms that part of the available tools are destroyed for the sake of increasing the global sway of the apparatus, viz., of the ability to devise fresh goals' (p. 105). Hence, he continues (p. 66), capitalism enters a stage of decline when, in an effort to tackle head-on confrontations between workers and employers or fend off competition from other nations, it starts using the technological means under the direction of modern science.

On closer analysis, the decline of the system is expedited by the capitalistic mode of action itself since business enterprises engaged in the competitive struggle 'make ever greater reliance on the latest technological breakthroughs and capitalists stop working towards profit maximisation as their ultimate goal and end up by magnifying the power of technology' (p. 35). In the end, the importance of a goal such as private profit maximisation is progressively eroded and eclipsed. Inasmuch as it is true that States (betraying their original mission) are ever more deeply involved in technology, they, too, will cease being masters of the techno-scientific apparatus and will become its servants (p. 63). Capitalists, he argues (p. 73), simultaneously further and employ technology, i.e. a tool which is designed to reduce scarcity and draws legitimisation from this ultimate goal.

For my part, I daresay that few economists will be prepared to subscribe to Severino's line of argument. Although it is evident that technology is achieving a burgeoning role in economic affairs, and that capitalism is more thoroughly dependent on it, it remains that capitalists make use of technology in an effort to achieve their prime aim, which is and remains profit maximisation. As a result, Severino's argument that the growing sway of technology is preventing business enterprises from pursuing profit maximisation is beside the point. The pursuit of profit maximisation by enterprises is still the main characteristic of capitalism.

On page 68 of his book, Severino adds that capitalism 'is its own enemy for two reasons: firstly, because it strives to destroy its own mainstay, competition, and, secondly, because *in essence*, due to its will to pursue profit through the use of technology, *it wages war against itself*'. On closer analysis, the claim that the tendency of companies to form monopolies conflicts with the essence of capitalism has nowhere been raised and business enterprises keep employing technology for their own ends without undergoing a change of nature. Further, on pp. 61–2, Severino argues that the sole, specific and ultimate objective of a business enterprise is to maximise profits, but that capitalism is obliged to deflect from this goal. Indeed, if the opponents of capitalism – for instance Islamic fundamentalists – should succeed in developing technological tools more efficiently and Western capitalists should suffer their adversaries to gain the upper hand, capitalistic countries would be doomed to extinction unless, in an effort to fend off this danger and gain supremacy, they resolved to drop the private profit maximisation goal.

In point of fact, Severino's line of reasoning boils down to arguing that *governments* wishing to leverage business firms may make decisions, for instance, tax increases, that may jeopardise, if not altogether reduce, corporate bottom-line results. In no way, however, does it demonstrate that companies have stopped pursuing profit maximisation as their ultimate goal. The distinctive characteristic of capitalism is and remains corporate business profit maximisation. 'Even today', Severino continues (p. 66), 'a great many economists hold that there is no economically relevant *difference* between building cars for the (sole) purpose of boosting private profit and building them for the (sole) purpose of providing jobs to workers (as Sylos Labini pointed out to me some time ago)'. As a matter of fact, we do not know of automotive works building cars for the sole purpose of providing employment opportunities and where the State should resolve to establish publicly run motorcar companies in an effort to create new jobs, this would not mark an end to capitalism unless such businesses were found to prevail in both quantitative and qualitative terms – which is definitely not the case today.

Therefore, while I am prepared to endorse both the claim that technology helps capitalistic countries combat scarcity and the assumption that capitalism would cease to exist if the scarcity problem were finally solved, let me emphasise that every economist knows all too well that the scarcity problem will never be solved once and for all.

7 CONCLUSION

Time and again, Marx and Engels argued the case for a transitional period to communism during which workers would be managing firms themselves. Considering the intrinsic advantages of self-management, however, such a system would be a major step forward on the road towards progress and democracy even if we should abstract from the opinions of these great classics.[177]

Starting from these considerations, two main queries were raised in this chapter: (a) whether a form of market socialism would be consistent

---

[177]   Galgano has highlighted the fact that the 'one head, one vote' principle arose first within the economic sphere and was extended to political life only later in time. At the meetings of the earliest joint-stock companies, i.e. the colonial enterprises set up in the seventeenth and eighteenth centuries, resolutions were passed by a majority of the votes cast. It was only in the nineteenth century that this kind of system was gradually replaced by the principle that resolutions were to be passed by a number of shareholders representing a majority of the shares owned. The exact opposite occurred in the political sphere, where the electoral systems vesting voting rights solely in people meeting certain property qualifications were gradually replaced by universal suffrage.

with Marx and Engels's thought; and (b) whether the transition to a new social order is possible. The basic premises for my line of reasoning were the definition of revolution as the turn to a different production mode – a notion which is not always correctly understood – and the awareness that Marx and Engels, far from theorising a sudden bound to communism, made it clear that the transition from one production mode to another was to be a long-term process.

In sum, in Marx's approach the reversal of the capitalistic capital–labour relation triggers a real and proper revolution because it entails changing actual production relations, instead of legal forms only. The moment we accept Marx's claim that the principal contradiction in capitalism is the capital–labour opposition, it naturally follows that the reversal of the respective roles of capital and labour causes a radical change in the existing production mode which amounts to a revolution. And, in our opinion, this transition to a new social order is possible.

10. The evolution of socialism from utopia to scientific producer cooperative economics

1 INTRODUCTION

'Reason is the Sovereign of the World' – Hegel wrote (1837, p. 10). But is this true?

Reviewing changes associated with the financiarisation of a globalised economy, the strong, though unexpressed need for community, as well as the 'unfulfilled promises of democracy', Norberto Bobbio, a well-known philosophical thinker, suggested that the world was heading towards one of those radical shifts in historical perspective which due to various – as yet not univocally definable – factors may mark a turning point comparable to the breakaway of Humanists from the culture of the Middle Ages or the triumph of the spirit of the Enlightenment over a conventional worldview (Bodei 2013, p. 175). In point of fact, few signs indeed indicate that the world is regulated by the spirit of the Enlightenment.[178]

Concerning the direction in which ways of thinking and living are evolving in the present day, I daresay that irrespective of whether it is true that reason governs the world the times are nevertheless ripe for the transition of the economy to a form of self-management socialism, whereas the existing political systems are as yet not prepared to work towards the attainment of this goal. In *Theses on the Philosophy of History*, Walter Benjamin pressed the need to review the 'time of the now' from the vantage point of the losers, rather than the winners, and to keep the memory of our oppressed ancestors. But is it reasonable to assume that such a development is forthcoming?

---

[178] The well-known Italian journalist Eugenio Scalfari remarked (2013, p. 23): 'the present era is fading out. Its agonies are sure to drag on for a fairly long period of time. As always happens in history, the changes in ways of thinking and living which are currently under way will remain unnoticed although they are not gradual, but radical and dramatic'.

A well-known work entitled *Socialism, Utopian and Scientific* offers Engels's brilliant outline of his own and Marx's basic contributions to political science. In Engels's words, both he and Marx offered ample evidence that (a) history is a sequence of different modes of production, and that (b) a new mode of production, far from being pre-ordained within the mind of a scholar and subsequently implemented in practice, is but the natural outgrowth of an earlier one.[179] Can these propositions justify the claim that a socialist revolution is at hand?

To answer this question it is necessary to establish whether it is realistic to assume that today, after the collapse of the Soviet-type centrally planned model, a new production mode may sprout from the ashes of capitalism as the natural outgrowth of the stepwise evolution of the present-day mode of production. In my opinion (and according to Schweickart 2002, and other authors), this new production mode is a system of worker-controlled firms – a model which is also consistent with Marx's argument that while 'political emancipation is, of course, a big step forward', rather than the final form of human emancipation in general it is just 'the final form of human emancipation within the hitherto existing world order' (Marx 1843, p. 85). Engels's view that the post-capitalistic production mode was to be a centrally planned system designated as 'socialism' was forcefully endorsed by Marxists until the collapse of the Soviet system, but is still widely shared today.[180]

In keeping with the line of reasoning adopted in this book, at this point it is necessary to raise the question as to whether centralised planning can be rated as a more or less natural outgrowth of capitalism and, most importantly, it can be described as a new production mode aimed to promote the interests of the working class.

The proposition I wish to put forth in this chapter is that while central planning may, admittedly, be the end result of the current tendency of capitalistic production to be ever more tightly controlled by a conscious

---

[179]   According to Engels (1882a, pp. 74–5), in the minds of leftist thinkers in France and Britain, socialism 'is the expression of absolute truth, reason and justice, and has only to be discovered to conquer all the world by virtue of its own power'. Given that 'absolute truth is independent of time, space and of the historical development of man', he argued, to make science of socialism one had to accept the two great insights that mankind owes to Marx. Specifically, it was necessary to: (1) 'present the capitalistic method of production, its historical connection and its inevitableness during a particular historical period'; and (2) 'lay bare its essential character'.

[180]   In part, its wide currency can probably be traced to an important book that Kolakowsky wrote in 1979 (see, inter alia, Yudt 2012, p. 193).

will, this is not enough to justify the assumption that central planning as such and, especially the centrally planned systems established in the Soviet Union and elsewhere, are designed to meet the needs of the working class. In point of fact, as workers in existing centrally planned systems are still denied any say in decision making, they will hardly have any incentive to increase their work input or raise productivity rates. Noam Chomsky has gone so far as to argue that Bolshevism and the ideology of liberalist technocrats have in common the firm belief that mass organisations and popular political movements are to be suppressed (see Chomsky 2013, p. 69). And no economic system can function effectively unless it is driven on by the private interest motive.[181]

In my opinion, it is much more realistic to assume that the new production mode to rise from the ashes of capitalism will be a system of worker-controlled firms, viz., a system in which production will be controlled by a conscious will, but where workers will find it in their interests to devote their best energies to production.[182] As this is not the place for an exhaustive analysis of the organisational structure of a system of worker-controlled firms, concerning this specific point the reader is referred to Jossa (2014d and 2016a).

The idea that what I term socialism is democratic firm management (rather than centralised planning) is gradually gaining ground thanks to advancements in economic science. According to Norberto Bobbio (1984, p. 136), the 'goalposts' of modern democracy are majority rule and the underlying principle that each head is entitled to one vote, and it is hard to see why this principle should hold good for politics, but not for economic processes as well. In Bobbio's view, the precondition for extending democracy today is proceeding from the political domain, the context where people are reckoned with as individuals, to the social sphere, where they act out multiple roles (Bobbio 1985, p. 147). And steps in this direction will be taken as soon as society starts working towards the establishment of a system of worker-controlled firms.

---

[181]   With regard to the advent of communism, Sartre, for instance, supported the view that change was impeded by theoretical shortcomings which, however, could not be blamed on Marx (see Chiodi 1973, p. 21).

[182]   Whereas the nation-wide British union for the protection of workers (General National Consolidated Trade Union, founded in 1834) had a correct appreciation of the role producer cooperatives 'as a key factor for the prompt establishment of a completely new social order' (see Cole 1953a, p. 136), few Marxists held this view in later years. An exception is Trower (1973, p. 138) who wrote: 'if freedom is our goal, industry will only become democratic when it is governed by those working in it'.

A socialist such as Walras did not believe that cooperation could bring about a socialist order. In 1900, he wrote (Walras 1990, p. 66):

> To think that social reform can be achieved through cooperation is like thinking that this goal can be achieved through a system of mutual insurance; it amounts to demeaning, if not altogether nullifying, the role of social reform and, conversely, escalating the importance of cooperative association to the point of impairing its actual potential.

Regrettably, Fitoussi argued (2013, p. 4), the current overemphasis on the role of competition and parallel understatement of the benefits of cooperation are impinging on solidarity. In *Le débat interdit* (1995) he observed that this amounted to undermining the social contract thanks to which job market inequalities had been kept within tolerable levels. On closer analysis, all this goes to confirm the importance of communitarianism in present-day theoretical thinking.

Paraphrasing Engels, it is possible to argue that the concept of socialism has been evolving from its utopian stage – the equation with centralised planning – to the stage of the modern economic theory of producer cooperatives.[183]

In the International Working Men's Association Marx stoutly opposed anarchism and Bakunin. Conversely, by the year that he wrote *The Civil War in France* under the strong impression of the Paris Commune (1871) he had made a U-turn towards anti-authoritarian stances, and this is why this work is sometimes described as an anti-Marxist pamphlet (Lehning 1969, p. 431).[184]

---

[183] Countries with strong cooperative traditions include Spain, Italy, US, Canada, the UK, France, Japan, Hungary, India, Chile, Argentina and Indonesia. The first producer cooperative was established in France and carried out business from 1834 to 1870 (see Dreyfus 2012, p. 42).

Some economists hold that the post-capitalistic system will neither be socialism nor communism, but a peer production model which is as yet in the making and is characterised by the individual production of socially owned goods made available for free use (see Benkler 2006; Kleiner 2010; and Rigi 2013).

[184] For Marx's ideas on firms run by workers see Jossa (2005a). Buchanan (1982, p. 24) has aptly argued that communism in Marx 'is not an ideal among competing ideals; it *is* the social form which *will* replace capitalism'.

Instead of pooling means of production in the State, the Paris Commune advocated a 'slimming State' in the tradition of Proudhon[185] and Bakunin and on 16 April it ordered projects for joining workers into cooperatives and having them run factories (see Engels 1891c, p. 19). In *The Civil War*, Marx made it absolutely clear that the main aim of the Commune – which he clearly endorsed – was to establish a system of self-governing producers to be coordinated by a federation of autonomous municipalities. My firm belief that the vision emerging from this critical reappraisal of Marx's theoretical edifice is still true to the spirit of Marxism is supported by Daniel Guerin's argument that anarchists and some Marxists share the same long-range goal: they concordantly plan to overthrow capitalism, to suppress the State, to get rid of all types of authoritarian protection and to place the management of social property in the hands of workers (see Guerin 1971, p. 445).[186]

Accordingly, there is good ground for describing Marx as the heir of the French Revolution, as a theorist who was planning to pass on to proletarians all the privileges conquered for themselves by the bourgeois (the place of radical liberalism in Marx's educational background is discussed in his biographies, particularly in Mehring 1918 (pp. 75–80) and Merker 2010 (ch. 3). And in my estimation this is a correct approach to Marxism today.[187]

One of the most radical critics of Marx was Simone Weil. 'As long as there is, on the surface of the globe, a struggle for power', she wrote (1955, pp. 15–17), 'and as long as the decisive factor in victory is industrial production, the workers will be exploited' because 'the power which the bourgeoisie has to exploit and oppress the workers lies at the very foundation of our social life and cannot be destroyed by any political and juridical transformation'. 'The very foundation of our culture, which is a culture of specialists', she concluded, 'implies the enslavement of those who execute to those who coordinate'. Faced with this apodictic argument, it comes as a surprise that Weil failed to consider situations in which workers allowed to run their firms on their own would

---

[185] In the opinion of Engels (1891a, p. 23), the policies of the Commune were mainly influenced by the Proudhonian movement.

[186] I agree with Cortesi that the broad outlines of the picture that the Paris Commune drew of the upcoming social order were more advanced than anything that Marx had prefigured in his writings (see Cortesi 2010, p. 76).

[187] For a dissenting view, see Virno's description of Marx as a stout anti-democrat critical of the liberty, equality and fraternity principles and, hence, of the French Revolution (see Virno 2008, p. 107).

manage to wrest themselves free from their subjection to the decisions made by others.

2 LENIN AND DEMOCRATIC CENTRALISM

The idea that socialism is connoted by centralised planning gained widespread recognition thanks to Engels's writings and the theoretical work that Lenin wrote before his change of focus in 1923, specifically the latter's theory of monopolistic state capitalism and imperialism as the last phase of capitalism.

The main points of Lenin's often quoted definition of imperialism can be summed up as follows:

(1) the concentration of production and capital reaches levels at which monopolies play a decisive role in economic life;
(2) bank capital merges with industrial capital and the resulting 'finance capital' gives rise to a financial oligarchy;
(3) capital exports acquire exceptional importance and begin to prevail over exports of commodities; and
(4) capitalists join to form monopolistic associations and partition the world among themselves (Lenin 1917a, p. 128).

The first two characteristics of imperialism, the rise of monopolies which puts an end to the competition-based phase of capitalism and the predominance of financial over industrial capital, are well-known points of Lenin's theoretical thinking and are basically in line with Hilferding's and Gramsci's analyses of the years from 1870 to 1914, approximately.[188] Accordingly, there is no need to expand on them here.

From the above-mentioned analysis of the ever closer interconnections between monopolistic concerns and the State, Lenin proceeded to focus on State intervention in the economy as a basic aspect of the closing stage of capitalism and presented state intervention as including a role in planning and the provision of funds and other forms of support to major concerns.

---

[188] Concerning the predominance of financial capital over industrial capital during the imperialistic period, see, for instance, Gramsci (1919–20, pp. 26 and 130).

According to Altvater (1982, p. 649), as Lenin's state capitalism theory has political implications, its analytical sections are followed up and completed not only by prognoses, but also by details of possible strategic actions. The core assumption behind this theory is that the closing stage of capitalism is the step that leads directly to a socialist revolution both because crises in the older system begin to escalate and, above all, because the typical processes of state capitalism prefigure the characteristics of the new system that will arise from the existing one. The point to be emphasised here is that the situation depicted by Lenin is a near proxy of the system that was to arise in the Soviet Union, namely state socialism with centralised planning.[189]

There is widespread agreement that Lenin describes the successive stages of capitalism objectively and shows how monopolistic concerns and state intervention in the economy pave the way for a form of organised socialism grounded on monopoly building and central planning. According to Lenin, at least in more advanced countries the assumptions for the takeover of the capitalist economic apparatus by the mass of workers had been created by the typically socialist measure of extending compulsory education to all, by the subjection of people to the discipline of industrial work and, finally, by simplified government and administration procedures (see Lorenz 1974, p. 762). In Lenin's state monopolism theory the prerequisite for the transition to socialism is the acquisition of political power: 'The whole question of control boils down to who controls whom, i.e. which class is in control and which is being controlled' (Lenin 1917a, p. 815).

In his biography of Lenin, Meyer reports that Lenin did not deny the fact that the system established in the Soviet Union was nothing but a tool to enable the party to exercise control over the masses (see Meyer 1957, p. 216).[190]

---

[189]   The charge that centralism proceeds from Lenin is usually traced to the well-known 1902 article *What Is to Be Done?*, which Lenin himself described as merely occasional and whose importance has probably been overrated (see Johnstone 1980, pp. 91–2).

[190]   Ragionieri (1965, pp. 129ff.) makes it clear that the socialism-centralised planning equation goes back not only to Lenin, but also to the powerful influence of Engels and his *Antidühring* on the Second International. Aron, too (1965, p. 2), holds that the main source of classical Marxism is Engels's *Antidühring*, though he emphasises that Marx did read and praise this book, but was barely aware of the problems associated with centralised planning (p. 3).

The main reasons explaining the association of Marxism with planning are obviously the success of the 1917 Bolshevik Revolution and the adoption of centralised planning in the USSR for over 60 years running. In this connection,

3 A CRITICAL APPROACH TO CENTRALISED PLANNING

Contemporary critics of the centralised planning model hold that production activities cannot be effectively organised without leveraging the private interest motive and, hence, markets. In the 1930s, neoclassical economists took the cue from Barone (1908) in speaking out against planning on account of the rejection of markets. During the ensuing socialist calculation debate, Marxist economists such as Dobb and Lange remarked that instead of suggesting that markets should be suppressed they were recommending actions designed to put the market in the service of planning. All the same, up to this day no economist has been able to explain how markets and Soviet-type central planning can be reconciled. Although Branko Horvat's book *The Political Economy of Socialism* is widely held to offer the most exhaustive account of all the attempts made to reconcile markets with planning, I stand firm by my belief that plan and market are antithetical. Historical experience has taught that the command economy model collapsed not only because the population rejected its non-democratic and authoritarian practices, but also in consequence of the poor performance of an economic system where the private profit motive was not allowed to be the mainspring of human action. Kornai (1980 and 1994) has shown that due to these difficulties a Soviet-type planned system tends to show chronic shortages and poor quality of production, waste and neglect of costs, perverse trends in quantitative indicators, lack of innovation, bargaining for lower plan targets, soft budget constraints, obstacles to the full attainment or overfulfilment of targets and other shortcomings.

The earliest criticisms of statism, even by the left, were raised many years ago. Marx spoke of the State as the 'lobbying group' of the bourgeoisie and a Marxist such as Antonio Labriola, much in the vein of

---

Bertrand Russell (1935, p. 263) remarked that socialism did not catch on immediately in political practice and remained the creed of a minority with no noticeable bearing on reality until 1917. Considering that all countries under socialism have so far adopted centralised planning, it will hardly come as a surprise that Marxism, the offshoot of scientific socialism, has always been associated with planning.

At the time when Lenin proclaimed the advent of State socialism, Pannekoek held antithetical views which are revealed, inter alia, by the following argument: 'Thus the fighting working class, basing itself upon Marxism, will find Lenin's philosophical work a stumbling block in its way, as the theory of a class that tries to perpetuate its serfdom' (Pannekoek 1938, p. 136).

Marx, dubbed German scholars 'old fogeys' stubbornly clinging to the idea that the State should perform an ethical mission (see Labriola 1896, p. 83).[191] Braudel, for his part, rightly argued that 'capitalism can only triumph when it is identified with the State, when it is the State' (see Braudel 1977, p. 64) and Marianne Weber reports that Max Weber mistrusted all metaphysical interpretations of the State on the assumption that they were just pretexts to shield the privileged classes from the risk of a redefinition of power spheres (see Marianne Weber 1984, p. 671). This means that Hobsbawm's argument that '"Socialism" as applied in the USSR and the other "centrally planned economies", that is to say theoretically market-less state-owned and -controlled command economies, has gone and will not be revived' should be unconditionally endorsed (see Hobsbawm 2011, p. 16).[192]

The most effective critique of centralised planning is doubtless implicit in the theory of public choice. The members of this current of thought tend to quote Hume's saying that 'in contriving any system of government, and fixing the several checks and controls of the constitution, every man ought to be supposed a knave, and to have no other end, in his actions, than private interest' (see Hume 1777, pp. 117–18). In effect, one of the central tenets of Buchanan and his school is that public choice theory cannot do without the *homo oeconomicus* model, i.e. the insight that each individual tends to act solely out of self-interest and that even those that exercise discretionary powers while holding public office will mostly use such power to attain their personal ends.[193]

---

[191]   The idea that the State was a system founded on class was enunciated by Engels even before Marx and is one of Engels's main contributions to the materialist conception of history (see Stedman Jones 1978, pp. 340–2).

[192]   For Veblen's opposition to State socialism, see Veblen 1892 and, inter alia, Hobson 1963, pp. 55–6. In the mind of Trotsky, statism has all the connotations of Stalinism, which he describes as 'a single clot of all monstrosities of the historical State, its most malicious caricature and disgusting grimace' (Trotsky 1938, p. 44).

[193]   Schopenhauer was basically of the same mind. Paraphrasing Thomas Mann (1918, p. 141), he thought that the State, far from combating self-interest, is the true offspring of the selfish drives of the citizens and that these, acting, as it were, in concert amongst them, have systematically developed an overall worldview which is the sum of their individual selfish drives and constitutes what can be termed the egotism of the community. The sole function and purpose of the State is to serve these egotistic interests on the assumption that the very idea of pure morals, i.e. the wish to work towards the general good for ethical reasons only, is unrealistic.

In fact, public choice theorists are not only critical of the foundations of modern finance, but also of 'Keynesians', 'monetarists', 'new classical macroeconomists', 'neo-Keynesians' and other economic schools on the assumption that they keep discussing the goals that governments are supposed to pursue instead of monitoring what governments are actually doing (see Kirchgassner 1989, pp. 11–12).[194] Today, the claim of public choice theorists that the primary concern of all humans is with their personal problems has gained currency to the point of being taken up even by non-liberalists as a possible key to the interpretation of public sector policies.[195]

In recent years, statism has come in for severe criticism from advocates of what is called a 'democracy with socially owned goods'. Departing from the European legal tradition, this movement opposes the central role of the sovereign State and its power to regulate the uses of tangible and intangible resources within the community over which it has jurisdiction. In liberalist and democratic regimes, the State has retained this central role while vesting in the citizens all the basic decisions concerning the way power is to be wielded. The moment assets and commodities are assumed to be socially owned (and, accordingly, title in them is thought to be held by the entire population), legislative choices and decision-making processes become increasingly complex. Up to that moment there were just two traditional actors: the State as the sovereign law maker, with its apparatus of executive, administrative and jurisdictional bodies, and society, viz. the citizens viewed as *donors* of the powers that the State takes over against the pledge to exercise them with self-discipline and in accordance with the resolutions of its jurisdictional, legislative and executive bodies. The 'third actor' that steps onto the stage at this point is the 'State as Community', i.e. the bulk of the citizens vindicating the status of active subjects (Galasso 2013, pp. 71–2).

In combination with the call for community life that capitalism fails to satisfy, the above-mentioned criticisms of statism as well as those raised against markets (with which readers are assumed to be familiar) point to

---

[194] In the minds of all liberalists, 'the rationale underlying constitutionalism is the belief that those in power tend to abuse their authority and that constitutionalism is a means of counteracting such temptation' (Zanone 2002, p. 132).

[195] According to some authors, with some differences this holds for lobbying groups because, the more powerful and active they are, the more their actions undermine efficiency, since they are 'free riders' against society (see, inter alia, Olson 1982).

a 'Third Way', i.e. a type of social organisation, other than free trade, which is founded on the rejection of centralised planning. In other words, critics of statism think that enemies of free market capitalism (who claim that a capitalistic system which is not sufficiently kept in check can only generate imbalance and injustice) do not have to accept massive State intervention if they choose the kind of control that comes with democratic firm management. A critic of centralised socialism such as Rosa Luxemburg warned that socialism, far from being decreed by a dozen officials from behind a few official desks, demanded 'a complete spiritual transformation of the masses degraded by centuries of bourgeois rule' (Luxemburg 1948, p. 590): and from my perspective, a full-fledged socialist order can only be achieved by establishing a system of democratically managed firms.

Some scholars have aptly remarked that most of the criticisms levelled by Yugoslav scholars against bureaucracy and statism are aimed against a process which was traditionally denounced by Marxists, i.e. the bureaucratisation of society as a clear sign of the split between the individual essence and sociality of man (in the spirit of Marx's early work), as a form of hired labour and part and parcel of a reified universe (Lukàcs), and as based on the expropriation of the working class (Trotsky) (see Arnason 1982, p. 180).[196] Consequently, I feel in synch with those Yugoslav scholars who claim that the 'Yugoslav road towards socialism' was antithetical to the centrally planned Soviet model and draw a parallel between it and Marx's theorisation of the death of the State (see p. 179).[197]

---

[196] It is widely held that the distinction between a State-oriented revolutionary movement and one pushing for an emphasis on individual transformation is nothing but the distinction between Marxism and anarchism – which should have general currency (see Wallerstein 2002, p. 309). From my perspective, this idea can barely hold and Wallerstein himself thinks that the anti-system movements of the future should and will not be statist in orientation (see pp. 37–8).

[197] In the opinion of Buchanan (1982, pp. 22–3), it is likely that Marx thought of post-capitalism as divided into three successive stages: the dictatorship of the proletariat, the early communist stage and the later communist stage – with *both* communist stages characterised by the absence of the State.

4 THE EVOLUTION OF SOCIALISM FROM UTOPIA TO SCIENTIFIC PRODUCER COOPERATIVE ECONOMICS

According to Bensaïd (2002, p. xi), after the collapse of the Soviet economy there was a strong temptation to revert from 'scientific socialism' to 'utopian socialism'.[198] From my perspective, instead, today it is possible to draw the broad outlines of the evolution of socialism as the passage from a fallacious centrally planned regime without true markets to the system developed by economic producer cooperative theorists. In the words of Screpanti (2007, p. 145):

> Marx and Engels remained strong advocates of centralisation until the advent of the Commune; in 1850, for instance, they argued the case for a revolutionary process entailing the most decisive centralization of power in the hands of the state authority ... It was the Commune that induced both Marx and Engels to rethink their previous position. (Referring to Marx & Engels 1850, p. 173)

In keeping with Roemer's approach (see 1994), the evolutionary process of socialism can be split into five steps.

At the first step, economists reached the conclusion that labour time is an inappropriate measure for rational economic calculus: even in socialism, they argued, the use of prices as scarcity indexes is, admittedly, the only way to prevent a waste of resources, but – they made clear – such prices cannot be determined by exclusive reference to the labour time needed to produce the commodities concerned.

The second step in the evolution of socialism is the phase in which it was demonstrated that general equilibrium theory can – viz. must – be the instrument for rational economic calculus even in socialist systems. This was the time when, more than a hundred years ago, Pareto and Barone proved that the prices the planning board had to use in striving to secure an efficient use of resources can only be determined by solving a complicated system of equations, i.e. Walras's general economic equilibrium system.

The third step was taken in the 1930s, when a number of renowned economists, including Marxists such as Lange (1936–37) and Lerner (1938), concordantly argued that the prerequisite for the proper functioning of a centrally planned system was a real and proper market, in terms

---

[198] For detailed information on the complex drafting of *Socialism, Utopian and Scientific*, see Prestipino (1973, ch. 1, note 3). For an analysis of this celebrated work of Engels's, see MacPherson (1984).

that it was not enough to solve a system of equations in order to determine the prices that were to be used for the relevant calculations. In a much praised contribution, Lange formulated two general laws that the planner was supposed to observe in order to vouchsafe a properly functioning plan: the first of these laws, which Lange took over from the neoclassical marginalist approach, can be enunciated by saying that the planning board is expected to instruct firms to increase the output volumes of each commodity produced to the level where its marginal cost will equate the corresponding market price.

Within the framework of what we now term the 'Lange-Lerner model of socialism', the prices of commodities are determined by the market, whereas the prices of capital goods are fixed by the planning board. The planning board fixes the initial prices of the capital goods produced and then waits for firms to submit their orders at the prices thus set. If demand for a given capital good exceeds supply, this is held to be a sign that the price that the planning board had provisionally fixed for that product is too low and will therefore have to be increased. The reverse will apply in the opposite situation, i.e. if supply is found to exceed demand. This process should be protracted until demand and supply are balanced out everywhere and for all the capital goods concerned. On closer analysis, however, the law which is being applied is nothing but the law of supply and demand which governs real markets and the planning board can be said to be ultimately acting in accordance with the laws of the market.

Let me specify that under the Lange-Lerner model the remuneration for any work done should be proportional to the associated disutility level, i.e. to the enervation caused by each job, so that the pay rates for sweated jobs would be higher than those for softer and more pleasant jobs.[199]

The fourth step in the evolution of socialism was marked by the introduction of self-management in Tito's Yugoslavia, in Hungary in connection with the reform of the planning system, in the Soviet Union during the tenure of Gorbachev and in post-Mao China. Although the systems established in these countries were not fully compliant with the Lange-Lerner model, they were a sign that the socialist establishment had acknowledged the validity of the economic debate conducted up to those years.

---

[199] For a description and analysis of the socialist calculation debate that took place in the 1930s, the reader should refer to Jossa and Cuomo (1997, chs 1–4).

The fifth step in this process is the debate on the market socialism models proposed by economists in more recent years (including a 1994 model by Roemer himself). At this point, however, in contrast with Roemer's approach I wish to advance the thesis that the fifth step in the debate on socialism started upon the publication of Ward's 1958 article and continued with a rich body of economic studies on producer cooperatives in the following 50+ year span. Ward's paper was one of the first attempts to explain how a worker-controlled firm wishing to conduct business rationally should fix the prices of its products and the later stages of this debate made it clear that a system of producer cooperatives can be rated as a correct implementation of a Marxian version of socialism (see Lowit 1962 and Jossa 2010).[200]

The main objection to a model of socialism with markets – the conflict between the material incentives required for markets to work effectively and the Marxist idea that work should be undertaken for the sake of the pleasure, not the personal profit, that may flow from it – is hardly convincing. Time and again, Lenin himself emphasised that socialism was expected to make the most of the impulse stemming from emulation and (as rightly remarked by Mészàros 1995, pp. 981–2) there is not much difference between the impulse stemming from the example of others and a material stimulus such as the profit motive.[201]

In contrast with other academics, I hold that the core idea behind self-management is neither anachronistic (see Hart & Moore 1996) nor

---

[200]   Zamagni (2005, p. 3) has remarked that 'the twentieth century witnessed a head-on confrontation between two principal socio-economic organisation models: capitalism and the system which is generally described as "state socialism". A far-reaching difference between these two systems is a different property regime of means of production, which are privately owned in the former and publicly (or collectively) owned in the latter. The past century ended with the victory of the capitalistic system.' In this connection, Fukuyama much too hurriedly pontificated that this was the 'end of history'. In fact, the property issue is neither the only difference between different types of economic organisation, nor the most important one. And as I am firmly persuaded that an even more crucial factor is control – i.e. establishing who is in control of the production process – I daresay that the twenty-first century will be the scene of a dialectical confrontation between two major ways to exercise control within firms: control by providers of capital versus control by providers of labour.

[201]   Among advocates of the prompt abolition of markets and its mechanisms in a socialist society let us mention the most renowned Japanese economist, K. Uno, who holds that socialism and markets cannot be reconciled by any means (see Makoto 2006, pp. 22–4).

destined to failure (see Chilosi 1992, p. 159 and Nuti 1992, p. 145)[202] or questionable because of its alleged grounding in the market as a *locus artificialis* or, for that matter, neutral (Amirante 2008, pp. xvii and 31–2). Self-management is a crucial issue of class struggle[203] and 'the primary goal of Marxism' (Garaudy undated, p. 187) and is therefore as topical as ever.[204] And today the economic theory of producer cooperatives, or self-management, is to be looked upon as the theorisation of scientific socialism which lays equal emphasis on its merits and its defects.

5 CONCLUSION

In this chapter, I have laid the claim that the Soviet-type centralised planning model that might be assumed to rise from the ashes of capitalism in consequence of the ever more tightly planned character of capitalistic production activities has markedly utopian overtones since it envisions a production system in which the day-to-day behaviour of workers is not governed by the personal profit motive. On this point, I fully agree with those authors who hold that 'this utopian prospect is to be purged of its unrealistic shades and accommodated within a long-term perspective' (see Losurdo 2005, p. 356).

An additional proposition put forth in this chapter is that the alternative assumption, i.e. the rise of a worker-controlled firm system as an offshoot of that self-same capitalistic dynamic (which taught workers to manage production on their own), has no such utopian overtones since the members of worker-controlled firms would engage in business with the aim of maximising the satisfaction associated with their work.

The classics of Marxism did not doubt that it was science that dictated the material conditions and lines of reasoning needed for political decision making;[205] and in my opinion science has made it sufficiently

---

[202]   The market socialism model that Chilosi and Nuti hold to have failed is a system that was launched in some countries in an abortive attempt to rectify the faults of the Soviet central planning model by reviving markets.

[203]   The movement for worker control in enterprises, Garson wrote in 1973 (p. 469), 'is the central issue of class struggle in our generation'.

[204]   This is what Anweiler wrote in 1958 (p. 472); and in 1973, Trower remarked that the pendulum of democracy had stopped swinging the other way and was now swinging in the direction of the establishment of democracy in the firm (p. 138).

[205]   This Marxist idea is associated with the claim of Enlightenment thinkers that 'man would by education become a rational being in a rational world', that the completion of this process 'would see the laws of his individual and social

clear that, while marketless planning is destined to failure, a system of producer cooperatives is not only viable, but even more efficient than capitalism (see, e.g. Vanek 1970).[206]

---

life all derived from his own autonomous judgment' and that 'the realization of reason thus implied an end to all external authority such as set man's existence at odds with the standards of free thought' (Marcuse 1954, p. 286).

[206] Criticising the State, political parties and political platforms of the present age for failing to vouchsafe democracy to the full, in *Liberalismo e democrazia* (2013, p. 73) Galasso summarily dismissed self-management as unwarranted by any record of positive experience because he looked upon the bullying attitudes of maximalist groups, irrespective of size, as persisting and recurring to the point that they could not be classed as occasional. As a result, he concluded that many strides forward were being taken out of excessive ambition and were eventually found to be marches without a goal. Be that as it may, anyone familiar with producer cooperative theory and, specifically, with the long drawn-out debate on Alchian and Demsetz's 1972 article will have difficulty imagining that episodes of prevarication and high-handedness may prove to be more frequent in a self-management system than they are in capitalism today.

11. The democratic firm in the estimation of intellectuals

1 INTRODUCTION

As we have seen, a system of worker-controlled firms is a possible new production mode which compared to capitalism would literally reverse the existing relation between capital and labour, spark off a true revolution and produce a variety of social benefits, including a major decline in unemployment.

At the beginning of the cooperative movement its potential of producing a variety of social benefits to spark off a true revolution was amply recognised by Mill and Marshall, as I have said in Chapter 3. In the light of these authoritative opinions, anyone analysing a system of cooperative firms in a distinctly Marxian key will have difficulty understanding why so many intellectuals not only ignore this prospect, but go so far as to dismiss it out of hand or openly declare their opposition to the revolutionary move it would entail.

Back in 2005, the awareness that ascertaining the opinions of intellectuals in matters of self-management was a fairly difficult undertaking induced me to interview some Neapolitan economists (see Jossa 2005b). The resulting material, which was used for a number of publications (see, in particular, Jossa 2006a and 2006b), will here be reproposed in a systematic manner along with reasoned comments of my own. My remarks will be grouped into five points, each of which will be addressed in a specific section of this chapter.

One more preliminary remark may be useful at this point.

The call for democratic firm management is closely associated with the defence of what is 'public' (as opposed to 'governmental') that the French Enlightenment thinker Condorcet put in his *Mémoires sur l'instruction publique* in the late eighteenth century. As no individual must be stripped of his natural right to make decisions, he argued, it follows that the citizens, while submitting to the authority of an established power, will at all times retain the right to weigh its resolutions day after day and reject them whenever they do not approve of them.

'Politics' has its roots in the public sphere, in judgements and exchanges of opinions which evolve at the same pace that knowledge is more widely circulated. As community life should at all times be guided by reason, rather than particular interests or even the authority of the State, Condorcet held that the paramount role of education could hardly be overstated. In his approach, ignorance carries in its track exposure to chance and error:

> Insofar as it is true that the more an individual knows, the more he will be able to predict the future, dismantling the barriers of ignorance via the generalised provision of education has been (and remains) the primary socio-political goal to be pursued by a community wanting to reduce the role of chance in the lives of individuals. (See Bodei 2013, p. 184)

In other words, Condorcet looked upon knowledge as the social good par excellence, as the rational language of the public sphere.[207]

In the words of Bascetta (2004, p. 104), 'this public sphere is not the State; nor is it the market or can it be identified with particular interests or the "general will"; it is the domain where the "general intellect" or "collective intelligence" of a community acts itself out'. Hence it follows that the knowledge we have to build on is a compound of the insights not only of intellectuals (who are seldom entirely free or courageous enough), but also of the community at large. Significantly enough, as soon as the terms of the issue are made absolutely clear, the man of the street is easily won over to the need that firms be run by workers. Engels once argued (1844, p. 460) that when 'a principle is set in motion, it works by its own impetus, through all its consequences, whether the economists like it or not'. And this may justify the hope that in due time both left- and right-leaning intellectuals will stop opposing this idea.[208]

---

[207] It is well known that Gramsci was the first thinker to address the role of intellectuals in society – an issue that Marxists had until then failed to tackle. As it is intellectuals that induce the masses to give the ruling bloc their ideological consensus (command plus hegemony), he argued, intellectuals can be defined as the 'agents of hegemony' and 'functionaries of the superstructure', acting as the linchpin between the base and the superstructure (see Macciocchi 1974, p. 261).

[208] Dissenting from this view, Hayek wrote that no far-reaching political changes could be achieved through mass propaganda. The appropriate strategy, he argued, was pressing ideas convincingly on intellectuals (Hayek 1983, p. 192; see also, Nik-Kah 2010 and Nik-Kah & van Horn 2012).

My starting point is the awareness that the 'organic' intellectuals that Gramsci set against traditional ones[209] and the 'specific' intellectuals that Foucault contrasted with universal ones are exactly the categories of intellectuals that have lately been increasing in number. For this reason, unlike other contemporary commentators, I endorse the claim of Adorno and Arendt that 'the classical role of the intellectual as the spokesman for universality is a thing of the past' (Auer 2004, p. 94).[210]

2 SOCIALISM AND MARKETS

During the well-known socialist calculation debate of the 1930s, socialist economists maintained that the creation of a socialist economy with publicly owned production means was rationally feasible, but that a socialist system was expected to imitate the working of markets. In response to criticisms from liberalists, they offered the demonstration that the central planning board was in a position to retrieve all the data needed to establish a rational price system and fine-tune it with consumer demand. And an interesting remark by Schumpeter runs that socialism 'does not necessarily – that is, by logical necessity – exclude the use of competitive mechanisms' (Schumpeter 1950, pp. 421–2).

Although they accepted this demonstration, the liberalist economists involved showed that it was not devoid of shortcomings. Among other things, they warned that continuing changes in consumer preferences and technological standards would prevent the planning board from securing all the necessary information in real time. Even though this difficulty might somehow be overcome, they argued, the number of commodities that would have to enter the requisite system of equations would be such as to rule out the very possibility of working out a satisfactory solution.

In reply to this criticism, Lange (1936–37) suggested constructing a supply curve for each commodity by setting a price and measuring the resulting levels of demand and supply. In this way, he maintained,

---

[209]   In the words of Macciocchi (1974, p. 262), the association that Gramsci establishes between the working class and 'intellectuals', specifically those he terms 'the organic intellectuals of the proletariat', is tantamount to a revolution in communist thought because it overturns the previous Marxist approach to this issue.

[210]   Since the true focus points of my critique are intellectuals, I do hope that my criticisms of them will neither sound arrogant nor excessively humble; my axiom is 'the Aristotelian criterion of magnanimity, a virtue which rules out both excessive self-esteem (presumption) and the understatement of one's merits (the Greeks looked upon humility as a vice)' (see Bodei 2013, p. 25).

consumers would be allowed freedom of choice and the planning board would simply have to cut prices in situations of overstocking and step them up in the opposite case. The same procedure, he added, can be adopted for the prices of production means, which are to be set as parametric indicators for the quantitative comparison of alternatives. The adoption of this model, he concluded, would relieve the central planning board from the need to compile huge lists of demand and supply functions or solve hundreds of thousands, if not millions of equations.

To solve the planning issue once and for all, Lange suggested obliging the managers of state-owned enterprises to observe two rules: firstly, to equalise the marginal productivity of factors in all firms; secondly, to fix the output volumes of the individual goods at the level where the marginal cost equalises the price.

In sum, based on Lange's model of a socialist market economy equilibrium prices can be set by recourse to an empirical trial and error process which recalls the mechanism governing the working of markets founded on competition. And while there is little doubt that Lange's model was fleshed out in order to refute the claim of Hayek and von Mises that no rational pricing system was available for use in a socialist economy with publicly owned enterprises, in point of fact it ends up by emphasising the need that markets be retained even in a socialist economy.

These reflections clear the field of the wrong assumption that no Marxist can accept the idea of a market economy.

Considering the advantages of self-management over capitalism (see, inter alia, Vanek 1970 and Jossa 2014a), it is difficult to account for the failure of anti-capitalists to espouse the theories that Ward and Vanek fleshed out in 1958 and 1970, to proclaim, as Lenin did back in 1923, that Marxists have to change their view of socialism or to admit that a forceful impulse to cooperation is all that is needed to implement socialism to the full – as will be argued in Section 3.

3 A SYSTEM OF PRODUCER COOPERATIVES AS A GENUINE SOCIALIST SYSTEM

Another point to confirmation that democratic firm management amounts to socialism can be put in perspective if we establish which of the contradictions of capitalism can be considered the fundamental one.

Discussing the active function of thought as the faculty enabling man not only to contemplate nature and society, but also to act upon them and work towards change, in *Theses on Feuderbach* Marx spelt it out that the precondition for changing and advancing society was solving its inherent contradictions. From this, it follows that identifying the farthest-reaching contradiction of capitalism is a process rich in important implications.

The first idea to cross the minds of Marxists and non-Marxists alike is the capital–labour polarity. Quoting Godelier, for instance,

> the first contradiction we come up against in capitalism is the conflict between capital and labour, between capitalists as a class and workers as a class. The former own capital; the latter are bereft of it. The profits of the former amount to the value of the work for which the latter have not been remunerated. (1966, p. 29)[211]

As Gramsci put it (1921, pp. 148–9), 'the control issue boils down to the question of industrial power, the question of deciding whether industrial production plans are to be framed in the interests of bankers and stockjobbers or, in contrast, in the interests of the masses; by the trustees of capitalists or those of the working class'. The workers' state (i.e. a state where workers are in control of both businesses and government) is specific to the transitional stage from capitalism to communism, he added, and

> the workers' state is not an arbitrary choice, nor is it a vain hope. It is a historical necessity which grows out of the very circumstances created by class conflict. When, in response to the errors or ineptitude of the bourgeoisie, individual categories of working people gain a sense of their joint interests, then communists claim that the social assumptions for the rise of a workers' state are given. (Gramsci 1921, p. 149)

---

[211]   Pareto (1926, pp. 73–4) rated the word 'socialism' as a vague term and recommended replacing it with a more trenchant one. Socialism has been variously defined, but the simplest and most widely used definition is 'an economic system where means of production are socially owned'. In the opinion of Dobb, for instance, to identify the main characteristic of a socialist economy with anything other than the social ownership of production means would amount to a break with the nineteenth-century tradition which inspired numerous attempts to establish a socialist order. According to him, Marx and Engels, the founders of socialism, were doubtless the first theorists to lay emphasis on the social ownership principle, but later theorists followed in their wake (see Dobb 1969; see also Pareto 1926, p. 74; Lange 1936–7, part I, para. 2, and 1958, p. 8; Sweezy 1963, p. 330; Landauer 1959, vol. 1, p. 5; Wiles 1962, ch. 1; Drewnowski 1961, para. 2; Kornai 1971, pp. 337–8; Dobb 1970, ch. 4). Steedman (1995, p. 1) describes socialism as a 'proteinic' notion whose analysis cannot be exhausted in a single book.

The idea that class struggle is the key problem of capitalistic economies is doubtless one of Marx's major contributions to the understanding of the social order in which we live. And as this idea was first stated in early writings not yet supported by a sound grounding in political economy, there are reasons for assuming that Marx did not take it over from any of the writers on whom he drew for his later studies. It features in such an early work as the *Critique of Hegel's Philosophy of Right*, which Marx wrote in the autumn of 1843 and issued in the early months of 1844, and it continued to take centre stage in his later theoretical approach.

Accordingly, there are reasons for arguing that the true precondition for superseding capitalism is solving the dialectical contradiction arising from the conflict between a class which wields all power and a class expected to obey passively, rather than the planning-markets opposition.[212] To look upon the plan–market option as the key problem, Bettelheim wrote, is a gross mistake which diverts attention towards side issues and, hence, away from the real crux of the issue: the existence of a class – the 'bourgeoisie' – whose primary aim is to prevent workers from attaining power. This is why an occasional acceleration or stalemate in market relations at one stage or other is, in itself, not enough to make us assume that the world is progressing towards socialism or moving away from it (see Bettelheim 1969b; and, among others, Poulantzas 1974; Marek 1982, p. 751).

In contrast, Engels and orthodox Marxists did not think of the capital–labour opposition as the basic contradiction of capitalism. In orthodox Marxist terms, the basic contradiction of capitalism originates from a mismatch between the socialised character of production in large-size industrial concerns (where hundreds and even thousands of workers see to their jobs side by side) and the private character of appropriation (the very underpinning of privately owned production means) (see, for example, Engels 1878, part 3, II; Tsuru 1969, pp. 364–5). According to Engels (and other Marxists), this contradiction sparks off an additional one: 'the contradiction between socialised production and capitalistic

---

[212] In quotes from Marcuse reported in Vacca (1969a, p. 333 and 1969b, p. 253), the key contradiction of capitalism is described as 'an oppressive relation opposing man to nature, subject to object, which is perceived at the root of our civilisation and which generates oppressive social relations', and industrial societies are said to be 'the outgrowth of a historical design aimed to establish control of man over man'.

appropriation now presents itself as an antagonism between the organization of production in the individual workshop and the anarchy of production in the society as a whole' (Engels 1878, pp. 260–1).[213]

Time and again, Engels argued that these contradictions were actually nothing but different ways of describing one and the same state of affairs. In *Antidühring*, he wrote (1878, pp. 260–1): 'The contradiction between socialised production and capitalistic appropriation now presents itself as an antagonism between the proletariat and the bourgeoisie'.

Commenting on this passage, Sève (1970, p. 145) appropriately objected that each such contradiction obeys a different logic and that Engels could therefore not be assumed to have described them as identical in purely abstract terms. But why is it important to distinguish between these two major contradictions of capitalism?

Lack of agreement on the basic contradiction of capitalism has a major bearing on the possibility to predict the kind of social order that will rise from the ruins of capitalism. Those looking on the capital–labour polarity as the main contradiction will argue that socialism – the social order of the transitional stage between capitalism and communism – arises when the capital–labour relation is reversed as a result of the replacement of a system controlled by capital owners with a system of worker-run firms. Conversely, those who think that the key contradiction of capitalism is the contrast between socialised production and private appropriation will contend that the social order to rise from the ashes of capitalism is a centrally planned system (Jossa 2014c).

To account for the rejection of this line of reasoning it is necessary to distinguish between two different Marxist stances. Some contend that the reversal of the capital–labour relation does not give rise to a genuine socialist order since it fails to do away with markets, the true underpinning of capitalism; others hold that the equation of socialism with a worker-controlled system shows that socialism can be implemented in practice although it is unable to come up with convincing objections against a system such as market socialism.[214]

---

[213] Panzieri, instead, highlights a conflict between book I of *Capital* and other Marxian works: whereas in *Capital* the opposition between 'despotism (planning) in factories and anarchy in society' is described as 'the general form of the law of value', he argues (see Panzieri 1964, p. 346), in other works we perceive the germs of a different approach (pp. 346ff. and 362).

[214] For a more extensive analysis of the claims advanced in this section, see Jossa 2009, 2010, pp. 262–9 and 2014a, ch. 13.

4 SOCIALISM AND ALIENATION

The issue of alienation, which is crucial to Marx's approach, is introduced in order to argue that (a) following the establishment of a self-managed system alienation would be scaled down in full keeping with Marx's approach, and that (b) this goes to confirm the claim that a system of LMF-type cooperatives would give rise to a new mode of production.

In his maturity, Marx identified different forms and levels of alienation, of which some were common to a variety of social organisations, while others were specific to capitalism only. In general terms, he made it clear that the categories of work to be described as 'alienated' were all those production activities which were not primarily aimed to meet human needs and, more generally, actions conditioned by external constraints. In all the societies of which we have knowledge, he argued, labour and productive life itself appeared to people not as a means of satisfying an inner urge, but only as a means of satisfying other people's needs.

In this wide meaning, any work done in a system characterised by productive specialisation – the division of labour – is alienated. In Marx's opinion, those finding pleasure in their work tend to diversify their activities, switch between jobs and eschew overspecialised occupations,[215] whereas the division of labour strips workmen of the intellectual potential inherent in any work process.

In a less wide and comprehensive sense, alienation comes in association with the working of the market, which has impersonal mechanisms whose effects can hardly ever be planned or wilfully contrived. The main alienation-generating market mechanism is competition, which impels people to behave in manners they would probably shun if they did not have to vie with competitors. A capitalistic market necessitates higher degrees of specialisation than would be needed in a competition-free environment.

Overall, market-related alienation is the effect of scarcity and the resulting need to renounce freedom of choice and act under compulsion.

These quotes are clear evidence that any work which is done for income-earning purposes is described as 'alienated' and that this point is a core assumption behind Marx's entire theoretical approach. Speaking of the worker, Marx raised the query: 'Is this 12 hours' weaving, spinning,

---

[215] The idea that work in systems organised in line with the principle of the division of labour becomes degrading was shared by a large number of eighteenth-century writers including Smith, Ferguson, Millar and Wallace (see West 1969, p. 137).

boring, turning, building, shovelling, stone-breaking, regarded by him as a manifestation of life, as life? Quite the contrary. Life for him begins where this activity ceases, at the table, at the tavern, in bed' (see Marx 1849, p. 34). And in *Grundrisse*, with reference to a tradesman or professional, he spelt it out in bold letters that the exchange relation confronts us like a power which is external to producers and independent of them:

> The social character of the activity, as also the social form of the product and the share of the individual in production, appear here as something alien to and existing outside the individuals; not as their relationship to each other, but as their subordination to relationships existing independently of them and arising from the collision between indifferent individuals. (See Marx 1857–58, p. 94)

A less general, but even more compelling definition of alienation is 'work which is subject to the sway of capital'. In Marx's *Manuscripts of 1844* we read: 'the more the worker exerts himself in his work, the more powerful the alien, objective world becomes which he brings into being over against himself, the poorer he and his inner world become, and the less they belong to him':

> The alienation of the worker in his product means not only that his labour becomes an object, an external existence, but that it exists outside him, independently, as something alien to him, and that it becomes a power on its own confronting him. It means that the life which he has conferred on the object confronts him as something hostile and alien. (Marx 1844a, p. 211)

In *Grundrisse*, we also read:

> No extraordinary intellectual power is needed to comprehend that, if the initial situation assumed is that of free labour arising from the dissolution of serfdom, or wage labour, the only way in which machines can originate is in opposition to living labour, as property alien to it and hostile power opposed to it, i.e., they must confront labour as capital. (Marx 1857–58, p. 577)[216]

From Marx's contention that hired labour is the main determinant of capitalistic alienation it follows that the suppression of hired labour in a system of self-managed firms would sweep away the primary form of alienation. As mentioned before, in a democratic firm system the

---

[216]   In a well-known monograph about alienation theory, Mészàros wrongly equated Marxian alienated labour with wage labour straightaway (see Mészàros 1970, ch. 4).

capitalistic relation between capital and labour is reversed since labour power ceases being bought by the owners of production means and workers become buyers of capital goods themselves. As a result, a democratic firm system is an effective means of counteracting that form of alienation that stems from the subordination of labour to capital:[217]

> The worker actually treats the social character of his work, its combination with the work of others for a common purpose, as a power which is alien to him; the conditions in which this combination is realized are for him property of another. It is quite different in factories that belong to the workers themselves, as at Rochdale. (Marx 1894, p. 179)[218]

An additional implication of these reflections is that alienation is much more common among workers than capitalists. 'The propertied class and the class of the proletariat present the same human self-estrangement. But the former class feels at ease and strengthened in this estrangement, it recognises estrangement as its own power and has in it the semblance of a human existence' (see Marx & Engels 1845, p. 36).

Considering the paramount role of alienation in Marx's theoretical approach, it must strike us as surprising that even those who rate alienation as a serious problem of modern society fail to see that a system of worker-controlled firms would outperform capitalism thanks to its potential for reducing alienation.

5 MARXISM AND DIALECTICS

As mentioned before, it is my belief that today analytical Marxism is the only acceptable theoretical approach to Marxism for two main reasons: firstly, because it refutes the idea that price is exclusively determined by the amount of labour incorporated in a commodity; secondly, because thanks to its use of a non-Hegelian form of dialectic (that is to say, a dialectic consistent with the non-contradiction principle) it does not cancel such a crucial element of Marx's approach as the dialectical view of reality. This necessitates going deeply into the subject of what Marx and Marxists mean by dialectics.

---

[217] For an interesting and exhaustive analysis of this point, see Reich and Devine (1981).

[218] In an outline of different levels of alienation, Sobel (2008) contends that alienation would outlast the end of capitalism, in terms of extending right into the early phases of the new social order.

Quoting Marx: 'if ever the time comes when such work is again possible, I should very much like to write two or three sheets making accessible to the common reader the rational aspect of the method which Hegel not only discovered but also mystified' (Marx 1858, p. 249). Unfortunately, he never turned this plan into practice and this is why his dialectical method is still interpreted in a variety of different ways (see Bhaskar 1991 and Reuten 2002, p. 28).[219]

The main point to be borne in mind when discussing the dialectical method is the awareness that the only way to avert the risk of an insoluble contrast between Marxism and orthodox economic science is reconciling dialectics with the non-contradiction principle; and Hegelian dialectics takes centre stage especially in Marx's writings on the subject of the labour theory of value.

Advocates of the labour theory of value tend to interpret Marx's dialectical method in Hegelian fashion, as a method which rules out the non-contradiction principle. According to them, the claim that commodities have both a use value and an exchange value is a dialectical contradiction. 'Commodities have characteristics that set them apart (because they are things and, as such, differ from each other quite obviously), but they have in common one element that makes them all alike. And this element is value' (Vinci 2008, p. 59).

Speaking of commodities as quantities, we abstract both from the material characteristics that satisfy given needs and from the nature of the work that went into their making. This is why Marx and Marxists think that labour turns into its opposite (from concrete to abstract) in any

---

[219]   In Oldrini (2007, p. 219) we read that 'no other term, in philosophy, is as vague and slippery as this. On the one hand, with the passing of time dialectics has come to acquire a wealth of mutually different meanings, so that its implications remain vague even in the works of philosophers – with Hegel the most prominent among them – who look upon it as a complex but unitary and organic process; on the other hand, its applications come in countless variables and its use is often understated, if not altogether concealed'. On this point, see also, Fineschi (2006, pp. 16–17).

In part, the different interpretations of the notion of dialectics can be traced to different views concerning Marx's theoretical approach to the issue of cognition. Some see Marx as a rationalist endorsing the need to apprehend reality through the exercise of reason, without regard to sensorial perception, while others have categorised him as an empiricist holding that cognition is the product of sensorial observation and consequently requires the aid of the inductive method of natural sciences. Others still characterise him as a pragmatist thinking that concepts are but cues to cognition and require the validation of concordant test results.

exchange transactions with capital and why they define the logic under-lying exchange (which Adam Smith saw as intrinsically associated with human nature) as a dialectical notion in which two opposites are concomitantly present.

In other words, it is widely held that according to Marx commodities are all alike (since they include abstract labour as a common component) and different as a result of their different values. And this is the foundation of dialectics. Concerning this point, Colletti commented (1979, pp. 124–5): 'One thing is certain. The analysis of commodities that Marx develops in the opening pages of *Capital* is a clear instance of the so-called "dialectical contradiction" method'.

For my part, I wish to press the point that the link between the notion of commodities and Hegelian dialectic is altogether dismantled by the demonstration that self-managed firms neither use labour power in commodity fashion nor turn concrete into abstract labour. As pointed out above, democratic firms do not employ any hired workers and, as work becomes abstract when it is acquired in exchange for wages, the work done in these firms will never be abstract.

Let me emphasise once again that democratic firm management theorists see no link between a Hegelian use of dialectics and the capitalism-as-a-reversed-world assumption of the labour theory of value. In their opinion, the link on which the reversed capital–labour relation of a labour-managed firm system provides focus is between the notion of the world as upside-down and the awareness that it is natural for man to use things and hold sway over capital (and not vice versa). And from this, it quite obviously follows that the view of the world as upside-down is no dialectical proposition.[220]

Our line of reasoning necessitates exploring the real implications of the term dialectics.

The well-known Italian political philosopher Norberto Bobbio holds that dialectics comes in two forms:

> Faced with two conflicting entities we may either opt for the 'compenetration-of-opposites' (or mutual-interaction) method or for a method founded on the 'negation of the negation'. When the former is adopted, both entities are kept firm and are assumed to mutually condition each other; when the latter is

---

[220] In part, the claim that the dialectical method is mainly aimed to tell appearance from reality and that the appearance–reality opposition is the principal Hegelian distinction in Marx is refuted by the demonstration that in labour-managed systems the appearance–reality distinction is unrelated to the labour theory of value and, hence, to dialectics.

adopted, we assume that the first entity is cancelled by the other at a first stage and the second by the third at a subsequent stage. (Bobbio 1958, p. 347)

Concerning these antithetical methods, Badaloni argued (1962, p. 110) that the former was the method adopted by Marx in his mature studies as an economist and scientist, while the latter was the method of the younger Marx.

According to Backhaus, one of the main editors of the Mega2 edition of Marx's works, Marx's theoretical approach can be explained in two ways: esoterically, as concerned with analysing a logical model of the contradictions perceived within a mode of production; exoterically (or in Hegelian fashion), as concerned with the diachronic analysis of the contradictions within an economic system and the way they evolve in time. This approach closely recalls Bobbio's, but Backhaus maintains that Marx was not fully aware of this distinction and that this is why he made less and less use of the dialectical method in his published works (see Backhaus 1997 and Fineschi 2008, pp. 24–8).

Today, Bobbio's view of dialectics is endorsed by a great many academics, including Marxist thinkers, who look upon dialectics as a way of thinking which tends to approach a problem with focus on two antithetical, though equally essential facets (Rothschild 1986, p. 188), as a process which aims to reconcile contradictions and is therefore described as the 'interpenetration of opposites' (see Sowell 1985, pp. 28–35), and as a method designed to expand our understanding of things by bringing to the fore both their evolution in time and the interactive context each of them is part of (Ollman 2003, p. 13 and Fay 1983, p. 560). Vidoni (2007, p. 260) has emphasised the major role that dialectics plays in the analysis of highly complex phenomena which are rich in mutual interactions, for example the complex links between organisms and their environment or social relations;[221] others have stressed the ability of dialectical thinking to identify a closely meshed web of internal links between different entities (Ollman 1976, p. 61) or revealing conflicts and contradictions in society (see, inter alia, Labriola 1902, p. 22; Gallino 1987, pp. 219–20; Volpi 1989, p. 29; and Sherman 1995, ch. 11). In this connection, Colletti has warned that this notion of

---

[221]   As pointed out by Cingoli (2001, p. 35), Marx embraced 'the romantic conception of nature as a living organism' in his early 20s.

dialectics is only acceptable if the contradictions involved are material, not just logical (on this distinction, see, specifically, Colletti 1974 and 1980).[222]

Lenin concerned himself extensively with dialectics (see Meyer 1957, p. 19) as 'a tool capable of disclosing links between one thing and all the others' (p. 21), i.e. as a notion which closely recalls Bernstein's (see Bernstein 1899, p. 52).

Hence, dialectics appears to be closely linked to the totality notion for two main reasons: firstly, because Marx and Engels's theorisation of the materialist conception of history was 'the very first attempt – and the greatest achievement to their credit in the history of social and historical science – to call attention to a unitary thread running through the entire span of social evolution' (Vorländer 1911, p. 248) and, secondly, because it is dialectical thinking that conceives of truth as a totality (Bell 1995, p. 112). In this connection, it has been remarked that logic becomes dialectical when the relations between its parts are devoid of meaning outside the global context (Sachs 1969, p. 355) and 'when the relations themselves are situated as moments of a totality' (Arthur 1998, p. 11).

The criticisms levelled against intellectuals in Section 4 receive fresh confirmation from these reflections. On closer analysis, to criticise Marxism because of its use of dialectics – for this is what Colletti and other intellectuals do – is nothing but a maladroit attempt to reject the revolutionary essence of Marx's approach. As mentioned above, modern producer cooperative theory demonstrates that it is possible to spark off a type of anti-capitalistic revolution which would defy the criticisms of even the most orthodox thinkers. This is why the tendency of many intellectuals to explain away as Marxist any idea of revolution and to interpret Marxism as a critique of the non-contradiction principle is actually instrumental to their attempt to avert the advent of a socialist revolution.

Colletti's argument that Hegelian dialectic is an essential component of Marxism is mainly based on his belief that the core element of Marx's approach, i.e. alienation theory, requires accepting dialectics in its Hegelian form (see Lissa 1982, p. 254). This is why he writes that alienation is caused by the fragmentation of what was once united, i.e. by the rupture of, or split in, an original whole (Colletti 1979, p. 47). In my opinion, rather, in Marx's theoretical approach only work that is done under compulsion, rather than for purposes of self-realisation, is

---

[222] Similarly, Struve wrote (1899, p. 140) that 'if reality is dialectical, logical thought – and therefore scientific thought – is *non-dialectical* by its very nature'.

described as alienated, and the resulting notion of alienation is not necessarily related to Hegel's dialectical method.[223]

6 CONCLUSION

As argued by Gramsci (1964, pp. 1246–7), the claim that the roots of Marxism lie in German classical philosophy, English political economy and French socialism is to be understood in the sense that the 'philosophy of praxis' (Gramsci's term to indicate Marxism) is the result of the merging of three movements which together constituted the whole coeval cultural heritage. The resulting combination, he went on to argue, is seen to have grown out of these three 'preparatory' movements irrespective of whether it is examined from the theoretical, economic or political viewpoint. In his opinion, the discovery of the formal logical principle underlying the 'laws of tendency' (which do not arise from natural causes in a deterministic sense, but are the product of historical evolution) amounts to the gnoseological discovery of a new type of 'immanence' and a new notion of 'necessity' (see p. 1247). This, Gramsci argued, is how Ricardo's insights were extended to history as a whole within the framework of the 'philosophy of praxis'. 'In the passage from economics to general history the concept of quantity is complemented by the concept of quality and by the concept of dialectical quantity which becomes quality' (p. 1248).

Like Gramsci, Lenin also held Marxism to be 'the legitimate successor to the best that man produced in the nineteenth century, as represented by German philosophy, English political economy and French socialism ... In one way or another all official and liberal science defends wage-slavery, whereas Marxism has declared relentless war on that slavery' (1902). The superiority of Marxism lies in its potential to shed light on the way a new mode of production grows out of the previous one. Lenin rated Marx's materialist conception of history as one of the greatest achievements in scientific thinking:

> The chaos and arbitrariness that had previously reigned in views on history and politics were replaced by a strikingly integral and harmonious scientific theory which shows how, in consequence of the growth of productive forces, out of one system of social life another and higher system develops – how capitalism, for instance, grows out of feudalism. (p. 477)

---

[223]   In this connection, Althusser wrote (1973, p. 76, footnote) that he did not see what good could come from a category such as the negation of the negation.

Capitalism, he claimed, has triumphed all over the world, 'but this triumph is only the prelude to the triumph of labour over capital' (p. 478).

In my estimation, this prompts the conclusion that democratic firm management amounts to a socialist revolution.

Let me add that insofar as Mondolfo and Garin are right when they argue that real humanism is the key to a correct understanding of the 'true Marx' (see Garin 1979 and 1983), a socialist revolution can be described as humanistic in essence. This view is not shared by Althusser.

Conceived of as the successor to classical German philosophy, English political economy and French socialism, Marxism fuses all human knowledge into one consistent whole, i.e. it fully realises the grand plan that Bacon termed *Instauratio Magna* and, as argued by Edward O. Wilson, constitutes the ultimate goal that humanity should strive to attain by all means (see Wilson 1998).

12. An involuntary antagonist of history and progress

1 INTRODUCTION

Kant defined history as 'steadily progressing development' (see Kant 1784, p. 174). Lukàcs, for his part, wrote that Marx's idea of world history 'as a unitary process and the highroad to liberation' was consistent with the approaches of the German philosophers and chiefly Hegel (1968a, p. 34). In *The German Ideology*, Marx and Engels described history as

> nothing but the succession of the separate generations, each of which exploits the materials, the capital funds, the productive forces handed down to it by all preceding generations; and thus, on the one hand, continues the traditional activity in completely changed circumstances and, on the other, modifies the old circumstances with a completely changed activity. (See Marx & Engels 1845–6, p. 27)[224]

In support of these statements suffice it to mention that an old-standing institution such as slavery was in due time replaced by serfdom in several countries, including Russia, or that universal suffrage, initially restricted to males only, was finally extended to women as well.

While these developments do suggest steady progress towards ever fuller freedom, it may well be that this process is grinding to a stop. Considering that the one step required to complete it is granting workers a say in production, there are grounds for arguing, with Fukuyama, that it will hardly be taken in the foreseeable future and that the final assertion of the present-day mode of production has brought historical progress to a halt.

---

[224] In this connection, Arendt (1978, p. 106) speaks of the 'sixteenth-century idea of an unlimited progress, which after a few centuries became the most cherished dogma of all men living in a scientifically oriented world'. Conversely, other theorists provide focus on the 'conception of a linear progression of time which is typical of Christianity and of the present-day worldview (as shaped by the spirit of the Enlightenment)' (Curi 2015, p. 15).

In other words, 50+ years of incessant concern with the history of socialism have taught me that the generalised view of history as steady development should probably be dropped for a reason which is usually overlooked[225] and will emerge from what follows.

2 ON THE CAPITAL–LABOUR RELATION

Establishing if, and in what manner, the management of firms by workers themselves might help cancel the 'contradiction' between capital and labour is no trivial issue and requires answering two questions: (a) whether this 'contradiction' reflects a conflict of interest between capitalists and workers which is impossible to eliminate or a contrast between the status quo and the conditions that would be desirable, and (b) whether the correct capital–labour relation, once restored, would solve the fundamental contradiction of capitalism by cancelling the grave injustice (stigmatised in the labour theory of value) inherent in the retention, by capitalists, of the greater part of the output of production.

In Marx's approach, the notion of contradiction is to be read through the lens of his dialectical vision, which entails that reality evolves at the same pace that its inherent contradictions are superseded. In other words, in Marx's approach a contradiction is a conflictual or disharmonious condition that is cured as historical development progresses.

In point of fact, the 're-reversed' capital–labour relation would not solve the conflict of interest associated with distribution, i.e. the fact that the greater part of the output of production is cashed by one class increases in inverse proportion to the part that is left to the other. This conflict of interest is bound to outlast the revolution discussed in this chapter.

On closer analysis, though, the capital–labour opposition is not only caused by this conflict of interest, but also and especially by the 'unnatural' subjection of man to capital, i.e. of man to an inanimate thing.

---

[225] In this connection, Fromm wrote (1962, p. 200): 'In contrast to the men of the eighteenth and nineteenth centuries who had an unfailing belief in the continuity of progress, we visualize the possibility that, instead of progress, we may create barbarism or our total destruction. The alternative of socialism or barbarism has become frighteningly real today'.

3 IS THE PROLETARIAT STILL A REVOLUTIONARY CLASS?

In the words of Marcuse (1967, p. 22), 'if Marx saw in the proletariat the revolutionary class, he did so also, and maybe even primarily, because the proletariat was free from the repressive needs of capitalist society, because the new needs for freedom could develop in the proletariat and were not suffocated by the old, dominant ones'. But is the proletariat still a revolutionary class?

Proletarians were no revolutionaries because they had not yet developed class consciousness; but things changed after the advent of machinery-based industry, when the work of ingenious individual inventors was replaced by scientific research as the true lever of technological progress and the one-time costly and time-consuming craftsmen training programmes became redundant. The resulting entry of women and children to the labour market produced a surge in labour supply exactly at a time when the brisk introduction of new machinery items was causing a sharp decline in demand. As wages fell and work rate rose (in proportion to rises in the working speed of machinery), labour became ever more dependent on capital, but due to the fact that 'the nature of work in the modern factory requires the organization and disciplining of the workers' and prepares them 'for organized and disciplined action in other fields', the proletariat concomitantly gained more political power (see Sweezy 1967, p. 323).

Consequently, the question that Marx failed to raise is whether the proletariat is likely to retain its revolutionary spirit under such circumstances. Before answering this question, Sweezy remarked that although the progress of technology reducing the size of the industrial labour force and scaling up the number of service-sector employees does not turn industrial workers into non-revolutionaries as a matter of course, there is no denying that in situations where shop floor workers become a minority they tend to adopt attitudes and embrace ideologies which are 'not totally different from those of the non-revolutionary majority of the working class which surround them' (see Sweezy 1967, p. 328).[226]

---

[226] According to Tronti (2008, p. 75), in Marx's approach it is only in periods when society moves towards industrial capitalism that workers can develop into a revolutionary class; the class struggle – he argues – is part and parcel of this social model and, in any way, Marx 'probably did not concern himself with other historical periods: neither with capitalistic tendencies arising prior to the emergence of industrial capitalism nor with capitalistic tendencies developing after the heyday of industry'.

Does this suggest that there are no more revolutionaries left?

Sweezy's answer is that all the industrialised countries of the capitalistic world system have started exploiting less developed nations. In his opinion, the revolutions in Vietnam, China and Cuba are clear evidence that this is one of the reasons why farmhands and industrial workers in exploited countries grow into revolutionaries. Hence, it is possible to conclude that the long-term effect of the Industrial Revolution is to radically change the revolutionary agent – in full keeping with Marx's claim that capitalism produces its own grave diggers.

4 CLASS 'IN ITSELF' VERSUS CLASS 'FOR ITSELF'

According to Kautsky, Lenin and Gramsci, 'class consciousness', the antagonistic worldview of workers, comes to them from the party, which means that in contexts without a workers' party workers would only develop trade union consciousness (for example, Poulantzas 1968, p. 258 and Gruppi 1970, pp. 44–9).[227]

In *What Is to Be Done?*, Lenin explained that the considerable background knowledge in philosophy, history and economics that is required to develop the doctrinal body of socialism was the preserve of the middle-class intelligentsia and concluded that socialism was to be looked upon as the child of bourgeois intellectuals who had developed into revolutionaries. Both Marx and Engels, he wrote, were representatives of this class, and even in revolutionary Russia the theoretical doctrine of social democracy arose independently of the spontaneous growth of the working-class movement, 'as a natural and inevitable outcome of the development of thought among the revolutionary socialist intelligentsia' (Lenin 1902, p. 63).

Indeed, Lenin added with much emphasis, Kautsky thought that modern economic science was as much a condition for socialist production as, say, modern technology, and that the proletariat, no matter how it might desire to do so, was unable to create either of them since both arise

---

[227]   In Hobsbawm 2011 (p. 325) we read that one of Gramsci's most brilliant insights is the idea that 'it is only through its movement and its organisation, i.e. in his view through the party, that the working class develops its consciousness and transcends the spontaneous "economic-corporative" or trade unionist phase'. Conversely, Hobsbawm argued that 'Marxist theorists from Kautsky to Lenin held that labour movements did not generate socialism spontaneously. Socialism had to be imported into them from outside' – and this '*was perhaps an exaggeration*' (see Hobsbawm 2011, p. 402, italics added).

out of the modern social process. 'The vehicle of science is not the proletariat, but the bourgeois intelligentsia', he claimed, and as 'it was in the minds of individual members of this stratum that modern socialism originated', the socialist conscience 'is something introduced into the proletarian class struggle from without ... and not something that arose within it spontaneously' (Lenin 1902, p. 72).

However much we may try 'to lend the economic struggle itself a political character', he added (p. 115), 'we shall never be able to develop the political consciousness of the workers (to the level of social-democratic political consciousness) by keeping within the framework of the economic struggle, for that framework is too narrow'. From the fact that debates at worker meetings and conferences are usually focused on economic issues and seldom, if ever, on the conditions of life of individual social classes, the history of the revolutionary movement or the economic trend under way in the country overall he deduced that the proletariat was unlikely to take the lead of a mass movement capable of imposing the transition to a different mode of production.

Lenin's approach is closely linked to Hegel's distinction between 'in itself' and 'for itself', from which Lenin held Marx to have drawn the idea for his distinction between 'class in itself' and 'class for itself'.

In Marx's approach, workers in a capitalistic system become a 'class in itself' when they gain an awareness of their true interests, set up a party of their own and develop their own intelligentsia. At that stage, they are ready to fight for better conditions within the existing production mode and often prove fairly successful in their efforts. However, on realising that any strides forward they take are not only far from permanent, but altogether incompatible with the capitalistic production mode, their enthusiasm tends to turn to frustration. As this is the stage when intellectuals can help proletarians realise that the precondition for add-itional and ever more lasting victories is changing the existing production mode, the proletariat will become a 'class for itself'. Subsequently, due to the awareness that an onslaught on capitalism is only justified if it serves the interests of society at large, the proletariat will join forces with other classes and thereby acquire the status of a 'class for others'.

The idea that the antagonistic worldview of the working class in a capitalistic society comes to it from the intelligentsia was shared by Gramsci, who had taken it over from Machiavelli,[228] but is hardly shared by those who think of socialism as democratic firm management.

---

[228] In the *Grundrisse*, Marx wrote that it was not at all contradictory to state that 'labour is absolute poverty as object, on one side, and is, on the other side,

While it is true that a major body of philosophical, historical and economic background knowledge is a necessary precondition for a correct appreciation of socialist theory, advocates of democratic firm management are aware that when workers secure ever higher incomes and educational levels they conceive the wish to progress from hired to own-account work without external advice.[229] It seems to me that provided the hoped-for new production mode envisages the transfer of firm control to workers, the working class will develop class consciousness spontaneously from within. Considering the sheer magnitude of the economic benefits that workers expect from self-management, there is a material chance that they will think them worth a revolution. Moreover, if they manage to spread the message that firm control by profit-seeking capitalists is an obstacle to the growth of democracy and the general good they may even obtain the help of the middle class and change a purely economic agenda into one with a distinctive political colouring.[230]

This does not mean that intellectuals do not play a major role or that revolution becomes impossible if the intelligentsia are not won over to the idea that starting a revolution means establishing democratic firm management.

5 TRADE UNIONISM AND SOCIALISM

The question to be raised at this point is why the democratic management of the firms has failed to assert itself to this day.

Trade unionism is true to its mission when it is organised as a worker movement consistently striving to change the existing industrial apparatus in ways that will bring it into line with a socially desirable model (see Touraine et al. 1984, pp. 59–61 and Baglioni 1995, p. 78). Nonetheless, democratic firm control is opposed by trade unions for the obvious reason that workers managing firms as 'their own masters' in an economic democracy would no longer need the services of organisations

---

the general possibility of wealth as subject and as activity' (Marx 1857–58, vol. 1, p. 280).

[229] According to Filippini, the discipline termed 'philosophy of praxis' was created by Machiavelli in order to train emergent classes in the art of political action. His work is the source on which Gramsci drew in order to flesh out new tools for a renewed political battle for the conquest of the right to rule over society (see Filippini 2011, p. 30).

[230] For a critical approach to the views of Kautsky and Lenin just reported, see Gorz (1973a) and Magri (1974, pp. 76–7).

for the protection of workers. Economic democracy would sweep away class divisions and, hence, the need for associations of employers and unions of workers defending the interests of their respective members. Both these reflections go to explain why trade unions do not welcome such a prospect (see Gorz 1973a, 1973b; Adler-Karlsson 1986, p. 45; Elster & Moene 1989, pp. 33–5; Moene & Wallerstein 1993, pp. 148–9; Kester & Pinaud 1996; and George 1997, pp. 59–60). Touraine holds that 'classical' trade unionism has ceased to exist because the main concern of trade unions is with framing union platforms, rather than with production relations.

Quite appropriately, Raniero Panzieri wrote (1960, p. 116):

> A more efficient distribution of tasks and delegates will barely help unions take roots within and outside factories. What really matters is an innovation process to be sparked off right within the factory at the cost of calling into question the role – and even the very existence – of trade unions themselves. Only a union which boldly offers collaboration in this direction can expect to play an appreciable role in a true innovation process.

At first sight, these conclusions would seem to be contradicted by the active involvement of trade unions in the Italian movement for self-management in the 1970s (see, inter alia, Giolitti 1977, p. 34), but on closer analysis it has to be admitted that unions never thought of producer cooperatives as the cells of a prospective new social order (see, inter alia, Castronovo 1987). In Gramsci's description, 'the essential nature of the union is competitive, it is not communist. The union cannot be an instrument for the radical renewal of society: it can offer the proletariat knowledgeable bureaucrats, technical experts in industrial questions of a general character, but it cannot be the base of proletarian power' (Gramsci 1919–20, p. 36).

A great many authors hold that trade unions oppose democratic firm control on the assumption that their members are not prepared to take business risks. One of these was Palmiro Togliatti, who rated workers as even more inimical to economic democracy than industrialists them-selves. In his opinion, the reason is that

> when Italian businessmen announce their intention to change capitalistic businesses into cooperatives, their true design is to turn the shareholders of these companies into creditors of the prospective cooperative firms. As soon as this is achieved, they will wash their hands of the management, production, marketing and other activities of these firms. Satisfied with cashing the fixed interest accruing on their credits, they will not spare a single thought for the fate of the industrial sector as a whole. (Togliatti 1920, p. 183)

From a certain angle, Tornquist argued (1973, p. 393), there is some truth in the argument that the democratic management of the firms appears to free workers for exclusive purpose of having them take over the uncongenial role of businessmen bent on earning profits – as Beatrice Webb suggested in a well-known book (Webb 1920, pp. 130–1).

Fromm held that workers were scared by the very prospect of freedom and, hence, were willing to submit to authority and to put up with existing conditions so long as this enabled them to stick to their everyday routine (see Fromm 1942, pp. 1ff.).

The idea that workers do not wish to become 'their own masters' is widely shared, but should be tested against reality in a manner never attempted before, for instance by polling workers after they have attended awareness-building programmes illustrating the findings on modern economic theory. In addition to this, it should be borne in mind that those workers who declare themselves hostile to democratic firm control are certainly influenced by trade union officials, i.e. those whom they rate as their representatives.

Hansmann reported the empirical finding that corporate governance researchers tended to overrate the role of risk takers in the day-to-day running of firms (see Hansmann 1996, p. 45). In my opinion, the objection that workers do not wish to take over the firms in which they work applies to the initial phases of capitalism and, probably, even to its current stage, but would cease to hold true at the same rate that workers manage to secure higher educational levels and incomes. As argued above, democratic firm management is tantamount to socialism and socialism is the post-capitalistic stage.

One explanation for the tepid support cooperation draws from the left is doubtless the fear that the simultaneous existence of two distinct movements striving to protect the interests of workers might produce a split within the working class. This is what the historian Gaetano Salvemini suggested in the years when Italy was ruled by cabinets presided over by Giolitti. As the cooperative movement had gained a firm foothold in central and northern Italy, but not in the south (much like today), he argued that its leaders were actively securing government contracts in the exclusive interests of northern versus southern workers and that this strategy had been chosen to please Giolitti (see Salvemini 1993, pp. 356–8 and 359–83).

To account for the tepid support for democratic firm management on the part of trade unions (rather than opposition proper), Braverman points to issues such as technological progress and labour productivity. In *Labor and Monopoly Capital* (1974, p. 10) he writes:

The unionized working class, intimidated by the size and complexity of capitalistic production, and weakened in its original revolutionary impetus by the gains afforded by the rapid increase in productivity, increasingly lost the will and ambition to wrest control of production from capitalistic hands and turned ever more to bargaining over labor's share in the product. This labor movement formed the immediate environment of Marxism; and Marxists were, in varying degrees, compelled to adapt themselves to it.

From this perspective, it can hardly come as a surprise that unions have been slowing down the progress of society in the direction of a system of worker-run business firms[231] or that, joining forces with other defenders of the status quo, they have played a part in preventing the system from gaining ground.

The fact that firms in financial distress are often let go instead of being taken over by the workers is an additional element in support of the conclusion that trade unions are not only hostile to worker management, but prefer to see enterprises flounder so long as this may enable them to avert their transfer to the workers.[232]

6 TWO ALTERNATIVE WAYS OF DEFENDING THE INTERESTS OF WORKERS

This conclusion is supported by historical evidence.

It is well known that even before the appearance of Marx's *Capital* authors such as Fourier, Owen, Blanc, Proudhon and others had – each of them in his own way – drawn the broad outlines of a social order founded on worker control of firms, and that their propositions had been well received by the coeval political left. In Germany, the political agenda of the Social Democratic Party included the plan to create a system of cooperatives, which were looked upon as genuinely socialist

---

[231] Engels once wrote (1846, p. 5) that democracy in his day was embodied in communism and that the forces that would battle for communism were sure to include the democratic-minded masses. Since workers suffering the oppression of capital can barely be expected to look forward to a centrally planned command economy, if the hoped-for new production mode is thought to be a system of this kind, Engels's statement can hardly be endorsed. In contrast, it will sound fully convincing if this new production mode is assumed to be a democratic form of business governance.

[232] Financing difficulties are the main obstacle to the success of the cooperative movement (see, inter alia, Zanotti 2016, p. 112). Although it is my personal belief that this is obviously a satisfactory explanation, unlike mainstream theorists, I also attach great importance to the opposition of trade unions.

firms and a viable alternative option to capital-managed business enterprises. Subsequently, the difficulties experienced by some cooperatives from the closing decade of the nineteenth century onwards, the criticisms levelled by Marx and some Marxists against Proudhon and, generally, 'utopian' socialist or anarchical approaches and the theories of liberalists such as Pantaleoni (who denied any appreciable differences between cooperatives and capitalistic businesses) slowed down the progress of cooperation and are probably responsible for the view that union action is a more effective means of protecting worker interests than worker control of firms.[233]

In all probability, the tendency to join workers into unions prevailed over the creation of cooperatives for two main reasons: firstly, because setting up a cooperative requires raising the funds needed to start up production (and cooperatives are known to have fundraising difficulties), it is easier, and less costly, to set up a union rather than a cooperative firm;[234] and secondly, because cooperation is barely supported by trade unions. To account for the opposition of trade unions from their own vantage point, it is worth considering that self-management and trade union bargaining are two alternative ways of defending the interests of workers, as I have said, and, even more importantly, that a system where worker-run firms are the rule would threaten the very existence of trade unionism. What sense would there be – I repeat – in defending the interests of workers in a society without masters where workers are free to structure their business activities as they like?[235]

---

[233] This view is refuted by Galgano (1982, pp. 83–4) on grounds that even in a cooperative with publicly owned production means the lofty aims pursued by cooperation can neither justify suspending the rights of workers, nor the decision of trade unions to adopt softer methods when championing the rights of the partners of cooperative firms rather than those of the employees of capital-owned businesses.

Leone described trade unionism and cooperation as complementary movements, i.e. inseparable forms of proletarian economic action (see Leone 1902, p. 288).

[234] In an analysis of the historical reasons why employment became the prevailing form of work, Offe and Lenhardt (1979, pp. 24–5) examined a number of alternative options open to workers, but not the establishment of cooperative enterprises.

[235] On this point, see, inter alia, Jossa (2002).

7 TRADE UNIONS AND SELF-MANAGEMENT SOCIALISM

Is there a material chance that self-management socialism may gain a firm foothold notwithstanding the failure of trade unions to support the necessary revolution?

Back in 1894, Franz Mehring wrote that the main task facing the proletariat was to engage in a concerted effort towards the overthrown, or 'liquidation' of capitalistic society (see Mehring 1893–94, p. 99).

> Proletarians are the chosen people of historical materialism for the very reason that they are denied access to the privileges of the dominant classes of society. Just as Sieyes, before the outbreak of the French Revolution, had postulated that the bourgeois was 'nothing' and therefore entitled to become 'everything', so Marx, fifty years after the victory of bourgeois society, postulated the universal mission of the proletariat which had developed from it. (Löwith 1949, p. 57)[236]

To trigger this process it is necessary to help workers develop the awareness that taking over defaulting firms and rescuing them from bankruptcy is in their own best interests (and in the interests of society) and persuade them to do without the collaboration of trade unions. And it is to be assumed that this goal will be ever more easily achieved, the more workers manage to secure higher education levels and incomes.[237]

The third transition scenario envisages the passing of a parliamentary act to enforce the compulsory conversion of the shares of existing companies into bonds of equal value and prohibit the use of hired workers in medium–large enterprises (to the extent this is deemed appropriate). Such an act would automatically disempower capitalists and turn capital-managed enterprises into worker-controlled firms.[238]

---

[236] 'This goes to disprove the long-standing and well-established socialist proposition that true understanding is not guaranteed by theoretical research and abstract reflection only, but needs the support of concrete political action' (Cunningham 1987, p. 318).

[237] Max Weber (1904–1905, p. 12) held access to the entrepreneurial functions to be conditional on 'some previous ownership of capital and generally an expensive education; often both'.

[238] In point of fact, Luxemburg made it clear (1913, p. 90) that political mass strikes do not 'fall from the clouds' and are only effective during a 'revolutionary situation'. As remarked by Agosti (1970, p. 13), discussing the general strikes that anarchists held to hasten the collapse of capitalism and the struggle under

As the third transitional process entails a ban on the creation of capital-managed enterprises using hired labour (specifically the use of hired workers in medium–large enterprises), the moneyed bourgeoisie is likely to dub it as a Marxist-type 'dictatorship of the proletariat'. In this connection, Bongiovanni has aptly suggested rewording this well-known Marxian phrase and speaking instead of a 'dictatorship of democracy'. Apparently an oxymoron, he adds, this phrase would convey the idea of a government which is temporarily strong in political terms and yet prepared to adopt socially oriented policies in favour of all those people, a vast majority, that had been oppressed and deprived of all rights until that stage (see Bongiovanni 2014, p. 132).[239]

The preconditions for setting in motion this process of change are, on the one hand, persuading the general public that the establishment of self-management socialism serves the interests of the community at large and, on the other, metamorphoses of capitalism that may act as the seeds from which the new system will sprout (Albuquerque 2015).[240]

According to Adler (1910, p. 291), as soon as we understand how the mechanisms governing social evolution work and how socialism can create solidarity relations consistent with humane ideals (not because believers in socialism are particularly noble-minded, but due to economic necessity), commitment to the establishment of socialism will become part and parcel of any educational approach (Adler 1910, p. 291). In the words of the Marshalls, 'co-operation is the child of confidence; and ignorance is the parent of mistrust' (Marshall & Marshall 1879, p. 276).

The third of the above transition scenarios can obviously not be set in motion without a parliamentary majority of worker representatives. On

---

way in existing bourgeois institutions day after day, Luxemburg argued that the former mode of struggle had been proved wrong by history.

[239]   In the estimation of Bell, the reason why trade unions do not seem to support this type of transitional process is that, though not devoid of an ideological underpinning of sorts, they differ from other progressive movements since they are not urged on by an unfailing confidence in the ultimate advancement of society and are consequently untouched by the grand ideals shaping the socialist doctrine (see Bell 1960, p. 148). It is interesting to note that Ichino's 2005 book *A che cosa serve il sindacato?* makes no mention of a potential role of trade unions in the conversion of defaulting companies into cooperative firms.

[240]   The transitional process suggested by Dow is a combination of the first and third processes just described. Specifically, Dow suggests polling the workers on this issue and, in the event of a democratic response in favour of a self-managed firm system, assigning subsidies to all those firms that are assumed to generate benefits for the community at large (see Dow 2003, ch. 12).

closer analysis, this was the rationale behind Engels's claim, in the mid-1890s, that the most effective tool available to the modern proletariat was universal suffrage, an institution that the German Social Democrats were using to advantage in their effort to bring about a revolution (see Steinberg 1979, p. 197).[241]

From a liberalist perspective, the crux of the matter is that being at the beck and call of a majority is barely more rewarding than obeying other people's commands. As argued by Popper, we are democrats not because the majority is always right, but because democratic traditions are the least evil that we know (see Zanone 2002, p. 131).[242]

8 CONCLUSION

The reflections developed in this chapter explain why socialism was identified with central planning at least throughout a whole century and why the failure of command economies in the USSR and elsewhere has been eroding the faith of most intellectuals that the transition to socialism would materialise at some point in time.

What else can we do but strongly hope that some day or other the intelligentsia will at last gain the awareness that (a) socialism coincides with democratic firm management and that (b) the main obstacle to the transition to socialism is trade union opposition.

The train of reasoning followed so far leads to the conclusion that Kant's definition of history as 'steadily progressive development' should be called into question. Indeed, unless and until intellectuals are made to understand that socialism coincides with democratic firm management and that its attainment would serve the interests of society at large, history might be prevented from taking its ultimate leap forward, i.e. progressing towards the abolition of capitalism.

Today, the belief that this ultimate step is unlikely to be taken in a foreseeable future is firmly entrenched in society.

---

[241] For other authors categorising the parliamentary road to socialism as authoritarian, see Nuti (2004, p. 201).

[242] As the former two transition scenarios envisage a stepwise process of change, it is hardly possible to agree with Magri that, however hard we may try, there are no means of sparking off the transition from capitalism to communism (see Magri 1967, p. 40).

References

Abendroth W., 1958, Il marxismo è 'superato'?, in Abendroth W., 1967, *Socialismo e marxismo da Weimar alla Germania Federale*, Ital. transl., La Nuova Italia, Florence, 1978.

Adler M., 1910, Il socialismo e gli intellettuali, in Adler M., 1974, *Il socialismo e gli intellettuali*, ed. L. Paggi, De Donato, Bari.

Adler-Karlsson G., 1986, Il socialismo 'minimale' e il dilemma delle uova, in Vv.Aa.*, eds, *Cooperare e competere*, Feltrinelli, Milan.

Agnoli J., 1975, *Lo Stato del capitale*, Feltrinelli, Milan.

Agosti A., 1970, Lo sciopero generale di massa, in Luxemburg R., ed., *Lo sciopero spontaneo di massa*, Musolini editore, Turin.

Albert M., 2003, *L'economia partecipativa*, Datanews, Rome.

Albert M. & Hahnel R., 1991, *Looking Forward*, South End, Boston, MA.

Albuquerque E., 2015, Visible Seeds of Socialism and Metamorphoses of Capitalism: Socialism after Rosdolsky, *Cambridge Journal of Economics*, vol. 39, no. 3.

Alchian A.A. & Demsetz H., 1972, Production, Information Costs and Economic Organization, *American Economic Review*, vol. 62, December.

Althusser L., 1965, *Per Marx*, Ital. transl., Editori Riuniti, Rome, 1969.

Althusser L., 1973, *Umanesimo e stalinismo*, Ital. transl., De Donato, Bari.

Althusser L. & Balibar E., 1965, *Leggere il Capitale*, Ital. transl., Feltrinelli, Milan, 1968.

Altvater E., 1968, L'attualità del Capitale, in Vv.Aa., eds, *Cent'anni dopo il Capitale*, Ital. transl., Samonà e Savelli, Rome, 1970.

Altvater E., 1982, La teoria del capitalismo monopolistico di Stato e le nuove forme di socializzazione capitalistica, in Hobsbawm E.J., Haupt G., Marek F., Ragionieri E., Strada V. & Vivanti C., eds, *Storia del marxismo*, 5 vols, Einaudi, Turin, vol. IV.

Amirante C., 2008, *Dalla forma Stato alla forma mercato*, Giappichelli, Turin.

---

* Vv.Aa. denotes Various Authors.

Angel P., 1975, *Stato e società borghese nel pensiero di Bernstein*, Istituto Giangiacomo Feltrinelli, Milan.

Ansart P., 1967, *La sociologia di Proudhon*, Ital. transl., Il Saggiatore, Milan, 1972.

Ansart P., 1969, *Marx e l'anarchismo*, Ital. transl., Il Mulino, Bologna, 1972.

Anweiler O., 1958, *Storia dei soviet, 1905–1921*, Ital. transl., Laterza, Bari, 1972.

Archer R., 1995, *Economic Democracy: The Politics of Feasible Socialism*, Oxford University Press, Oxford.

Arendt H., 1978, *La vita della mente*, Ital. transl., Il Mulino, Bologna, 2009.

Arnason J.P., 1982, Prospettive e problemi del marxismo critico nell'Est europeo, in Hobsbawm E.J., Haupt G., Marek F., Ragionieri E., Strada V. & Vivanti C., eds, *Storia del marxismo*, 5 vols, Einaudi, Turin.

Aron R., 1965, The Impact of Marxism in the Twentieth Century, in Drachkovitch M.M., ed., *Marxism in the Modern World*, Oxford University Press, Oxford.

Aron R., 1969, Equivoco e inesauribile, in Vv.Aa., 1969b. Vv.Aa., 1969b, *Sviluppo economico e rivoluzione*, Bari, De Donato.

Arthur C.J., 1998, Engels, Logic and History, in Bellofiore R., ed., *Marxian Economics: A Reappraisal*, Palgrave Macmillan, New York.

Arthur C.J., 2001, Value, Labour and Negativity, *Capital and Class*, no. 73, spring.

Arthur C.J., 2009, The Possessive Spirit of Capital: Subsumption/Inversion/Contradiction, in Bellofiore R. & Fineschi R., eds, *Rereading Marx; New Perspectives after the Critical Edition*, Palgrave Macmillan, New York.

Auer D., 2004, Paria contro voglia. Adorno, Arendt e la condizione degli intellettuali, in Pastore L. & Gebur T., eds, 2008, *Teodoro Adorno, il maestro ritovato*, Manifestolibri, Rome.

Avineri S., 1968, *Il pensiero politico e sociale di Marx*, Ital. transl., Il Mulino, Bologna, 1972.

Backhaus H.G., 1997, *Dialektik der Wertform. Untersuchungen zur marxschen Ökonomiekritik*, Çaira, Freiburg im Breisgau.

Backhouse R., 1985, *A History of Modern Economic Analysis*, Blackwell, Oxford.

Badaloni N., 1962, *Marxismo come storicismo*, Feltrinelli, Milan.

Badaloni N., 1972, *Il marxismo italiano degli anni sessanta*, Editori Riuniti, Rome.

Baglioni G., 1995, *Democrazia impossibile?*, Il Mulino, Bologna.

Bahro R., 1977, *Eine Dokumentation*, Europäische Verlagsanstalt, Frankfurt am Main.

Balibar E., 1974, *Cinq études du matérialisme historique*, Maspero, Paris.

Balibar E., 1976, *Sulla dittatura del proletariato*, Ital. transl., Feltrinelli, Milan, 1978.

Balibar E., 1993, *La filosofia di Marx*, Ital. transl., Manifestolibri, Rome, 1994.

Baran P.A. & Sweezy P.M., 1966, *Monopoly Capital*, Monthly Review Press, New York.

Barcellona P., 1980, *Oltre lo Stato sociale; economia e politica nella crisi dello Stato keynesiano*, De Donato, Bari.

Bardhan P. & Roemer J.E., eds, 1993, *Market Socialism: The Current Debate*, Oxford Economic Press, New York.

Barone E., 1908, Il Ministro della produzione in uno stato collettivista, *Giornale degli economisti*, vol. 34.

Barreto T., 2011, Penser l'entreprise cooperative: au delà du réduction-isme du mainstream, *Annals of Public and Cooperative Economics*, vol. 82, no. 2.

Barro R.J., 1996, Democracy and Growth, *Journal of Economic Growth*, vol. 1.

Bartlett W., Cable J., Estrin S., Derek C. & Smith S., 1992, Labour-Managed versus Private Firms: An Empirical Comparison of Co-operatives and Private Firms in Central Italy, *Industrial and Labour Relations Review*, vol. 46, no. 1.

Bascetta M., 2004, *La libertà dei postmoderni*, Manifestolibri, Rome.

Basso L., 1969, Appunti sulla teoria rivoluzionaria in Marx and Engels, in Vv.Aa., eds, *Sviluppo economico e rivoluzione*, De Donato, Bari.

Basso L., 1971, Introduction to Luxemburg R., *Lettere ai Kautsky*, Editori Riuniti, Rome.

Bauman Z. & Bordoni C., 2014, *Stato di crisi*, Ital. transl., Einaudi, Turin, 2015.

Bell D., 1960, *Violenza e politica*, Ital. transl., Edizioni di Comunità, Milan, 1964.

Bell J.R., 1995, Dialectics and Economic Theory, in Albritton R. & Sekine T.T., eds, *A Japanese Approach to Political Economy*, Palgrave, New York.

Bellas C., 1972, *Industrial Democracy and the Worker-Owned Firm: A Study of Twenty-One Plywood Companies in the Pacific Northwest*, Praeger, New York.

Bellofiore R., 1993, Per una teoria monetaria del valore-lavoro. Problemi aperti nella teoria marxiana, tra radici ricardiane e nuove vie di ricerca, in Lunghini G., ed., *Valori e prezzi*, UTET, Turin.

Bellofiore R., 2005, Marx dopo Hegel. Il capitale come totalità e la centralità della produzione, in Musto M., ed., *Sulle tracce di un fantasma*, Manifestolibri, Rome.

Bellofiore R. & Finelli R., 1998, Capital, Labour and Time: The Marxian Monetary Labour Theory of Value as a Theory of Exploitation, in Bellofiore R., ed., *Marxian Economics: A Reappraisal*, Palgrave Macmillan, New York.

Ben-Ner A., 1987, Producer Cooperatives: Why Do They Exist in Market Economies?, in Powell W., ed., *The Non-Profit Sector: A Research Handbook*, Yale University Press, New Haven, CT.

Ben-Ner A., 1988, The Life-Cycle of Worker-Owned Firms in Market Economies: A Theoretical Analysis, *Journal of Economic Behavior and Organization*, vol. 10, no. 3.

Ben-Ner A., Hahn T. & Jones D.C., 1996, The Productivity Effects of Employee Participation in Control and in Economic Returns: A Review of Empirical Evidence, in Pagano U. & Rowthorn R., eds, *Democracy and Efficiency in Economic Enterprise*, Routledge, London.

Benjamin W., 1995, *Angelus Novus: saggi e frammenti*, Einaudi, Turin.

Benkler Y., 2006, *The Wealth of Networks: How Social Production Transforms Markets and Freedom*, Yale University Press, New Haven, CT.

Bensaïd D., 2002, *Marx for Our Times*, Verso, London.

Berlin I., 1963, *Marx*, Ital. transl., La Nuova Italia, Florence, 1967.

Berman K.V. & Berman M.D., 1989, An Empirical Test of the Theory of the Labour-Managed Firm, *Journal of Comparative Economics*, vol. 13, no. 2.

Berman M.D., 1977, Short Run Efficiency in the Labour-Managed Firm, *Journal of Comparative Economics*, vol. 1, no. 3.

Bernstein E., 1899, *I presupposti del socialismo e i compiti della socialdemocrazia*, Ital. transl., Laterza, Bari, 1969.

Bernstein E., 1918, *Völkerbund oder Staatenbund*, P. Cassirer, Berlin.

Bernstein P., 1980, *Workplace Democratization: Its Internal Dynamics*, Transaction Books, New Brunswick, NJ.

Bettelheim C., 1969a, *La transizione all'economia socialista*, Ital. transl., Jaca Books, Milan, 1969.

Bettelheim C., 1969b, On the Transition between Capitalism and Socialism, *Monthly Review*, March–April.

Bettelheim C., 1974, *Class Struggles in the USSR; 1917–1923,* Engl. transl., Harvester Press, Hertford, 1977.

Bhaskar R., 1991, Dialectics, in Bottomore T.B., ed., *A Dictionary of Marxist Thought*, 2nd edn, Blackwell, Oxford.

Bidet J., 1998, *Que faire du Capital?*, Presses Universitaires de France, Paris.

Bidet J., 2004, '*Il Capitale*', *spiegazione e ricostruzione*, Ital. transl., Manifestolibri, Rome, 2010.

Bidet J., 2005, La ricostruzione metastrutturale del *Capitale*, in Musto M., ed., *Sulle tracce di un fantasma*, Manifestolibri, Rome.

Birchall J., 2012, The Comparative Advantages of Member-Owned Businesses, *Review of Social Economy*, vol. 70, no. 3, September.

Bloch E., 1968, *Karl Marx*, Ital. transl., Il Mulino, Bologna, 1972.

Bloom S.F., 1943, Man of His Century: A Reconsideration of the Historical Significance of Karl Marx, in Wood J.C., ed., 1988, *Karl Marx's Economics: Critical Assessments*, Croom Helm, Sydney.

Blumberg P., 1968, *Industrial Democracy: The Sociology of Participation*, Constable, London.

Blumberg P., 1973, On the Relevance and Future of Workers' Management, in Hunnius G., Garson G.D. & Case J., eds, *Workers' Control*, Random House, New York.

Blundell-Wignall A., 1976, On Exposing the Transformation Problem, *Australian Economic Papers*, vol. 15, no. 27.

Bobbio N., 1958, Nota sulla dialettica in Gramsci, in Vv.Aa., eds, *Studi gramsciani*, 2nd edn, Editori Riuniti, Rome, 1973.

Bobbio N., 1976, *Quale socialismo?*, Einaudi, Turin.

Bobbio N., 1977, *Dalla struttura alla funzione; nuovi studi di teoria del diritto*, Edizioni di Comunità, Milan.

Bobbio N., 1984, *Il futuro della democrazia*, Einaudi, Turin.

Bobbio N., 1985, *Stato, governo, società; frammenti di un dizionario politico*, 2nd edn, Einaudi, Turin, 1995.

Bobbio N., 1995, *Eguaglianza e libertà*, Einaudi, Turin.

Bodei R., 2013, *Immaginare altre vie; realtà, progetti, desideri*, Feltrinelli, Milan.

Boffa G., 1976, *Storia dell'Unione Sovietica*, Mondadori, Milan.

Bolaffi A., 2002, *Il crepuscolo della sovranità*, Donzelli editore, Rome.

Bonefeld W., 2010, Abstract Labour: Against Its Nature and on Its Time, *Capital and Class*, vol. 34, no. 2.

Bonefeld W., 2011, Debating Abstract Labour, *Capital and Class*, vol. 35, no. 3.

Bongiovanni B., 2014, Afterword to Marx K. & Engels F., [1848], *Manifesto del partito comunista*, Einaudi, Turin.

Bonin J.P. & Putterman L., 1987, *Economics of Cooperation and the Labor-Managed Economy: Fundamentals of Pure and Applied Economics*, Harvard Academic Publishing, Cambridge, MA.

Bonin J.P., Jones D.C. & Putterman L., 1993, Theoretical and Empirical Studies of Producer Cooperatives: Will the Twain Ever Meet?, *Journal of Economic Literature*, vol. 31.

Bourdet Y., 1974, *Pour l'autogestion*, Antropos, Paris.

Bowles S. & Gintis H., 1996a, Is the Demand for Workplace Democracy Redundant in a Liberal Economy?, in Pagano U. & Rowthorn R., eds, *Democracy and Efficiency in Economic Enterprise*, Routledge, London.

Bowles S. & Gintis H., 1996b, The Distribution of Wealth and the Viability of the Democratic Firm, in Pagano U. & Rowthorn R., eds, *Democracy and Efficiency in Economic Enterprise*, Routledge, London.

Bowles S. & Gintis H., 2002, Social Capital and Community Governance, *Economic Journal*, vol. 112, November.

Brachet P., 1975, *L'Ètat-patron. Théories et réalites*, Editions Syros, Paris.

Braudel F., 1977, *Afterthoughts on Material Civilization and Capitalism*, Johns Hopkins University Press, Baltimore, MD.

Braverman H., 1974, *Lavoro e capitale monopolistico*, Ital. transl., Einaudi, Turin, 1978.

Brewer A.A., 1995, A Minor Post-Ricardian? Marx as an Economist, *History of Political Economy*, vol. 27, no. 1.

Brewer A.A. & Browning M.J., 1982, On the Employment Decision of a Labour-Managed Firm, *Economica*, vol. 49, no. 194.

Briganti W., ed., 1982, *Il movimento cooperativo in Italia. Scritti e documenti, dal 1854 al 1980*, Editrice cooperativa, Rome.

Bronfenbrenner M., 1967, Marxian Influences in 'Bourgeois' Economics, in Wood J.C., ed., *Karl Marx's Economics: Critical Assessments*, Croom Helm, Sydney, vol. III.

Bronfenbrenner M., 1970, The Vicissitudes of Marxian Economics, in Wood J.C., ed., *Karl Marx's Economics: Critical Assessments*, Croom Helm, Sydney, vol. 3.

Buchanan A.E., 1979, Revolution, Motivation and Rationality, *Philosophy and Public Affairs*, vol. 9, no. 1.

Buchanan A.E., 1982, *Marx and Justice: The Radical Critique of Liberalism*, Rowman & Allanheld, Totowa, NJ.

Bukharin N.I., 1982, *Selected Writings on the State and the Transition to Socialism*, Spokesman, Nottingham.

Burczak T., 2006, *Socialism after Hayek*, University of Michigan Press, Ann Arbor, MI.

Bush P.D., 2009, The Neoinstitutionalist Theory of Value, *Journal of Economic Issues*, vol. 153, no. 2.

Cacciatore G., 1987, Il Marx di Gramsci. Per una rilettura del nesso etica-teoria politica nel marxismo, in Cacciatore G. & Lomonaco F., eds, *Marx e i marxisti cent'anni dopo*, Guida Editori, Naples.

Campbell A., 2011, The Role of Workers in Management: The Case of Mondragón, *Review of Radical Political Economics*, vol. 43, no. 3.

Candela G., 2014, *Economia, Stato, anarchia*, Elèuthera, Milan.

Canfora L., 2004, *La democrazia; storia di un'ideologia*, Laterza, Bari.

Carandini G., 1971, *Lavoro e capitale nella teoria di Marx*, Marsilio, Padua.

Carandini G., 1973, *La struttura economica della società nelle opere di Marx*, Marsilio, Padua.

Carandini G., 2005, *Un altro Marx*, Laterza, Rome.

Carchedi G., 1984, The Logic of Prices and Values, *Economy and Society*, vol. 13, no. 4.

Carchedi G., 2011, A Comment on Bonefeld's 'Abstract Labour: Against Its Nature and on Its Time', *Capital and Class*, vol. 35, no. 2.

Carr E.H., 1953, *La rivoluzione bolscevica, 1917–1923*, Ital. transl., Einaudi, Turin, 1964.

Carver T., 1984, Marxism as Method, in Ball T. & Farr J., eds, *After Marx*, Cambridge University Press, Cambridge.

Cassano F., 1973, *Marxismo e filosofia in Italia, 1958–1971*, De Donato, Bari.

Castoriadis C., 1975, *L'institution imaginaire de la société*, Le Seuil.

Castronovo V., 1987, Dal dopoguerra ad oggi, in Zangheri R., Galasso G. & Castronovo V., eds, *Storia del movimento cooperativo in Italia*, Einaudi, Turin.

Chilosi A., ed., 1992, *L'economia del periodo di transizione: dal modello di tipo sovietico all'economia di mercato*, Il Mulino, Bologna.

Chiodi G., 2008, Beyond Capitalism: Sraffa's Economic Theory, in Chiodi G. & Ditta L., eds, *Sraffa or an Alternative Economics*, Palgrave Macmillan, London.

Chiodi P., 1973, *Sartre e il marxismo*, Feltrinelli, Milan.

Chitarin A., ed., 1973, *Lenin e il controllo operaio*, Savelli, Rome.

Chomsky N., 1971, *Conoscenza e libertà*, Ital. transl., Il Saggiatore, Milan, 2010.

Chomsky N., 2013, *I padroni dell'umanità*, Ital. transl., Salani, Milan, 2014.

Cingoli M., 2001, *Il primo Marx (1835–1841)*, Edizioni Unicopli, Milan.

Citati P., 2010, *Leopardi*, Mondadori, Milan.

Cliff T. & Barker C., 1966, *Income Policy, Legislation and Shop Stewards*, Industrial Shop Stewards Defence Committee, London.

Codignola T., 1944, La libertà del lavoro, in Rossi M., ed., 2015, *La libertà; periodico toscano del Partito d'Azione, 1943–44*, Il Ponte Editore, Florence.

Cole G.D.H., 1920, *Guild Socialism Re-stated*, Leonard Parson, London.

Cole G.D.H., 1953a, *Attempts at General Union*, Macmillan, London.

Cole G.D.H., 1953b, *Socialist Thought*, vol. 1, *The Forerunners (1789–1850)*, Macmillan, London.

Colletti L., 1958, Lettera di Colletti a Gerratana, in Cassano F., ed., 1973, *Marxismo e filosofia in Italia, 1958–1971*, De Donato, Bari.

Colletti L., 1968, Bernstein e il marxismo della seconda internazionale, Preface to Bernstein E., [1899], *I presupposti del socialismo e i compiti della socialdemocrazia*, Ital. transl., Laterza, Bari.

Colletti L., 1969, *Il marxismo e Hegel*, Laterza, Bari.

Colletti L., 1974, *Intervista politico-filosofica*, Laterza, Bari.

Colletti L., 1979, *Tra marxismo e no*, Laterza, Bari.

Colletti L., 1980, *Tramonto dell'ideologia*, Laterza, Bari.

Conte M.A., 1982, Participation and Performance in U.S. Labour-Managed Firms, in Jones D.C. & Svejnar J., eds, *Participatory and Self-Managed Firms: Evaluating Economic Performance*, Heath, Lexington, MA.

Cortesi L., 1970, *La rivoluzione leninista*, De Donato, Bari.

Cortesi L., 2010, *Storia del comunismo; da utopia al Termidoro sovietico*, Manifestolibri, Rome.

Craig B. & Pencavel I., 1995, Participation and Productivity: A Comparison of Worker Cooperatives and Conventional Firms in the Plywood Industry, *Brookings Papers: Microeconomics*, I.

Croce B., 1899, *Materialismo storico ed economia marxista*, Laterza, Bari, 1968.

Crouch C., 2003, *Post-democracy*, Polity Press, Cambridge.

Cugno F. & Ferrero M., 1992, L'efficienza delle cooperative nella produzione di servizi pubblici, in Gramaglia E. & Sacconi L., eds, *Cooperazione, benessere e organizzazione economica*, F. Angeli, Milan.

Cunningham F., 1987, *Teoria della democrazia e socialismo*, Ital. transl., Editori Riuniti, Rome, 1991.

Cuomo G., 2003, La cooperativa di produzione italiana e i modelli teorici di riferimento, in Buonocore V. & Jossa B., eds, *Organizzazioni economiche non capitalistiche*, Il Mulino, Bologna.

Cuomo G., 2004, Il finanziamento esterno delle imprese gestite dai lavoratori, in Jossa B., ed., *Il futuro del capitalismo*, Il Mulino, Bologna.

Curi U., 1975, *Sulla 'scientificità' del marxismo*, Feltrinelli, Milan.

Curi U., 2015, L'Occidente tra compimento e tramonto, in De Giovanni L. & Donisi C., eds, *Convergenza dei saperi e direttive dell'umano*, ESI, Naples.

Dahl R.A., 1989, *Democracy and Its Critics*, Yale University Press, New Haven, CT.

Dahrendorf R., 1957, *Classi e conflitto di classe nella società industriale*, Ital. transl., Laterza, Bari, 1963.

Dal Pra M., 1972, *La dialettica in Marx*, 2nd edn, Laterza, Bari.

Damjanovic P., 1962, Les conceptions de Marx sur l'autogestion sociale, *Praxis*, no. 1.

De Angelis M., 1995, Beyond the Technological and Social Paradigms: A Political Reading of Abstract Labour as the Substance of Value, *Capital and Class*, no. 57, autumn.

De Bonis R., Manzone B. & Trento S., 1994, La proprietà cooperativa: teoria, storia e il caso delle banche popolari, Banca d'Italia, *Temi di discussione*, no. 238, December.

de Paula J.A., de Gama Cerqueira H.E.A., Cunha A.M., Suprinyak C.E., Gomes de Deus L. & Albuquerque E., 2013, Notes on a Crisis: The Exzerpthefte and Marx's Method of Research, *Review of Radical Political Economics*, vol. 45, no. 2.

De Vroey M., 1982, On the Obsolescence of Marxian Theory of Value, *Capital and Class*, vol. 17, summer.

Defourny J., 1992, Comparative Measures of Technical Efficiency for 500 French Workers' Cooperatives, in Jones D.C. & Svejnar J., eds, *Advances in the Economic Analysis of Participatory and Labor-Managed Firms*, vol. IV, JAI Press, Greenwich, CT.

Defourny J., Estrin S. & Jones D.C., 1985, The Effects of Workers' Participation on Enterprise Performance, *International Journal of Industrial Organization*, vol. 3, no. 2.

della Volpe G., 1964, *Rousseau e Marx*, Editori Riuniti, Rome.

Derrida J., 1993, *Spettri di Marx*, Ital. transl., Raffaello Cortina, Milan, 1994.

Deutscher I., 1970, *Lenin; frammento di una vita e altri saggi*, Ital. transl., Laterza, Bari.

Di Marco G.A., 2005, *Dalla soggezione all'emancipazione umana*, Soveria Mannelli, Rubettino.

DiQuattro A.R., 1981, Alienation and Justice in the Market, in Burke J.P., Crocker L. & Legters L.H., eds, *Marxism and the Good Society*, Cambridge University Press, Cambridge.

DiQuattro A., 2011, Market Socialism Is Not Market Capitalism. Remarks on Robin Hahnel's 'Theory of Justice', *Review of Radical Political Economics*, vol. 43, no. 4.

Dobb M., 1954, Una conferenza su Marx, in *Teoria economica e socialismo*, Ital. transl., Editori Riuniti, Rome, 1974.

Dobb M., 1969, *Welfare Economics and the Economics of Socialism*, Cambridge University Press, Cambridge.

Dobb M., 1970, *Argument on Socialism. Socialist Planning: Some Problems*, Lawrence & Wishart, London.

Domar E.D., 1996, The Soviet Collective Farm as a Producer Co-operative, *American Economic Review*, vol. 56, no. 4.

Doucouliagos C., 1995, Worker Participation and Productivity in Labor-Managed and Participatory Capitalist Firms: A Meta-Analysis, *Industrial and Labour Relations Review*, vol. 49, no. 1.

Dow G., 1993, *Why Capital Hires Labor: A Bargaining Perspective, American Economic Review*, vol, 83, no. 1.

Dow G., 2003, *Governing the Firm: Workers' Control in Theory and Practice*, Cambridge University Press, Cambridge.

Drewnowski J., 1961, The Economic Theory of Socialism: A Proposal, in Bornstein M., ed., 1969, *Comparative Economic Systems: Models and Cases*, Richard D. Irwin, London.

Dreyfus M., 2012, La cooperazione di produzione in Francia dalle origini alla Grande guerra, *Il Ponte*, vol. 68, no. 5–6.

Drèze J.H., 1976, Some Theory of Labour Management and Participation, *Econometrica*, vol. 44, no. 6.

Drèze J.H., 1989, *Labour-Management, Contracts and Capital Markets: A General Equilibrium Approach*, Basil Blackwell, Oxford.

Drèze J.H., 1993, Self-Management and Economic Theory: Efficiency, Funding and Employment, in Bardhan P. & Roemer J.E., eds, *Market Socialism: The Current Debate*, Oxford Economic Press, New York.

Duffield J., 1970, The Value Concept in Capital in Light of Recent Criticism, reprinted in Wood J.C., ed., 1988, *Karl Marx's Economics: Critical Assessments*, Croom Helm, Sydney.

Duménil G. & Lévy D., 2001, Old Theories and New Capitalism: The Actuality of Marxian Economics, in Bidet J. & Kouvélakis S., eds, *Critical Companion to Contemporary Marxism*, Engl. transl., Brill, Leiden, 2008.

Dunayevskaya R., 1988, *Marxism and Freedom: From 1776 until Today*, Columbia University Press, New York.

Dunlap L.A., 1979, Social Production in Karl Marx, *Review of Social Economy*, vol. 37, no. 3.

Dunn J., 2005, *Il mito degli uguali. La lunga storia della democrazia*, Ital. transl., Egea, Milan, 2006.

Dworkin R., 2006, *La democrazia possibile*, Ital. transl., Feltrinelli, Milan, 2007.

Easton L.D., 1994, Marx and Individual Freedom, in Patsuras L., ed., *Debating Marx*, Lewiston, New York.

Eldret M. & Hanlon M., 1981, Reconstructing the Value-Form Analysis, *Capital and Class*, vol. 13.

Elster J. & Moene K.O., eds, 1989, *Alternatives to Capitalism*, Cambridge University Press, Cambridge.

Engels F., 1844, *La sacra famiglia*, Ital. transl., Editori Riuniti, Rome, 1969.

Engels F., 1846, Lettera al Comitato comunista di corrispondenza a Bruxelles del 23 ottobre, in Marx K. & Engels F., 1844–51, *Opere Complete*, Ital. transl., Editori Riuniti, Rome, 1972, vol. 38.

Engels F., 1847a, Principles of Communism, in Marx K. & Engels F., 1975–2001, *Collected Works*, vols 1–49, Lawrence & Wishart, London, vol. 6.

Engels F., 1847b, Draft of a Communist Confession of Faith, in Marx K. & Engels F., 1975–2001, *Collected Works*, vols 1–49, Lawrence & Wishart, London, vol. 6.

Engels F., 1859, Review of *Per la critica dell'economia politica*, in Marx K., *Per la critica dell'economia politica*, Ital. transl., Editori Riuniti, Rome, 1969.

Engels F., 1871, Lettera a Cafiero del 1–3 luglio, in Basevi P., ed., 1951, Le prime tre lettere di Engels a Carlo Cafiero, *La società*, December.

Engels F., 1878, *Antidühring*, in Marx K. & Engels F., 1975–2001, *Collected Works*, vols 1–49, Lawrence & Wishart, London, vol. 25.

Engels F., 1882a, *Socialism: Utopian and Scientific*, in Marx K. & Engels F., 1975–2001, *Collected Works*, vols 1–49, Lawrence & Wishart, London, vol. 24.

Engels F., 1882b, Additions to the Text of *Antidühring*, in Marx K. & Engels F., 1975–2001, *Collected Works*, vols 1–49, Lawrence & Wishart, London, vol. 25.

Engels F., 1884, Preface to Marx K., 1847, *Miseria della filosofia*, Ital. transl., Editori Riuniti, Rome, 1969.

Engels F., 1886, Letter to Bebel, 20–23 January, in Marx K. & Engels F., 1975–2001, *Collected Works*, vols 1–49, Lawrence & Wishart, London, vol. 27.

Engels F., 1890, Farewell Letter to the Readers of the Sozialdemokrat, in Marx K. & Engels F., 1975–2001, *Collected Works*, vols 1–49, Lawrence & Wishart, London, vol. 27.

Engels F., 1890–91, In the Case of Brentano versus Marx. Regarding Alleged Falsification of Quotation, in Marx K. & Engels F., 1975–2001, *Collected Works*, vols 1–49, Lawrence & Wishart, London, vol. 27.

Engels F., 1891a, Introduction to Marx K., 1849, *Lavoro salariato e capitale*, Ital. transl., Editori Riuniti, Rome, 1971.

Engels F., 1891b, Introduzione, in Marx K., *La Guerra civile in Francia*, Ital. transl., Editori Riuniti, Rome, 1974.

Engels F., 1891c, *Socialism: Utopian and Scientific*, in Marx K. & Engels F., 1975–2001, *Collected Works*, vols 1–49, Lawrence & Wishart, London.

Engels F., 1894a, On Authority, reprinted in Engels F., 1959, *Basic Writings on Political and Philosophy*, ed. L. Feuer, Doubleday, Garden City, NY.

Engels F., 1894b, Preface to Marx K., *Il capitale*, vol. III, Ital. transl., Editori Riuniti, Rome, 1965.

Engels F., 1895, Introduction to Karl Marx's *The Class Struggle in France, 1848 to 1850*, in Marx K. & Engels F., 1975–2001, *Collected Works*, vols 1–49, Lawrence & Wishart, London, vol. 27.

Estrin S., 1985, The Role of Producer Co-operatives in Employment Creation, *Economic Analysis and Workers' Management*, vol. 19, no. 4.

Estrin S., 1991, Some Reflections on Self-Management, Social Choice and Reform in Eastern Europe, *Journal of Comparative Economics*, vol. 15, no. 2.

Estrin S. & Jones D.C., 1992, The Viability of Employee-Owned Firms: Evidence from France, *Industrial and Labor Relations Review*, vol. 45, no. 2.

Estrin S. & Jones D.C., 1995, Worker Participation, Employee Ownership and Productivity: Results from French Producer Cooperatives, *Advances in the Economic Analysis of Participatory and Labor-Managed Firms*, vol. 5.

Estrin S., Jones D.C. & Svejnar J., 1987, The Productivity Effects of Worker Participation: Producer Cooperatives in Western Europe, *Journal of Comparative Economics*, vol. 11, no. 1.

Eswaran M. & Kotwal A., 1989, Why Are Capitalists the Bosses?, *Economic Journal*, vol. 99, March.

Faccioli D. & Fiorentini G., 1998, Un'analisi di efficienza comparata tra imprese cooperative e for profit, in Fiorentini G. & Scarpa C., eds, *Cooperative e mercato*, Carocci, Rome.

Fanelli R., 1997, Introduzione. Una soggettività immaginaria, in Althusser L., ed., 1969 and 1995, *Lo Stato e i suoi apparati*, Ital. transl., Laterza, Bari.

Favilli P., 2001, Socialismo e marginalismo. La 'battaglia delle idee': una lettura, in Guidi M.E.L. & Michelini L., eds, *Marginalismo e socialismo nell'Italia liberale, 1870–1925*, Feltrinelli, Milan.

Fawcett H., 1863, *Manual of Political Economy*, 1888 edn, London.

Fay M., 1983, The Influence of Adam Smith on Marx's Theory of Alienation, in Wood J.C., ed., *Karl Marx's Economics: Critical Assessments*, Croom Helm, Sydney, vol. 1.

Ferrarotti F., 1960, Attualità di Proudhon, *Tempo presente*, no. 2.

Filippini M., 2011, Nicolò Machiavelli: la grande politica, in D'Orsi A., ed., *Il nostro Gramsci; Antonio Gramsci a colloquio con i protagonisti della storia d'Italia*, Viella, Rome.

Fine B., Jeon H. & Gimm G.H., 2010, Value Is as Value Does: Twixt Knowledge and the World Economy, *Capital and Class*, vol. 34, no. 1.

Fine R., 2001, The Marx-Hegel Relationship: Revisionist Interpretations, *Capital and Class*, special issue, no. 75, autumn.

Finelli R., 2004, *Un parricidio mancato. Hegel e il giovane Marx*, Bollati Boringhieri, Turin.

Finelli R., 2007, Un marxismo 'senza Capitale', in Bellofiore R., ed., *Da Marx a Marx?*, Manifestolibri, Rome.

Fineschi R., 2005, Teoria della storia e alienazione in Marx, in Fineschi R., ed., *Karl Marx: Rivisitazioni e prospettive*, Mimesis, Milan.

Fineschi R., 2006, *Marx e Hegel; contributi a una rilettura*, Carocci, Rome.

Fineschi R., 2008, *Un nuovo Marx; filologia ed interpretazione dopo la nuova edizione storico-critica (Mega2)*, Carocci, Rome.

Finocchiaro M.A., 1988, *Gramsci and the History of Dialectical Thought*, Cambridge University Press, Cambridge.

Fitoussi J.P., 1995, *Le débat interdit*, Arléa, Paris.

Fitoussi J.P., 2013, *Il teorema del lampione*, Ital. transl., Einaudi, Turin.

Fitzroy F.R. & Kraft K., 1987, Cooperation, Productivity and Profit Sharing, *Quarterly Journal of Economics*, vol. 102, no. 1.

Fleetwood S., 2006, Rethinking Labour Market: A Critical-Realist-Socioeconomic Perspective, *Capital and Class*, vol. 89, summer.

Freeman A. & Carchedi G., 1996, *Marx and Non-Equilibrium Economics*, Edward Elgar Publishing, Cheltenham, UK and Brookfield, VT, USA.

Frölich P., 1967, *Rosa Luxemburg*, Ital. transl., La Nuova Italia, Florence, 1969.

Fromm E., 1942, *Fear of Freedom*, Routledge, London.

Fromm E., 1962, *Marx e Freud*, Ital. transl., Il Saggiatore, Milan, 1968.

Fukuyama F., 1992, *La fine della storia e l'ultimo uomo*, Ital. transl., Rizzoli, Milan, 1992.

Furubotn E.G., 1976, The Long-Run Analysis of the Labor-Managed Firm: An Alternative Interpretation, *American Economic Review*, vol. 66, no. 1.

Furubotn E.G., 1980, The Socialist Labor-Managed Firm and Bank-Financed Investment: Some Theoretical Issues, *Journal of Comparative Economics*, vol. 4, no. 2.

Furubotn E.G. & Pejovich S., 1970a, Tax Policy and Investment Decision of the Yugoslav Firm, *National Tax Journal*, vol. 23, no. 3.

Furubotn E.G. & Pejovich S., 1970b, Property Rights and the Behavior of the Firm in a Socialist State: The Example of Yugoslavia, *Zeitschrift für Nationalökonomie*, vol. 30, no. 5.

Furubotn E.G. & Pejovich S., 1973, Property Rights, Economic Decentralization and the Evolution of the Yugoslav Firm, 1965–72, *Journal of Law and Economics*, vol. 16, October.

Galasso G., 2013, *Liberalismo e democrazia*, Salerno editrice, Rome.

Galgano F., 1974, *Le istituzioni della società capitalistica*, Zanichelli, Bologna.

Galgano P., 1974, *Le istituzioni della'economia capitalistica*, Zanichelli, Bologna.

Galgano P., 1982, L'autogestione cooperativa e il sistema organizzato d'imprese, in Lega nazionale cooperative e mutue, ed., *L'impresa cooperativa negli anni 80*, De Donato, Bari.

Gallino L., 1987, Su alcuni fraintendimenti di Marx e intorno a Marx in tema di evoluzione delle società, in Cacciatore G. & Lomonaco F., eds, *Marx e i marxisti cent'anni dopo*, Guida Editori, Naples.

Garaudy R., 1969, Il concetto di struttura in Marx e le concezioni alienate della struttura, in Vv.Aa., eds, *Marx vivo*, Mondadori, Milan.

Garaudy R., undated, *L'alternativa; cambiare il mondo e la vita*, Ital. transl., Cittadella editrice, Assisi, 1972.

Garegnani P., 1981, *Marx e gli economisti classici*, Einaudi, Turin.

Garegnani P. & Petri F., 1982, Marxismo e teoria economica d'oggi, in Vv.Aa., eds, *Storia del marxismo*, vol. IV: *Il marxismo oggi*, Einaudi, Turin.

Garin E., 1979, *Filosofia e marxismo nell'opera di Rodolfo Mondolfo*, La Nuova Italia, Florence, 1979.

Garin E., 1983, Rodolfo Mondolfo, in Garin E., *Tra due secoli. Socialismo e filosofia in Italia dopo l'Unità*, Laterza, Bari.

Garson G.D., 1973, Beyond Collective Bargaining, in Hunnius G., Garson G.D. & Case J., eds, *Workers' Control*, Random House, New York.

Gattei G., 2007, La *via crucis* dei marxismi italiani, in Bellofiore R., ed., *Quelli del lavoro vivo*, Manifestolibri, Rome.

Geary R.J., 1974, Difesa e deformazione del marxismo in Kautsky, in Istituto Giangiacomo Feltrinelli, ed., *Storia del marxismo contemporaneo*, Feltrinelli, Milan.

George D.A.R., 1997, Self-Management and Ideology, *Review of Political Economy*, vol. 9, no. 1, January.

Gerratana V., 1972, L'estinzione dello Stato nella concezione marxiana e la tematica consiliare, in Vv.Aa., eds, *I consigli operai*, Samonà e Savelli, Rome.

Gibson-Graham J.K., 2003, Enabling Ethical Economies: Cooperativism and Class, *Critical Sociology*, vol. 29, no. 2.

Gilbert A., 1984, Marx's Moral Realism: Eudaimonism and Moral Progress, in Ball T. & Farr J., eds, *After Marx*, Cambridge University Press, Cambridge.

Gintis H., 1976, The Nature of Labor Exchange and the Theory of Capitalistic Production, *Review of Radical Political Economics*, vol. 8, no. 2.

Gintis H. & Bowles S., 1981, Structure and Practice in the Labour Theory of Value, *Review of Radical Political Economics*, vol. 12, no. 4, winter.

Giolitti A., 1977, L'autogestione, in La Ganga G., ed., *Socialismo e democrazia economica*, F. Angeli, Milan.

Gobetti P., 1929, Rassegna di questioni politiche, reprinted in Gobetti P., 1969, *Scritti politici*, Einaudi, Turin.

Godelier M., 1966, Sistema, struttura e contraddizione nel *Capitale*, Ital. transl., in Godelier M. & Sève L., eds, 1970, *Marxismo e strutturalismo*, Einaudi, Turin.

Gordon D.M., 1976, Capitalist Efficiency and Socialist Efficiency, *Monthly Review*, vol. 28, no. 3.

Gorz A., 1973a, Workers' Control Is More than Just That, in Hunnius G., Garson G.D. & Case J., eds, *Workers' Control*, Random House, New York.

Gorz A., 1973b, The Politics of Workers' Control: A Review Essay, in Hunnius G., Garson G.D. & Case J., eds, *Workers' Control*, Random House, New York.

Gramsci A., 1914–18, *Scritti giovanili (1914–18)*, Einaudi, Turin, 1958.

Gramsci A., 1917, La rivoluzione contro il 'Capitale', in Gramsci A., 1914–1918, *Scritti giovanili (1914–18)*, Einaudi, Turin, 1958.

Gramsci A., 1918, Individualismo e collettivismo, in Gramsci A., 1958, *Scritti giovanili (1914–18)*, Einaudi, Turin.

Gramsci A., 1919–20, *L'ordine nuovo*, Einaudi, Turin, 1955.

Gramsci A., 1921, Inganni, in Gramsci A., 1971, *Socialismo e fascismo: l'Ordine Nuovo, 1921–1922*, Einaudi, Turin.

Gramsci A., 1948, *Il materialismo storico*, Einaudi, Turin.

Gramsci A., 1964, *Il materialismo storico e la filosofia di Benedetto Croce*, 7th edn, Einaudi, Turin.

Gramsci A., 1975, *Quaderni del carcere*, ed. V. Gerratana, Einaudi, Turin.

Grossman H., 1940, *Marx, l'economia politica classica e il problema della dinamica*, Ital. transl., Laterza, Bari, 1971.

Gruppi L., 1970, *Il pensiero di Lenin*, Editori Riuniti, Rome.

Guerin D., 1971, Le marxisme libertaire, in Vv.Aa., eds, *Anarchici e anarchia nel mondo contemporaneo, Atti del convegno promosso dalla Fondazione Luigi Einaudi*, Einaudi, Turin.

Gui B., 1982, Imprese gestite dal lavoro e diritti patrimoniali dei membri: una trattazione economica, *Ricerche economiche*, vol. 36, no. 3.

Gui B., 1985, Limits to External Financing: A Model and an Application to Labour-Managed Firm, in Jones D.C. & Svejnar J., eds, *Advances in the Economic Analysis of Participatory and Labor-Managed Firms*, vol. I, JAI Press, Greenwich, CT.

Gui B., 1993, The Chances for Success of Worker Managed Form Organization: An Overview, *Associazione Italiana per lo Studio dei Sistemi Economici Comparati*, 9th scientific meeting, preprint.

Gui B., 1996, Is There a Chance for the Worker-Managed Form of Organization?, in Pagano U. & Rowthorn R., eds, *Democracy and Efficiency in Economic Enterprise*, Routledge, London.

Gunn C.E., 2006, Cooperative and Market Failure: Workers' Cooperatives and System Mismatch, *Review of Radical Political Economics*, vol. 38, no. 3, summer.

Habermas J., 1969, La tecnica e la scienza come ideologie, in Vv.Aa., eds, *Marx vivo*, Mondadori, Milan.

Hahnel R., 2004, Economic Justice, *Review of Radical Political Economics*, vol. 37, no. 2.

Hansmann H., 1996, *The Ownership of Enterprise*, Belknap Press, Harvard University Press, Cambridge, MA.

Hart O. & Moore J., 1996, The Governance of Exchanges: Members' Cooperatives versus Outside Ownership, working paper, available at http//ssrn.com/abstract=60039.

Haug F.W., 2005, Sul processo di apprendimento di Marx: dai *Grundrisse* alla traduzione francese del primo libro del *Capitale*, in Musto M., ed., *Sulle tracce di un fantasma*, Manifestolibri, Rome.

Haupt G., 1978, Marx e il marxismo, in Hobsbawm E.J., Haupt G., Marek F., Ragionieri E., Strada V. & Vivanti C., eds, 1978–82, *Storia del marxismo*, 5 vols, Einaudi, Turin, vol. 1.

Hayek F.A., 1960, *The Constitution of Liberty*, University of Chicago Press, London.

Hayek F.A., 1983, The Rediscovery of Liberty: Personal Recollections, in Hayek F.A., 1992, *The Fortunes and the Ideal of Freedom*, Routledge & Kegan, London.

Hegedus A., 1980, La costruzione del socialismo in Russia: il ruolo dei sindacati, la questione contadina, la Nuova politica economica, in Hobsbawm E.J., Haupt G., Marek F., Ragionieri E., Strada V. & Vivanti C., eds, 1978–82, *Storia del marxismo*, 5 vols, Einaudi, Turin, vol. 3.

Hegel G.W.F., 1831, *Scienza della logica*, 2nd edn, Ital. transl., Laterza, Bari, 1974.

Hegel G.W.F., 1837, *Lezioni sulla filosofia della storia*, Ital. transl., Laterza, Bari, 2003.

Heilbroner R.L., 1980, *Marxismo pro e contro*, Armando, Rome, 1982.

Hobsbawm E.J., 1994, *Il secolo breve*, Ital. transl., Rizzoli, Milan, 1995.

Hobsbawm E.J., 2005, *La fine dello Stato*, Ital. transl., Rizzoli, Milan, 2007.

Hobsbawm E.J., 2011, *Come cambiare il mondo*, Ital. transl., BUR, Milan, 2012.

Hobson J.A., 1963, *Veblen*, Augustus M. Kelley, New York.

Hodges D.C., 1965, The Value Judgement in *Capital*, reprinted in Wood J.C., ed., 1988, *Karl Marx's Economics: Critical Assessments*, Croom Helm, Sydney.

Hodges D.C., 1970, Marx's Concept of Value and Critique of Value Fetishism, reprinted in Wood J.C., ed., 1988, *Karl Marx's Economics: Critical Assessments*, Croom Helm, Sydney.

Hodgson G.M., 1982, Marx without the Labor Theory of Value, reprinted in Wood J.C., ed., 1988, *Karl Marx's Economics: Critical Assessments*, Croom Helm, Sydney, vol. II.

Hofmann W., 1971, *Da Babeuf a Marcuse*, Ital. transl., Mondadori, Milan.

Hollas D. & Stansell S., 1988, An Examination of the Effect of Ownership Form on Price Efficiency: Proprietary, Cooperative, and Municipal Electric Utilities, *Southern Economic Journal*, vol. 50, October.

Holloway J., 2001, Why Read *Capital?*, *Capital and Class*, special issue, no. 75, autumn.

Horvat B., 1969, *An Essay on Yugoslav Society*, International Arts and Science Press, Armonk, NY.

Horvat B., 1975, On the Theory of the Labor-Managed Firm, reprinted in Prychitko D.L. & Vanek J., eds, 1996, *Producer Cooperatives and Labor-managed Systems*, Edward Elgar Publishing, Cheltenham, UK and Brookfield, VT, USA.

Horvat, B., 1976, *The Yugoslav Economic System*, New York, M.E. Sharpe.

Howard M.C. & King J.E., 1975, *L'economia politica di Marx*, Ital. transl., Liguori, Naples, 1980.

Hudis P., 2013, *Marx's Concept of the Alternative to Capitalism*, Haymarket Books, Chicago.

Hume D., 1777, Enquiry Concerning the Principles of Morals, in Hume D., *Essays*, Macmillan, London, vol. 2.

Hutchison T.W., 1978, Friedrich Engels and Marxist Economic Theory, in Wood J.C., ed., 1988, *Karl Marx's Economics: Critical Assessments*, Croom Helm, Sydney.

Hyppolite J., 1969, Lo 'scientifico' e l''ideologico' in una prospettiva marxista, in Vv.Aa., eds, *Marx vivo*, Mondadori, Milan.

Ichino P., 2005, *A che cosa serve il sindacato?*, Mondadori, Milan.

Ilyenkov E.V., 1960, *La dialettica dell'astratto e del concreto nel Capitale di Marx*, Ital. transl., Feltrinelli, Milan, 1961.

Ishibashi S., 1995, The Demonstration of the Law of Value and the Uno-Sekine Approach, in Albritton R. & Sekine T.T., eds, *A Japanese Approach to Political Economy*, Palgrave, New York.

Jacobsson F., Johannesson M. & Borgquist L., 2007, Is Altruism Paternalistic?, *Economic Journal*, vol. 117, no. 520.

Jahn W. & Noske D., 1980, Ist das Aufsteigen vom Abstrakten zum Konkreten die wissenschaftlich richtige Methode?, *Arbeitsblätter zur Marx-Engels-Forschung*, vol. 2.

Jay P., 1980, The Workers' Cooperative Economy, in Clayre A., ed., *The Political Economy of Cooperation and Participation: A Third Sector*, Oxford Economic Press, Oxford.

Jensen M.C. & Meckling W.H., 1976, Theory of the Firm: Managerial Behavior, Agency Costs and Ownership Structure, *Journal of Financial Economics*, vol. 3, no. 4, October.

Jensen M.C. & Meckling W.H., 1979, Rights and Production Functions: An Application to Labor-Managed Firms and Codetermination, *Journal of Business*, vol. 52, no. 4.

Johnstone M., 1980, Lenin e la rivoluzione, in Hobsbawm E.J., Haupt G., Marek F., Ragionieri E., Strada V. & Vivanti C., eds, 1978–1982, *Storia del marxismo*, 5 vols, Einaudi, Turin.

Jones D.C. & Backus D.K., 1977, British Producer Cooperatives in the Footwear Industry: An Empirical Evaluation of the Theory of Financing, *Economic Journal*, vol. 87, no. 9.

Jones D.C. & Pliskin J., 1991, The Effects of Worker Participation, Employee Ownership and Profit Sharing on Economic Performance: A Partial Review, in Russel R. & Rus V., eds, *International Handbook of Participation in Organizations*, Oxford University Press, Oxford.

Jossa B., 1978, *Socialismo e mercato; contributi alla teoria economica del socialismo*, Etas Libri, Milan.

Jossa B., 1981, L'equilibrio di breve periodo in un'impresa autogestita, *Rassegna Economica*, vol. 45, no. 4.

Jossa B., 1982, Sulla teoria economica dell'impresa autogestita, paper for the Meeting of Würzburg (Germany) of 16–17 December, published in *Rivista Internazionale di Scienze Sociali*, January–March 1983.

Jossa B., 1985, Due opinioni sulla teoria dell'impresa cooperativa; con una conclusione sulla definizione del socialismo, *Rivista internazionale di Scienze Sociali*, vol. 93.

Jossa B., 1986, Considerazioni su di un tipo ideale di cooperative di produzione, *Studi economici*, vol. 41, no. 28.

Jossa B., 1988, Teoria economica e cooperative di produzione, in Jossa B., ed., *Autogestione, cooperazione e partecipazione agli utili*, Il Mulino, Bologna.

Jossa B., ed., 1989, *Teoria dei sistemi economici*, UTET, Turin.

Jossa B., 1992, Socialismo di mercato e distribuzione del reddito, in Chilosi A., ed., *L'economia del periodo di transizione; dal modello di tipo sovietico all'economia di mercato*, Il Mulino, Bologna.

Jossa B., 1993, Is There an Option to Denationalization of Eastern European Enterprises?, in Baldassarri M., Paganetto L. & Phelps E.S., eds, *Privatization Processes in Eastern Europe*, Macmillan, London.

Jossa B., 1994, Hayek and Market Socialism, in Colonna M., Hagemann H. & Hamouda O.F., eds, *Capitalism, Socialism and Knowledge*, vol. II, Edward Elgar Publishing, Cheltenham, UK and Brookfield, VT, USA.

Jossa B., 1997, *The Economic Theory of Socialism and the Labour Managed Firm*, in collaboration with G. Cuomo, Edward Elgar Publishing, Cheltenham, UK and Lyme, NH, USA.

Jossa B., 1999, *La democrazia nell'impresa*, Edizioni Scientifiche, Naples.

Jossa B., 2001, L'impresa gestita dai lavoratori e la disoccupazione classica e keynesiana, *Rivista italiana degli economisti*, no. 1, April.

Jossa B., 2002, Il marxismo e le imprese gestite dai lavoratori, *Economia Politica*, vol. 19, no. 3.

Jossa B., 2004, Schweickart and Economic Democracy, *Review of Radical Political Economics*, vol. 36, no. 4, autumn.

Jossa B., 2005a, Marx, Marxism and the Cooperative Movement, *Cambridge Journal of Economics*, no. 1, January.

Jossa B., 2005b, *La teoria economica delle cooperative di produzione e la possibile fine del capitalismo*, Giappichelli, Turin.

Jossa B., 2006a, Gli intellettuali e la democrazia nell'impresa, *Studi e Note di Economia*, no. 1.

Jossa B., 2006b, L'economia politica della rivoluzione democratica, *Politica Economica*, vol. 22, no. 3.

Jossa B., 2008, *L'impresa democratica*, Carocci, Rome.

Jossa B., 2009, Unemployment in a System of Labour-Managed Firms, in Salvadori N. & Opocher A., eds, *Long-Run Growth, Social Institution and Living Standard*, Edward Elgar Publishing, Cheltenham, UK and Northampton, MA, USA.

Jossa B., 2010, *Esiste un'alternativa al capitalismo?*, Manifestolibri, Rome.

Jossa B., 2012a, Cooperative Firms as a New Production Mode, *Review of Political Economy*, vol. 24, no. 3.

Jossa B., 2012b, Una nuova stella polare per la sinistra?, *Nuova Logos*, April.

Jossa B., 2014a, *A System of Cooperative Firm as a New Mode of Production*, Routledge, London.

Jossa B., 2014b, Marx, Lenin and the Cooperative Movement, *Review of Political Economy*, vol. 26, no. 2.

Jossa B., 2014c, The Key Contradiction in Capitalism, *Review of Radical Political Economics*, vol. 46, no. 1, March.

Jossa B., 2014d, The Joint-Stock Company as a Springboard for Socialism, *Rivista internazionale di Scienze Sociali*, vol. 122, January–March.

Jossa B., 2016a, *Un marxismo rinnovato*, Manifestolibri, Rome.

Jossa B., 2016b, *Labour-Managed Firms and Post-Capitalism*, Routledge, London.

Jossa B. & Casavola P., 1993, The Problem of Under-Investment in Firms Managed by Workers, in Atkinson A.B., ed., *Alternatives to Capitalism: The Economics of Partnership*, Macmillan, London.

Jossa B. & Cuomo G., 1997, *The Economic Theory of Socialism and the Labour-Managed Firm*, Edward Elgar Publishing, Cheltenham, UK and Lyme, NH, USA.

Kant I., 1784, Idea per una storia universale dal punto di vista cosmo-politico, in Kant I., 1965, *Scritti politici e di filosofia della storia e del diritto*, UTET, Turin.

Kautsky K., 1892, *Il Programma di Erfurt*, Ital. transl., Samonà e Savelli, Rome, 1971.

Kautsky K., 1907, *Ethics and the Materialist Conception of History*, C.H. Kerr, Chicago.

Kautsky K., 1960, *Erinnerungen und Erörterungen*, Gravenhage, Berlin.

Kester G. & Pinaud H., 1996, *Trade Unions and Democratic Participation: A Scenario for the 21st Century*, Averbury, Aldershot.

Keynes J.M., 1926, La fine del *laissez-faire*, in Keynes J.M., *Laissez-Faire and Communism*, New Republic, New York.

Keynes J.M., 1931, *Esortazioni e profezie*, Ital. transl., Il Saggiatore, Milano, 1968.

Keynes J.M., 1979, *The Collected Writings of John Maynard Keynes*, vol. 29: *The General Theory and After: A Supplement*, Macmillan, London.

Kicillof A. & Starosta G., 2007, Value Form and Class Struggle: A Critique of the Autonomist Theory of Value, *Capital and Class*, no. 92, summer.

Kicillof A. & Starosta G., 2011, On Value and Abstract Labour: A Reply to Werner Bonefeld, *Capital and Class*, vol. 35, no. 2.

Kirchgassner G., 1989, On the Political Economy of Economic Policy, *Economia delle scelte pubbliche*, vol. 7, no. 1–2.

Kleiner D., 2010, *The Telecommunist Manifesto*, Institute of Network Cultures, Amsterdam.

Kliman A.J., 1998, Value, Exchange Value and the Internal Consistency of Volume III of *Capital*: A Refutation of Refutations, in Bellofiore R., ed., *Marxian Economics: A Reappraisal*, Palgrave Macmillan, New York.

Kolakowsky, L., 1979 *Nascita, sviluppo, dissoluzione del marxismo*, Ital. transl., Milano, SugarCo, 1980–85.

Kornai J., 1971, *Anti-Equilibrium*, North-Holland, Amsterdam.

Kornai J., 1980, *Economics of Shortage*, North-Holland, Amsterdam.

Kornai J., 1994, *Over-Centralization in Economic Administration*, 2nd edn, Oxford University Press, Oxford.

Kouvélakis S., 2005, Marx e la critica della politica, in Musto M., ed., *Sulle tracce di un fantasma*, Manifestolibri, Rome.

Kramer-Badoni R., 1972, *Anarchia. Passato e presente di un'utopia*, Bietti, Milan.

Krugman P., 2009, How Did Economists Get It So Wrong?, www.ny times.com/2009/09/06/magazine/06Economict.html/pagewanted=all&_r=0.

Labriola A., 1895, In memoria del Manifesto dei Comunisti, in Labriola A., 1965, *La concezione materialistica della storia*, ed. E. Garin, Laterza, Bari.

Labriola A., 1896, Del materialismo storico; delucidazione preliminare, in Labriola A., 1902, *Discorrendo di socialismo e di filosofia*, Edizioni Millennium, Bologna, 2006.

Labriola A., 1965, *La concezione materialistica della storia*, ed. E. Garin, Laterza, Bari.

Labriola A., 1970, *Scritti politici*, ed. V. Gerratana, Laterza, Bari.

Laibman D., 2006, The Future within the Present: Seven Theses for a Robust Twenty-First Century Socialism, *Review of Radical Political Economics*, vol. 18, no. 3, summer.

Laibman D., 2013, Market Socialism: Design, Prerequisites, Transition, *Review of Radical Political Economics*, vol. 45, no. 4.

Landauer C., 1959, *European Socialism: A History of Ideas and Movements*, University of California Press, Berkeley, CA.

Landauer G., 1985, *Ein Weg zur Befreiung der Arbeiterklasse*, Verlag von Adolf Marreck, Berlin.

Lange O., 1935, Marxian Economics and Modern Economic Theory, *Review of Economic Studies*, vol. 2, no. 3, June.

Lange O., 1936–37, Sulla teoria economica del socialismo, Ital. transl., in Vv.Aa., eds, *Teoria economica ed economia socialista*, Savelli, Rome.

Lange O., 1957, Alcuni problemi riguardanti la via polacca al socialismo, in Lange O., 1958, *The Political Economy of Socialism*, Erasmus University, Rotterdam.

Lange O., 1966, *Socialismo ed economia socialista*, Ital. transl., La Nuova Italia, Florence.

Lawler J., 1994, Marx's Theory of Socialism: Nihilistic and Dialectical, in Patsouras, L., ed., *Debating Marx*, Lewiston, New York.

Lawler J., 1998, Marx as Market Socialist, in Ollman B., ed., *Market Socialism: The Debate among Socialists*, Routledge, London.

Lazonick W., 1978, The Subjection of Labour to Capital: The Rise of the Capitalist System, *Review of Radical Political Economics*, vol. 10, no. 1.

Lehning A., 1969, Anarchisme et bolscevisme, in Vv.Aa., eds, *Anarchici e anarchia nel mondo contemporaneo, Atti del convegno promosso dalla Fondazione Luigi Einaudi*, Einaudi, Turin.

Lenin V.I., 1902, *Che fare?*, Editori Riuniti, Rome, 1974.

Lenin V.I., 1917a, *L'imperialismo, fase suprema del capitalismo*, Editori Riuniti, Rome, 1969.

Lenin V.I., 1917b, *Stato e rivoluzione*, 2nd edn, Editori Riuniti, Rome, 1974.

Lenin V.I., 1917c, Primo congresso dei soviet deputati operai, in Lenin V.I., 1957–70, *Opere complete*, Editori Riuniti, Rome, vol. 25.

Lenin V.I., 1917d, La catastrofe imminente e come lottare contro di essa, in

Lenin V.I., 1918, I compiti immediati del potere sovietico, in Lenin V.I., 1957–70, *Opere complete*, Editori Riuniti, Rome, vol. 27.

Lenin V.I., 1921a, La nuova politica economica, in Lenin V.I., 1972, *La costruzione del socialismo*, Editori Riuniti, Rome.

Lenin V.I., 1921b, Rapporto sulla sostituzione dei prelevamenti alle eccedenze con l'imposta in natura, in Lenin V.I., 1957–70, *Opere complete*, Editori Riuniti, Rome, vol. 32.

Lenin V.I., 1922a, La funzione e i compiti dei sindacati nelle condizioni della Nuova politica economica, in Lenin V.I., 1965, *Opere scelte*, Editori Riuniti, Rome.

Lenin V.I., 1922b, Cinque anni di rivoluzione russa e le prospettive della rivoluzione mondiale, in Lenin V.I., 1965, *Opere scelte*, Editori Riuniti, Rome.

Lenin V.I., 1923, Sulla cooperazione, in Lenin V.I., 1965, *Opere scelte*, Editori Riuniti, Rome.

Lenin V.I., 1957–70, *Opere complete*, Editori Riuniti, Rome.

Lenin V.I., 1965, *Opere scelte*, Editori Riuniti, Rome.

Leone E., 1902, Sul principio di cooperazione nei suoi rapporti con il socialismo, *Critica sociale*, vol. 12, no. 18.

Leone E., 1906, *Il sindacalismo*, Remo Sandron, Milan.

Lerner A.P., 1938, Theory and Practice in Socialist Economics, *Review of Economic Studies*, vol. 6, no. 1.

Levine D.J., 1995, *Reinventing the Workplace: How Business and Employees Can Both Win*, Brookings Institution, Washington, DC.

Levine D.J. & Tyson L., 1990, Participation, Productivity and the Firm's Environment, in Blinder A., ed., *Paying for Productivity: A Look at the Evidence*, Brookings Institution, Washington, DC.

Levine D.P., 1998, The Structure of Marx's Argument in *Capital*, in Bellofiore R., ed., *Marxian Economics: A Reappraisal*, Palgrave Macmillan, New York.

Lewin M., 1974, *Economia e politica nella società sovietica*, Ital. transl., Editori Riuniti, Rome.

Libertini L. & Panzieri R., 1969, Sette tesi sul controllo operaio, in Vv.Aa., eds, *La sinistra e il controllo operaio*, Feltrinelli, Milan.

Lichtheim G., 1965, *Marxism: An Historical and Critical Study*, F.A. Praeger, New York.

Lipietz A., 1982, The So-Called 'Transformation Problem' Revisited, *Journal of Economic Theory*, vol. 50, no. 26.

Lippi M., 1976, *Marx; il valore come costo sociale reale*, Etas Libri, Milan.

Lissa G., 1982, Il marxismo italiano tra scienza e filosofia, in Bobbio N., ed., *La cultura filosofica italiana dal 1945 al 1980*, Guida Editori, Naples.

Lombardo Radice L., 1972, Intervento, in Istituto Gramsci, ed., *Il marxismo italiano degli anni sessanta e la formazione teorico-politica delle nuove generazioni*, Editori Riuniti, Rome.

Lorenz R., 1974, La costruzione del socialismo in Lenin, in Istituto Giangiacomo Feltrinelli, ed., *Storia del marxismo contemporaneo*, Feltrinelli, Milan.

Losurdo D., 2005, Marxismo, globalizzazione e bilancio storico del socialismo, in Musto M., ed., *Sulle tracce di un fantasma*, Manifestolibri, Rome.

Lowit T., 1962, Marx et le mouvement cooperatif, *Cahiers de l'institut de science èconomique appliquée*, no. 129, September.

Löwith K., 1949, *Significato e fine della storia*, Ital. transl., Edizioni di Comunità, Milan.

Lukàcs G., 1922, *Storia e coscienza di classe*, Ital. transl., Sugarco Edizioni, Milan, 1974.

Lukàcs G., 1923, *Storia e coscienza di classe*, Ital. transl., Sugarco Edizioni, Milan, 1974.

Lukàcs G., 1968a, *Marxismo e politica culturale*, Einaudi, Turin.

Lukàcs G., 1968b, *Scritti politici giovanili, 1919–1928*, Laterza, Bari.

Lukàcs G., 1971, Vecchia kultur e nuova kultur, *Quaderni Piacentini*, vol. 43, no. 4.

Lukàcs G., 1972, *L'uomo e la rivoluzione*, Ital. transl., Editori Riuniti, Rome, 1973.

Lukàcs G., 1976, *Ontologia dell'essere sociale*, vol. 1, Editori Riuniti, Rome.

Luxemburg R., 1913, *L'accumulazione del capitale*, Ital. transl., Einaudi, Turin, 1960.

Luxemburg R., 1919, Discorso sul programma, in Luxemburg R., 1967, *Scritti politici*, ed. L. Basso, Editori Riuniti, Rome.

Luxemburg R., 1948, La rivoluzione russa, in Luxemburg R., 1967, *Scritti politici*, ed. L. Basso, Editori Riuniti, Rome.

Macciocchi M.A., 1974, *Per Gramsci*, Il Mulino, Bologna.

MacGregor D., 1984, *The Communist Ideal in Hegel and Marx*, University of Toronto Press, Toronto.

MacPherson I., 1984, Democracy: Utopian and Scientific, in Ball T. & Farr J., eds, *After Marx*, Cambridge University Press, Cambridge.

Magri L., 1967, A cinquant'anni da 'Stato e Rivoluzione', reprinted in Vv.Aa., eds, *Classe, consigli, partito*, Alfani editore, Rome.

Magri L., 1974, 'Via italiana' e strategia consiliare, in Vv.Aa., eds, *Classe, consigli, partito*, Alfani editore, Rome.

Maione G., 1975, *Il biennio rosso*, Il Mulino, Bologna.

Makoto I., 2006, Marx's Economic Theory and the Prospect for Socialism, in Uchida H., ed., *Marx for the 21st Century*, Routledge, London.

Mandel E., 1973, The Debate on Workers' Control, in Hunnius G., Garson G.D. & Case J., eds, *Workers' Control*, Random House, New York.

Mann T., 1918, *Considerazioni di un impolitico*, Ital. transl., Adelphi, Milan.

Marcuse H., 1954, *Ragione e rivoluzione*, Ital. transl., Il Mulino, Bologna, 1966.

Marcuse H., 1964, *L'uomo ad una dimensione*, Ital. transl., Einaudi, Turin, 1967.

Marcuse H., 1967, *Fine dell'utopia*, Ital. transl., Laterza, Bari, 1968.

Marek F., 1982, Teorie della rivoluzione e fasi della transizione, in Hobsbawm E.J., Haupt G., Marek F., Ragionieri E., Strada V. & Vivanti C., eds, 1978–82, *Storia del marxismo*, 5 vols, Einaudi, Turin.

Marglin S.A., 1974, What Do Bosses Do?, *Review of Radical Political Economics*, vol. 6, no. 2.

Marković M., 1969, Marx e il pensiero critico-scientifico, in Vv.Aa., eds, *Marx vivo*, Mondadori, Milan.

Marramao G., 1977, *Austromarxismo e socialismo di sinistra tra le due guerre*, La Pietra, Milan.

Marramao G., 1980, Tra bolscevismo e socialdemocrazia: Otto Bauer e la cultura politica dell'austromarxismo, in Hobsbawm E.J., Haupt G., Marek F., Ragionieri E., Strada V. & Vivanti C., eds, 1978–82, *Storia del marxismo*, 5 vols, Einaudi, Turin, vol. IV.

Marshall A., 1889, Cooperation, in Marshall A., 1925, *Memorials of Alfred Marshall*, ed. A.C. Pigou, Macmillan, London.

Marshall A., 1890, *Principles of Political Economy*, 9th edn, Macmillan, London, 1961.

Marshall A., 1925, *Memorials of Alfred Marshall*, ed. A.C. Pigou, Macmillan, London.

Marshall A. & Marshall M.P., 1879, *Economia della produzione*, ed. G. Becattini, ISEDI, Milan, 1975.

Marx K., 1843, Critica della filosofia hegeliana del diritto pubblico, in Marx K. & Engels F., 1966, *Opere scelte*, ed. L. Gruppi, Editori Riuniti, Rome.

Marx K., 1844a, *Manoscritti economico-filosofici del 1844*, Einaudi, Turin, 1968.

Marx K., 1844b, Sulla questione ebraica, in Marx K. & Engels F., 1966, *Opere scelte*, ed. L. Gruppi, Editori Riuniti, Rome.

Marx K., 1847, *Miseria della filosofia*, Ital. transl., Editori Riuniti, Rome, 1969.

Marx K., 1849, *Lavoro salariato e capitale*, Ital. transl., Editori Riuniti, Rome, 1971.

Marx K., 1857, Introduzione a *Per la critica dell'economia politica*, in Marx K., 1859, *Per la critica dell'economia politica*, Ital. transl., Editori Riuniti, Rome, 1969.

Marx K., 1857–58, *Lineamenti fondamentali della critica dell'economia politica*, vol. II, Ital. transl., La Nuova Italia, Florence, 1970.

Marx K., 1858, A Letter to Engels dated January 14, Ital. transl, in Marx K. & Engels F., 1972, *Carteggio Marx–Engels*, vols 1–6, Editori Riuniti, Rome.

Marx K., 1859, *Per la critica dell'economia politica*, Ital. transl., Editori Riuniti, Rome, 1969.

Marx K., 1861–63, Economic Manuscript of 1861–63, in Marx K. & Engels F., 1975–2001, *Collected Works*, vols 1–49, Lawrence & Wishart, London, vols 30–4.

Marx K., 1863–66, *Il Capitale: libro I, capitolo VI inedito*, La Nuova Italia, Firenze, 1969.

Marx K., 1864, Inaugural Address of the Working Men's International Association, in Marx K. & Engels F., 1975–2001, *Collected Works*, vols 1–49, Lawrence & Wishart, London, vol. 20.

Marx K., 1866, Lettera ad Engels del 18 agosto, in Marx K. & Engels F., 1972, *Carteggio Marx-Engels*, vols 1–6, Editori Riuniti, Rome.

Marx K., 1867, *Capital*, vol. 1, Penguin Books, Harmondsworth, 1986.

Marx K., 1868, Letter to Kugelmann of 6 March, in Marx K. & Engels F., 1975–2001, *Collected Works*, vols 1–49, Lawrence & Wishart, London, vol. 42.

Marx K., 1871, *La Guerra civile in Francia*, Ital. transl., Editori Riuniti, Rome, 1974.

Marx K., 1873, Poscritto alla seconda edizione del *Capitale*, in Marx, K., *Capital*, Penguin Books, Harmondsworth.

Marx K., 1875a, Critique of the Gotha Programme, in Marx K. & Engels F., 1975–2001, *Collected Works*, vols 1–49, Lawrence & Wishart, London, vol. 24.

Marx K., 1875b, Notes on Bakunin's 'Statehood and Anarchy', in Marx K. & Engels F., 1975–2001, *Collected Works*, vols 1–49, Lawrence & Wishart, London, vol. 24.

Marx K., 1885, *Il capitale*, vol. II, Ital. transl., Editori Riuniti, Rome, 1965.

Marx K., 1894, *Il capitale*, vol. III, Ital. transl., Editori Riuniti, Rome, 1965.

Marx K. & Engels F., 1845, *La sacra famiglia*, Ital. transl., Editori Riuniti, Rome, 1969.

Marx K. & Engels F., 1845–46, *L'ideologia tedesca*, Ital. transl., Editori Riuniti, Rome, 1969.

Marx K. & Engels F., 1848, *Manifesto del partito comunista*, Editori Riuniti, Rome.

Marx K., Engels F., 1850, Indirizzo al Comitato centrale della Lega dei comunisti del marzo 1850, in Marx ed Engels, 1978.

Marx K. & Engels F., 1972, *Carteggio Marx-Engels*, vols 1–6, Editori Riuniti, Rome.

Marx K., Engels F., 1978, *Proletariato e comunismo*, ed. by G. M. Bravo, Editori Riuniti, Rome.

Marx K. & Engels F., 2014 [1848], *Manifesto del partito comunista*, Einaudi, Turin.

Massari R., 1974, *Le teorie dell'autogestione*, Jaca Book, Milan.

Mattick P., 2002, Class, Capital and Crisis, in Campbell M. & Reuten G., eds, *The Culmination of Capital: Essays on Volume III of Marx's Capital*, Palgrave, London.

Mavroudeas S.D., 2004, Forms of Existence of Abstract Labour and Value-Form, in Freeman A., Kliman A. & Wells J., eds, *The New Value Controversy and the Foundations of Economics*, Edward Elgar Publishing, Cheltenham, UK and Northampton, MA, USA.

Mayer T., 1994, *Anaytical Marxism*, SAGE, London.

Mazzini G., 1862, Il socialismo e la democrazia, in Mazzini G., *Politica ed Economia*, Sonzogno, Milan.

Mazzini G., 1935, *Scritti editi ed inediti*, Galeati, Imola.

McGlone T. & Kliman A., 1996, One System or Two? The Transformation of Values into Prices of Production versus the Transformation Problem, in Freeman A. & Carchedi G., eds, *Marx and Non-Equilibrium Economics*, Edward Elgar Publishing, Cheltenham, UK and Brookfield, VT, USA.

McMurtry J.J., 2004, Social Economy as a Social Practice, *International Journal of Social Economics*, vol. 31, no. 9–10.

Meade J.E., 1972, The Theory of Labour-Managed Firms and of Profit Sharing, *Economic Journal*, vol. 82, March, supplement.

Meade J.E., 1979, The Adjustment Processes of Labour Cooperatives with Constant Returns to Scale and Perfect Competition, *Economic Journal*, vol. 89, December.

Meek R., 1956, *Saggi sulla teoria del valore-lavoro*, Ital. transl., Feltrinelli, Milan, 1973.

Mehring F., 1893–94, Der Festtag der Arbeit, *Neue Zeit*, vol. 12, no. 2.

Mehring F., 1918, *Vita di Marx*, Ital. transl., Editori Riuniti, Rome, 1966.

Mellor M., Hannah J. & Stirling J., 1988, *Worker Cooperatives in Theory and Practice*, Open University Press, Philadelphia, PA.

Merker N., 2010, *Karl Marx: vita e opera*, Laterza, Bari.

Mészàros I., 1970, *La teoria dell'alienazione in Marx*, Ital. transl., Editori Riuniti, Rome, 1976.

Mészàros I., 1995, *Beyond Capital*, Merlin Press, London.

Meyer A.G., 1957, *Il leninismo*, Ital. transl., Edizioni di Comunità, Milan, 1965.

Meyer T., 1994, *Analytical Marxism*, vol. 1, SAGE, London.

Michels R., 1909, L'uomo economico e la cooperazione, *La Riforma sociale*, vol. 16, no. 20.

Miconi B., 1981, Valori e prezzi nell'analisi marxiana e nella letteratura economica, in Panizza R. & Vicarelli S., eds, *Valori e prezzi nella teoria di Marx*, Einaudi, Turin.

Mill J.S., 1859, *La libertà*, Ital. transl., RCS libri, Milan.

Mill J.S., 1871, *Principi di economia politica*, 3rd edn, Ital. transl., UTET, Turin, 1953.

Miller R.W., 1984, Producing Change: Work, Technology and Power in Marx's Theory of History, in Ball T. & Farr J., eds, *After Marx*, Cambridge University Press, Cambridge.

Miyazaki H. & Neary H.N., 1983, The Illyrian Firm Revisited, *Bell Journal of Economics*, vol. 14, no. 1.

Moene K.O. & Wallerstein, M., 1993, Unions versus Cooperatives, in Bowles S., Gintis H. & Gustafsson B., eds, *Markets and Democracy: Participation, Accountability and Efficiency*, Cambridge University Press, Cambridge.

Mohun S., 1991, Abstract Labour, in Bottomore T.B., ed., *A Dictionary of Marxist Thought*, 2nd edn, Blackwell, Oxford.

Mondolfo R., 1923, *Sulle orme di Marx*, Cappelli, Bologna.

Mondolfo R., 1952, *Il materialismo storico in Federico Engels*, La Nuova Italia, Florence.

Montias J.M., 1976, *The Structure of Economics Systems*, Yale University Press, New Haven, CT.

Mordenti R., 2007, *Gramsci e la rivoluzione necessaria*, Editori Riuniti, Rome, 2011.

Morishima M., 1973, *La teoria economica di Marx*, Ital. transl., ISEDI, Milan, 1974.

Morris J., 1966, Commodity Fetishism and the Value Concept: Some Contrasting Point of View, reprinted in Wood J.C., ed., 1988, *Karl Marx's Economics: Critical Assessments*, Croom Helm, Sydney.

Moseley F., 1982, The 'New Solution' to the Transformation Problem: A Sympathetic Critique, *Review of Radical Political Economics*, vol. 32, no. 2.

Moseley F., 1993, Marx's Logical Method and the Transformation Problem, in Moseley F., ed., *Marx's Method in 'Capital': A Re-examination*, Humanities Press, Atlantic Highlands, NJ.

Moseley F., 1998, *Marx's Logic in Capital and the 'Transformation Problem'*, in Bellofiore R., ed., *Marxian Economics: A Reappraisal*, Palgrave Macmillan, New York.

Mumford L., 1934, *Tecnica e cultura*, Ital. transl., Il Saggiatore, Milan, 1961.

Murgescu C., 1969, Alcune riflessioni sommarie in occasione di un anniversario, in Vv.Aa., eds, *Marx vivo*, Mondadori, Milan.

Murray P., 2002, The Illusion of Economic: The Trinity Formula and the 'Religion of Everyday Life', in Campbell M. & Reuten G., eds, *The Culmination of Capital; Essays on Volume III of Marx's Capital*, Palgrave, London.

Musgrave R.A., 1958, On Merit Goods, in Musgrave R.A., *Public Finance in a Democratic Society: Collected Papers of Richard A. Musgrave*, vol. 1, Wheatsheaf Books, Brighton.

Musgrave R.A., 1986, *Public Finance in a Democratic Society: Collected Papers of Richard A. Musgrave*, vol. 1, Wheatsheaf Books, Brighton.

Musto M., 2011, *Ripensare Marx e i marxismi*, Carocci, Rome.

Mygind N., 1997, Employee Ownership in Baltic Countries, in Uvalic M. & Vaughan-Whitehead D., eds, Privatization Surprises in Transition Economies: Employee Ownership in Central and Eastern Europe, Edward Elgar Publishing, Cheltenham, UK and Lyme, NH, USA.

Napoleoni C., 1985, *Discorso sull'economia politica*, Boringhieri, Turin.

Natoli S., 2008, *Felicità*, Feltrinelli, Milan.

Naville P., 1948, Psychologie, Marxisme, Matérialisme. Essais critiques, Rivière, Paris.

Negt O., 1979, Il marxismo e la teoria della rivoluzione nell'ultimo Engels, in Hobsbawm E.J., Haupt G., Marek F., Ragionieri E., Strada V. & Vivanti C., eds, 1978–82, *Storia del marxismo*, 5 vols, Einaudi, Turin, vol. 2.

Nicolaus M., 1973, Introduzione ai *Grundrisse*, in Vv.Aa., eds, *Dialettica e proletariato. Dibattito sui 'Grundrisse' di Marx*, Ital. transl., La Nuova Italia, Florence, 1978.

Nik-Kah E., 2010, Georg Stigler, in Emmett R.B., ed., *The Elgar Companion to the Chicago School of Economics*, Edward Elgar Publishing, Cheltenham, UK and Northampton, MA, USA.

Nik-Kah E. & van Horn R., 2012, Inland Empire: Economics Imperialism as an Imperative of the Chicago School of Economics, *Journal of Economic Methodology*, vol. 19, no. 3.

Nordhal R.A., 1982, Marx on the Use of History in the Analysis of Capitalism, in Wood J.C., ed., 1988, *Karl Marx's Economics: Critical Assessments*, Croom Helm, Sydney, vol. 1.

Nuti D.M., 1992, Il socialismo di mercato. Il modello che avrebbe potuto esserci, ma che non c'è mai stato, in Chilosi A., ed., *L'economia del periodo di transizione; dal modello di tipo sovietico all'economia di mercato*, Il Mulino, Bologna.

Nuti D.M., 2004, I sistemi economici post-comunisti, ovvero 2001 odissea nella transizione, in Jossa B., ed., Schweickart and Economic Democracy, *Review of Radical Political Economics*, vol. 36, no. 4, autumn.

O'Boyle B., 2013, Reproducing the Social Structure: A Marxist Critique of A. Giddens's Structuration Methodology, *Cambridge Journal of Economics*, vol. 17, no. 5.

Offe C., 1972, *Strukturprobleme des kapitalistischen Staates*, Suhrkamp Verlag, Frankfurt am Main.

Offe C., 1977, *Lo Stato nel capitalismo maturo*, Ital. transl., Etas Libri, Milan.

Offe C. & Lenhardt G., 1979, *Teoria dello stato e politica sociale*, Feltrinelli, Milan.

Oldrini G., 2007, Lukàcs e il dilemma della dialettica, in Burgio A., ed., *Dialettica; tradizioni, problemi sviluppi*, Quodlibet Studio, Macerata.

Ollman B., 1976, *Alienation; Marx's Conception of Man in Capitalistic Society*, 2nd edn, Cambridge University Press, Cambridge.

Ollman B., 1998, Market Mystification in Capitalist and Market Socialist Societies, in Ollman B., ed., *Market Socialism: The Debate among Socialists*, Routledge, London.

Ollman B., 2003, *Dance of the Dialectic: Steps in Marx's Method*, University of Illinois Press, Chicago.

Olson M., 1965, *The Logic of Collective Action*, Harvard University Press, Cambridge, MA.

Olson M., 1982, *The Rise and Decline of Nations*, Yale University, New Haven, CT.

Pagano U., 2006, Marx fra autoritarismo e democrazia economica, in Jossa B. & Lunghini G., eds, *Marxismo oggi*, Il Ponte Editore, Florence.

Panayotakis C., 2009, Individual Differences and the Potential Tradeoffs between the Value of a Participatory Economy, *Review of Radical Political Economics*, vol. 41, no. 1.

Panico C., 2015, Teoria economica, scelte legislative e giustizia distributiva, in De Giovanni L. & Donisi C., eds, *Convergenza dei saperi e direttive dell'umano*, ESI, Naples.

Pannekoek A., 1938, *Lenin filosofo*, Ital. transl., Feltrinelli, Milan, 1972.

Pantaleoni M., 1898, Esame critico dei principi teorici della cooperazione, republished in Pantaleoni M., 1925, *Erotemi di Economia politica*, Cacucci, Bari.

Panzieri R., 1960, Intervento sui temi per il Congresso della CGIL, in Panzieri R., 1975, *La ripresa del marxismo leninismo in Italia*, Sapere edizioni, Milan.

Panzieri R., 1964, Plusvalore e pianificazione (appunti di lettura del capitale), in Panzieri R., 1975, *La ripresa del marxismo leninismo in Italia*, Sapere edizioni, Milan.

Panzieri R., 1976, *Lotte operaie nello sviluppo capitalistico*, Einaudi, Turin.

Panzieri R., 1994, *Spontaneità ed organizzazione. Gli anni dei 'Quaderni Rossi', 1959–1964*, Pisa, BFS edizioni.

Pareto V., 1926, *I sistemi socialisti*, Ital. transl., UTET, Turin, 1963.

Pejovich S., 1975, The Firm, Monetary Policy and Property Rights in a Planned Economy, in Horvat B., Markovic M. & Supek R., eds, *Self-governing Socialism: A Reader*, International Arts and Science Press, New York.

Pelikan J., 1977, Il socialismo e l'Europa orientale, in ARA, ed., *Quale socialismo; quale Europa*, Feltrinelli, Milan.

Pellicani L., 1976, Socialismo e economia di mercato, *Mondoperaio*, June.

Pellicani L., 1987, La dialettica marxiana: scienza o gnosis?, in Cacciatore G. & Lomonaco F., eds, *Marx e i marxisti cent'anni dopo*, Guida Editori, Naples.

Pérotin V., 2006, Entry, Exit, and the Business Cycle: Are Cooperatives Different?, *Journal of Comparative Economics*, vol. 34, no. 2.

Perri S., 1998, *Prodotto netto e sovrappiù*, UTET, Turin.

Pesciarelli E., 1981, *Un nuovo modo di produrre*, Clua editrice, Ancona.

Pivetti M., 2006, *Marx e lo sviluppo dell'economia critica*, in Jossa B. & Lunghini G., eds, *Marxismo oggi*, Il Ponte Editore, Florence.

Plechanov G.V., 1911, *Anarchismo e socialismo*, 3rd edn, Ital. transl., Samonà e Savelli, Rome, 1971.

Poletti L., 1905, Un cimitero di cooperative, *Giornale degli economisti*, vol. 11, no. 31, September.

Potter B., 1893, *The Cooperative Movement in Great Britain*, Swan Sonnershein, London.

Poulantzas N., 1968, Brevi note sull'oggetto del Capitale, in Vv.Aa., eds, *Cent'anni dopo il Capitale*, Ital. transl., Samonà e Savelli, Rome, 1970.

Poulantzas N., 1973, *Classes in Contemporary Capitalism*, London, New Left Books.

Poulantzas N., 1974, *Classi sociali e capitalismo oggi*, Ital. transl., Etas Libri, Milan, 1975.

Prandergast C., 1999, The Provisions of Incentives on Firms, *Journal of Economic Literature*, vol. 37.

Preobrazhensky E.A., 1926, *The New Economics*, Clarendon Press, Oxford, 1965.

Prestipino G., 1973, *Natura e società*, Editori Riuniti, Rome.

Proudhon P.J., 1846, *Système des Contradictions économiques ou Philosophie de la Misère*, Michel Rivière, Paris, 1926.

Prychitko D.L. & Vanek J., eds, 1996, *Producer Cooperatives and Labor-managed Systems*, Edward Elgar Publishing, Cheltenham, UK and Brookfield, VT, USA.

Putterman L., 1982, Some Behavioural Perspectives on the Dominance of Hierarchical over Democratic Form of Enterprise, *Journal of Economic Behaviour and Organization*, vol. 3.

Putterman L., 1984, On Some Explanations of Why Capital Hires Labor, *Economic Inquiry*, vol. 22, no. 2.

Putterman L., Roemer J.E. & Silvestre J., 1998, Does Egalitarianism Have a Future?, *Journal of Economic Literature*, vol. 36, no. 2.

Quarter J., 1992, *Canada's Social Economy*, J. Lorimer & Co, Toronto.

Rabbeno U., 1889, Le società cooperative di produzione. Contributo allo studio della questione operaia, *La rivista della cooperazione*, no. 1, Rome.

Ragionieri E., 1965, Il marxismo e la Prima Internazionale, in Ragionieri E., 1968, *Il marxismo e l'Internazionale*, Editori Riuniti, Rome.

Ramos-Martinez A. & Rodriguez-Herrera A., 1996, The Transformation of Values into Prices of Production: A Different Reading of Marx's

Text, in Freeman A. & Carchedi G., eds, *Marx and Non-Equilibrium Economics*, Edward Elgar Publishing, Cheltenham, UK and Brookfield, VT, USA.

Rapone L., 2011, *Cinque anni che paiono secoli; Antonio Gramsci dal socialismo al comunismo (1914–1919)*, Carocci Editore, Rome.

Rawls J., 1971, *A Theory of Justice*, Harvard Economic Press, Cambridge, MA.

Reed J., 1920, Come funziona il soviet, *L'Ordine nuovo*, no. 8, reprinted in Vv.Aa., eds, 1970, *Marxismo ed etica*, Ital. transl., Feltrinelli, Milan.

Reich M. & Devine J., 1981, The Microeconomics of Conflict and Hierarchy in Capitalist Production, *Review of Radical Political Economics*, vol. 13, January.

Resnick S. & Wolff R.D., 1982, Classes in Marxian Theory, *Review of Radical Political Economics*, vol. 13, no. 4.

Reuten G., 2002, Marx's *Capital III*, the Culmination of *Capital*, in Campbell M. & Reuten G., eds, *The Culmination of Capital; Essays on Volume III of Marx's* Capital, Palgrave, London.

Rigi J., 2013, Peer Production and Marxian Communism: Contours of a New Emerging Mode of Production, *Capital and Class*, vol. 37, no 3.

Riguzzi B. & Porcari R., 1925, *La cooperazione operaia*, Libreria Pontremoli, Turin.

Robinson J., 1942, *Marx e la scienza economica*, Ital. transl., La Nuova Italia, Florence, 1951.

Robinson J. & Eatwell, J., 1973, *Economia Politica*, Ital. transl., Etas Libri, Milan, 1974.

Rockmore T., 2005, Lukàks tra Marx e il marxismo, in Fineschi R., ed., *Karl Marx: Rivisitazioni e prospettive*, Mimesis, Milan.

Rodinson M., 1969, Sociologia marxista e ideologia marxista, in Vv.Aa., eds, *Marx vivo*, Mondadori, Milan.

Roelants B., 2000, Worker Cooperatives and Socio-economic Development: The Role of Mesolevel Institutions, *Economic Analysis*, vol. 3, no. 1.

Roemer J.E., 1982, *A General Theory of Exploitation and Class*, Harvard University Press, Cambridge, MA.

Roemer J.E., ed., 1986, *Analytical Marxism*, Cambridge University Press, Cambridge.

Roemer J.E., 1988, *Free To Lose: An Introduction To Marxist Economic Philosophy*, Harvard University Press, Cambridge, MA.

Roemer J.E., 1993, Can There Be Socialism after Communism?, in Bardhan P. & Roemer J.E., eds, *Market Socialism: The Current Debate*, Oxford Economic Press, New York.

Roemer J.E., 1994, *Egalitarian Perspectives: Essays in Philosophical Economics*, Cambridge Economic Press, Cambridge.

Roemer J.E., 2008, Socialism vs. Social Democracy as Income-Equalizing Institutions, *Eastern Economic Journal*, vol. 34, no. 1.

Rosanvallon P., 1976, *L'age de l'autogestion*, Seuil/Politique, Paris.

Rosdolsky R., 1955, *Genesi e struttura del 'Capitale' di Marx*, Ital. transl., Laterza, Bari, 1971.

Rosenthal J., 1988, *The Myth of Dialectics: Reinterpreting the Marx–Hegel Relation*, Macmillan, London.

Rosselli C., 1930, *Socialismo liberale*, Einaudi, Turin, 1973.

Rothschild K.W., 1986, Capitalist and Entrepreneurs: Prototypes and Roles, in Wagener H.J. & Drukker J.W., eds, *The Economic Law of Motion of Modern Society*, Cambridge University Press, Cambridge.

Rovatti P.A., 1973, *Critica e scientificità in Marx*, Feltrinelli, Milan.

Rubel M., 1974, *Marx critico del marxismo*, Ital. transl., Cappelli, Bologna, 1981.

Rubin I.I., 1928, *Saggi sulla teoria del valore di Marx*, Ital. transl., Feltrinelli, Milan, 1976.

Russel R. & Hanneman R., 1992, Cooperatives and the Business Cycle: The Israeli Case, *Journal of Comparative Economics*, vol. 16, no 4.

Russell B., 1935, *Storia delle idee del secolo XIX*, Ital. transl., Mondadori, Milan, 1970.

Saad-Filho A., 1996, The Value of Money, the Value of Labour Power and the Net Product: An Appraisal of the 'New Approach' to the Transformation Problem, in Freeman A. & Carchedi G., eds, *Marx and Non-Equilibrium Economics*, Edward Elgar Publishing, Cheltenham, UK and Brookfield, VT, USA.

Saad-Filho A., 1997, Concrete and Abstract Labour in Marx's Theory of Value, *Review of Political Economy*, vol. 9, no. 4.

Sacconi L., 1992, I costi di governo e i benefici della proprietà dei lavoratori, in Gramaglia E. & Sacconi L., eds, *Cooperazione, benessere e organizzazione economica*, F. Angeli, Milan.

Sachs I., 1969, Marx e i fondamenti della previsione economico-sociale, in Vv.Aa., eds, *Marx vivo*, Mondadori, Milan.

Salvadori M.L., 1979, La socialdemocrazia tedesca e la rivoluzione russa del 1905. Il dibattito sullo sciopero di massa e sulle 'differenze' tra Oriente e Occidente, in Salvadori M.L., 1981, *Dopo Marx*, Einaudi, Turin.

Salvadori M.L., 2015, Perché è debole e divisa la grande eredità del Novecento, *La Repubblica*, 3 April.

Salvemini G., 1993, *Movimento socialista e questione meridionale*, ed. Arfè, Feltrinelli, Milan.

Samuelson P.M., 1967, Marxian Economics and Economics, *American Economic Review*, vol. 57, May.

Sapelli G., 1982, Necessità di una teoria dell'impresa cooperativa, in Lega nazionale cooperative e mutue, ed., *L'impresa cooperativa negli anni 80*, De Donato, Bari.

Sapelli G., 1998, *La cooperazione: impresa e movimento sociale*, Edizioni Lavoro, Rome.

Sapelli G., 2006, *Coop: il futuro dell'impresa cooperativa*, Einaudi, Turin.

Sartori G., 1995, *Elementi di teoria politica*, 3rd edn, Il Mulino, Bologna.

Sartori G., 2006 [1993], *Democrazia. Cos'è*, Rizzoli, Milan.

Sartre J.P., 1960, *Critica della ragione dialettica*, Ital. transl., Il Saggiatore, Milan, 1963.

Scalfari E., 2013, La fragile armonia di una politica ambigua, *La Repubblica*, 27 October.

Schaff A., 1965, *Il marxismo e la persona umana*, Ital. transl., Feltrinelli, Milan, 1966.

Schaff A., 1974, Marxismo, strutturalismo e il metodo della scienza, Ital. transl., Feltrinelli, Milan, 1976.

Schlicht E. & Von Weizsäcker C.C., 1977, Risk Financing in Labour Managed Economies: The Commitment Problem, *Zeitschrift fúr die Gesamte Staatswissenschaft*, special issue.

Schumpeter J.A., 1950, The March into Socialism, *American Economic Review*, vol. 60, no. 2.

Schumpeter J.A., 1954, *Storia dell'analisi economica*, Ital. transl., Einaudi, Turin, 1959.

Schumpeter J.A., 1976, *Capitalism, Socialism and Democracy*, 5th edn, Unwin, London, 1987.

Schweickart D., 1992, Socialism, Democracy, Market Planning: Putting the Pieces Together, *Review of Radical Political Economics*, vol. 24, no. 3–4.

Schweickart D., 1993, *Against Capitalism*, Cambridge University Press, Cambridge.

Schweickart D., 2002, *After Capitalism*, Rowman & Littlefield, Lanham, MD.

Schweickart D., 2005, Marx's Democratic Critique of Capitalism, and Its Implications for China's Development Strategy, *Teaching and Research*, no. 10.

Screpanti E., 2001, *The Fundamental Institutions of Capitalism*, Routledge, London.

Screpanti E., 2002, Contratto di lavoro, regimi di proprietà e governo dell'accumulazione: verso una teoria generale del capitalismo, in Fausto D., Jossa B. & Panico C., eds, *Teoria economia e riformismo politico*, F. Angeli, Milan.

Screpanti E., 2003, Value and Exploration: A Counterfactual Approach, *Review of Political Economy*, no. 1.

Screpanti E., 2007, *Comunismo libertario*, Manifestolibri, Rome.

Screpanti E., 2011, *Marx dalla totalità alla moltitudine (1841–1843)*, ed. Petite plaisance, Pistoia.

Sekine T.T., 1995a, A Uno School Seminar on the Theory of Value, in Albritton R. & Sekine T.T., eds, *A Japanese Approach to Political Economy*, Palgrave, New York.

Sekine T.T., 1995b, The Necessity of the Law of Value, Its Demonstration and Significance, in Albritton R. & Sekine T.T., eds, *A Japanese Approach to Political Economy*, Palgrave, New York.

Selucky R., 1974, Marxism and Self-Management, reprinted in Nove A. & Thatcher I.D., eds, 1994, *Markets and Socialism*, Edward Elgar Publishing, Aldershot, UK and Brookfield, VT, USA.

Sertel M.R., 1982, *Workers and Incentives*, North-Holland, Amsterdam.

Sève L., 1970, Metodo strutturale e metodo dialettico, in Godelier M. & Sève L., eds, *Marxismo e strutturalismo*, Einaudi, Turin.

Severino E., 1978, *Gli abitatori del tempo. Cristianesimo, marxismo, tecnica*, Armando, Rome.

Severino E., 2012, *Capitalismo senza futuro*, Rizzoli, Milan.

Sgrò G., 2016, *Mega-Marx, studi sulla edizione e sulla recezione di Marx in Germania e in Italia*, Orthotes, Naples.

Sherman H., 1995, *Reinventing Marxism*, Johns Hopkins University Press, London.

Sidoti F., 1987, Parlamento e governo in Marx. Alcune 'verità sociologiche' di un centenario, in Nassisi A.M., ed., *Marx e il mondo contemporaneo*, Editori Riuniti, Rome.

Sinha A., 1982, The Transformation Problem: Is the Standard Commodity a Solution?, *Review of Radical Political Economics*, vol. 32, no. 2.

Skillman G.L., 2013, The Puzzle of Marx's Missing 'Results': A Tale of Two Theories, *History of Political Economy*, vol. 48, no. 3.

Smith A., 1776, *Indagine sulla natura e le cause della ricchezza delle nazioni*, Ital. transl., Milan, ISEDI, 1973.

Smith A, 1790, *Teoria dei sentimenti morali*, 6th edn, Ital. transl., Rizzoli, Milan, 2001.

Smith S.C. & Rothbaum J., 2013, *Cooperatives in a Global Economy: Key Economic Issues, Recent Trends, and Potential for Development*, IZA policy paper no. 68.

Sobel R., 2008, Travail et justice dans la société communiste chez Marx. Un commentaire à propos de quelques ambiguïtés naturalistes de 'l'etage du bas' de la 'phase superieure' du communisme, *Economies et Sociétés*, vol. 40, no. 5.

Sombart W., 1894, Zur Kritik des oekonomischen Systems von Karl Marx, *Archiv für Soziale Gesetzgebung und Statistik*, vol. 7, no. 4.

Southworth G., 1972, Samuelson on Marx: A Note, *Review of Radical Political Economics*, vol. 4, no. 5.

Sowell T., 1985, *Marxism; Philosophy and Economics*, Quill William Morris, New York.

Sraffa P., 1960, *Produzione di merci a mezzo di merci*, Einaudi, Turin.

Srinivasan R. & Phansalkar, S.J., 2003, Residual Claims in Cooperatives: Design Issues, *Annals of Public and Cooperative Economics*, vol. 74, no. 3, September.

Stauber L.G., 1987, Capitalism vs. Socialism: Some General Issues and the Relevance of Austrian Experience, reprinted in Nove A. & Thatcher I.D., eds, 1994, *Markets and Socialism*, Edward Elgar Publishing, Aldershot, UK and Brookfield, VT, USA.

Stauber L.G., 1989, Age-Dependence and Historical Effects on the Failure Rates of Worker Cooperatives: An Event-History Analysis, *Economic and Industrial Democracy*, vol. 10, no. 1.

Stedman Jones G., 1978, Ritratto di Engels, in Hobsbawm E.J., Haupt G., Marek F., Ragionieri E., Strada V. & Vivanti C., eds, 1978–82, *Storia del marxismo*, Einaudi, Turin.

Steedman I., 1995, Socialism and Marginalism in Economics, 1870–1930. A Brief Overview, in Steedman I., ed., *Socialism and Marginalism in Economics, 1870–1930*, Routledge, London.

Steinberg H.J., 1979, Il partito e la formazione dell'ortodossia marxista, in Hobsbawm E.J., Haupt G., Marek F., Ragionieri E., Strada V. & Vivanti C., eds, 1978–82, *Storia del marxismo*, 5 vols, Einaudi, Turin, vol. 2.

Steinherr A., 1975, Profit-Maximizing vs. Labor-Managed Firms: A Comparison of Market Structure and Firm Behavior, *Journal of Industrial Economics*, vol. 24, no. 1.

Steinherr A. & Thisse J.F., 1979a, Are Labour-Managers Really Perverse?, *Economic Letters*, vol. 2, no. 2.

Steinherr A. & Thisse J.F., 1979b, Is There a Negatively-Sloped Supply Curve in the Labour-Managed Firm?, *Economic Analysis and Workers' Management*, vol. 13, 35.

Sterner T., 1990, Ownership, Technology and Efficiency: An Empirical Study of Cooperatives, Multinationals, and Domestic Enterprises in the Mexican Cement Industry, *Journal of Comparative Economics*, vol. 4, no. 2.

Stiglitz J.E. & Weiss A., 1981, Credit Rationing in Markets with Imperfect Competition, *American Economic Review*, vol. 71, June.

Struve P., 1899, La théorie marxienne de l'évolution sociale, reprinted in *Cahiers de l'Institut de science économique appliquée*, vol. 129, September, 1962.

Sweezy P.M., 1942, *Teoria dello sviluppo capitalistico*, Boringhieri, Turin.

Sweezy P.M., 1963, Communism as an Ideal, *Monthly Review*, October.

Sweezy P.M., 1967, Marx and the Proletariat, in Wood J.C., ed., 1988, *Karl Marx's Economics: Critical Assessments*, Croom Helm, Sydney, vol. 4.

Sweezy P.M., 1968, Cecoslovacchia, capitalismo e socialismo, *Monthly Review*, November.

Sweezy P.M., 1969, A Reply to Bettelheim, *Monthly Review*, March–April.

Sweezy P.M., 1971, Sulla teoria del capitalismo monopolistico, in Sweezy P.M., 1972, *Il capitalismo moderno*, Ital. transl., Liguori, Naples, 1975.

Sylos Labini P., 2004, *Torniamo ai classici*, Laterza, Bari.

Sylos Labini P., 2006, Perché gli economisti debbono fare i conti con Marx, in Jossa B. & Lunghini G., eds, *Marxismo oggi*, Il Ponte Editore, Florence.

Tarrit F., 2006, A Brief History, Scope and Peculiarities of 'Analytical Marxism', *Review of Radical Political Economics*, vol. 38, no. 4.

Tasca A., 1950, *Nascita e avvento del fascismo*, Universale Laterza, Bari, 1965.

Tawney R.H., 1918, The Conditions of Economic Liberty, in Hinden R., ed., 1964, *The Radical Tradition*, Pantheon Books, New York.

Thomas H. & Logan C., 1982, *Mondragon: An Economic Analysis*, George Allen and Unwin, London.

Thomas P., 1984, Alien Politics: A Marxian Perspective on Citizenship and Democracy, in Ball T. & Farr J., eds, *After Marx*, Cambridge University Press, Cambridge.

Thompson W., 1827, *Labour Rewarded: The Claims of Labour and Capital Conciliated by One of the Idle Classes, or, How to Secure to Labour the Whole Products of Its Exertions*, August McKelley, New York, 1969.

Togliatti P., 1920, Cooperative o schiavitù, reprinted in Togliatti P., 1967, *Opere*, ed. E. Ragionieri, Editori Riuniti, Rome.

Tornquist D., 1973, Workers' Management: The Intrinsic Issues, in Hunnius G., Garson G.D. & Case J., eds, *Workers' Control; A Reader on Labor and Social Change*, Vintage Books, New York.

Tortia E., 2008, *Le determinanti dello sforzo lavorativo nelle imprese sociali*, Università di Trento, Trento.

Tosel A., 1996, *Études sur Marx (et Engels). Vers un communisme de la finitude*, Kimé, Paris.

Tosel A., 2005, Perché la proposta del comunismo della finitudine?, in Musto M., ed., *Sulle tracce di un fantasma*, Manifestolibri, Rome.

Touraine A., Wieviorka M. & Dubet F., 1984, *Il movimento operaio*, Ital. transl., Franco Angeli, Milan, 1988.

Tronti M., 1962, La fabbrica e la società, in *Quaderni Rossi*, II, ristampa, Sapere, Milano-Roma, 1974.

Tronti M., 1977, *Sull'autonomia del politico*, Feltrinelli, Milan.

Tronti M., 1978, Operaismo e centralità operaia, in Vv.Aa., eds, *Operaismo e centralità operaia*, Editori Riuniti, Rome.

Tronti M., 2008, Classe, in Vv.Aa., eds, *Lessico marxiano*, Manifestolibri, Rome.

Trotsky L., 1938, *La loro morale e la nostra*, Ital. transl., De Donato, Bari, 1967.

Trower C., 1973, Collective Bargaining and Industrial Democracy, in Hunnius G., Garson G.D. & Case J., eds, *Workers' Control; A Reader on Labor and Social Change*, Vintage Books, New York.

Tseo G.K.Y., Hou Gui Sheng, Zhang Peng-Zhu & Zang Libain, 2004, Employee Ownership and Profit Sharing as Positive Factors in the Reform of Chinese State-Owned Enterprises, *Economic and Industrial Democracy*, vol. 25, no. 1.

Tsuru S., 1969, Marx e l'analisi del capitalismo. Un nuovo studio della contraddizione fondamentale?, in Vv.Aa., eds, *Marx vivo*, Mondadori, Milan.

Tucker R.C., 1961, *Philosophy and Myth in Karl Marx*, Cambridge University Press, Cambridge.

Turati F., 1897, Il miraggio delle cooperative, *Critica sociale*, 1 August, 16 August and 1 September.

Turchetto M., 2001, From 'Mass Worker' to 'Empire': The Disconcerting Trajectory of Italian Operaismo, in Bidet J. & Kouvelakis S., eds, 2008, *Critical Companion to Contemporary Marxism*, Brill, Leiden.

Vacca G., 1969a, *Lukàcs o Korsch?*, De Donato, Bari.

Vacca G., 1969b, *Marxismo e analisi sociale*, De Donato, Bari.

Vahabi M., 2010, Integrating Social Conflict into Economic Theory, *Cambridge Journal of Economics*, vol. 34, no. 4, July.

Valenti G., 1902, L'associazione cooperativa e la distribuzione della ricchezza. Contributo alla teoria economica della cooperazione, in *Archivio giuridico 'Filippo Serafini'*, Mucchi editore, Modena.

Van Parijs P., 1993, Envoi: The Greening of Marx, in Van Parijs P., *Marxism Recycled*, Cambridge University Press, Cambridge.

Vanek J., 1970, *The General Theory of Labour-Managed Market Economies*, Cornell University Press, Ithaca, NY.

Vanek J., 1971a, Some Fundamental Considerations on Financing and the Form of Ownership under Labor Management, reprinted in Vanek J., 1977, *The Labor Managed Economy: Essays by J. Vanek*, Cornell University Press, Ithaca, NY.

Vanek J., 1971b, The Basic Theory of Financing of Participatory Firms, reprinted in Vanek J., 1977, *The Labor Managed Economy: Essays by J. Vanek*, Cornell University Press, Ithaca, NY.

Vanek J., 1972, *The Economics of Workers' Management: A Yugoslav Case Study*, Allen and Unwin, London.

Vanek J., 1977, Educazione alla pratica dell'autogestione, in Vanek J., 1985, *Imprese senza padrone nelle economie di mercato*, Edizioni Lavoro, Rome.

Vanek J., 1993, From Partnership with Paper to Partnership among Human Beings, in Atkinson A.B., ed., *Alternatives to Capitalism: The Economics of Partnership*, Macmillan, London.

Vanek J., 2006, The Future, Dynamics and Fundamental Principles of Growth of Economic Democracy, mimeo.

Vaughan-Whitehead D., 1999, Employee Ownership on the Policy Agenda: Lessons from Central and Eastern Europe, *Economic Analysis*, vol. 2, February.

Veblen T., 1892, Some Neglected Points in the Theory of Socialism, *Annals of the American Academy of Political and Social Science*, vol. 2.

Vidoni F., 2007, Sulla presenza della dialettica nell'epistemologia recente, in Burgio A., ed., *Dialettica; tradizioni, problemi sviluppi*, Quodlibet Studio, Macerata.

Vinci P., 2008, Astrazione determinata, in Vv.Aa., eds, *Lessico marxiano*, Manifestolibri, Rome.

Virno P., 2008, Forza lavoro, in Vv.Aa., eds, *Lessico marxiano*, Manifestolibri, Rome.

Volpi F., 1989, Sistema economico e modo di produzione, in Jossa B., ed., *Teoria dei sistemi economici*, UTET, Turin.

Vorländer C., 1911, Kant e Marx, in Vv.Aa., eds, *Marxismo ed etica*, Ital. transl., Feltrinelli, Milan.

Vygodsky V.S., 1967, *Introduzione ai 'Grundrisse' di Marx*, Ital. transl., La Nuova Italia, Florence, 1974.

Wallerstein I., 2002, New Revolts against the System, *New Left Review*, November–December.

Walras L., 1865, *Les associations populaires*, Dentu, Paris.

Walras L., 1987, *Oeuvres économiques complètes*, ed. C. Hebert & J.P. Potier, Economica, Paris.

Walras L., 1990 [1866–67], Etudes d'économie sociale. Théorie de la répartition de la richesse sociale. Œuvres économiques complètes d'Auguste et Léon Walras, in *Economica*, vol. 9.

Ward B.N., 1958, The Firm in Illyria: Market Syndicalism, *American Economic Review*, vol. 48, no. 4, September.

Ward B.N., 1967, *The Socialist Economy*, Random House, New York.

Webb B., 1891, *The Cooperative Movement in Great Britain*, Swan Sonnenschein & Co, London.

Webb B., 1920, *The Cooperative Movement in Great Britain*, London, Forgotten Books, 2012.

Weber Marianne, 1984, *Max Weber, una biografia*, Ital. transl., Il Mulino, Bologna, 1995.

Weber Max, 1904–1905, *L'etica protestante e lo spirito del capitalismo*, Ital. transl., RCS Quotidiani, Milan, 2010.

Weil S., 1955, *Riflessioni sulle cause della libertà e dell'oppressione sociale*, Ital. transl., Adelphi, Milan, 2008.

Weitzman M. & Kruse D.L., 1990, Profit Sharing and Productivity, in Blinder A., ed., *Paying for Productivity: A Look at the Evidence*, Brookings Institution, Washington, DC.

Wennerlind C., 2002, The Labor Theory of Value and the Strategic Role of Alienation, *Capital and Class*, no. 77, spring.

West E.G., 1969, The Political Economy of Alienation: Karl Marx and Adam Smith, reprinted in Wood J.C., ed., 1988, *Karl Marx's Economics: Critical Assessments*, Croom Helm, Sydney, vol. 1.

Westra R., 2002, Marxian Economic Theory and an Ontology of Socialism: A Japanese Intervention, *Capital and Class*, no. 78, autumn.

Wetter G.A., 1948, *Il materialismo dialettico sovietico*, Einaudi, Turin.

Wiles P., 1962, *The Political Economy of Communism*, Harvard University Press, Cambridge, MA.

Williamson O.E., 1975, *Markets and Hierarchies: Analysis and Anti-Trust implications*, Free Press, New York.

Wilson E.O., 1998, *L'armonia meravigliosa*, Ital. transl., Mondadori, Milan, 1999.

Wolff R., 2012, *Democracy at Work: A Cure for Capitalism*, Haymarket Books, Chicago.

Wolff R., Callari A. & Roberts B., 1982, Marx's (not Ricardo's) Transformation Problem: A Radical Reconceptualization, *History of Political Economy*, vol. 14, no 4.

Wolff R., Callari A. & Roberts B., 1984, A Marxian Alternative to the Traditional Transformation Problem, *Review of Radical Political Economics*, vol. 16, no. 2–3.

Wolff R., Callari A. & Roberts B., 1998, The Transformation Trinity: Value, Value Form and Price, in Bellofiore R., ed., *Marxian Economics: A Reappraisal*, Palgrave Macmillan, New York.

Woltmann L., 1898, *System des moralischen Bewußtseins*, Michels, Düsseldorf.

Wright E. O., 1985, What is Analytical Marxism?, in Carver and Thomas, 1995. Carver T., Thomas P. 1995, eds, *Rational Choice Marxism*, Macmillan, London.

Wright E.O., 1995, What Is Analytical Marxism?, in Carver T. & Thomas P., eds, *Rational Choice Marxism*, Macmillan, London.

Wright Mills C., 1962, *I marxisti*, Ital. transl., Feltrinelli, Milan, 1969.

Yudt T., 2012, *Novecento; il ruolo degli intellettuali e della politica*, Ital. transl., Laterza, Bari, 2012.

Yunker J.A., 1992, *Socialism Revised and Modernised*, Praeger, New York.

Yunker J.A., 1995, Post-Lange Market Socialism: An Evolution of Profit Oriented Proposal, *Journal of Economics Issues*, vol. 29, no. 3, September.

Zamagni S., 2005, Per una teoria economico-civile dell'impresa cooperativa, in Mazzoli E. & Zamagni S., eds, *Verso una nuova teoria economica della cooperazione*, Il Mulino, Bologna.

Zamagni S., 2006, Promozione cooperativa e civilizzazione del mercato, in Bulgarelli M. & Viviani M., eds, *La promozione cooperativa: Copfond tra mercato e solidarietà*, Il Mulino, Bologna.

Zamagni S., 2008, Sul nesso causale tra economia e sviluppo economico, in Quadrio Curzio A. & Marseguerra G., eds, *Democracy, Institutions and Social Justice*, Libri Scheiwiller, Milan.

Zamagni V. & Felice E., 2006, *Oltre il secolo: le trasformazioni del sistema cooperativo Legacoop alla fine del secondo millennio*, Il Mulino, Bologna.

Zangheri R., Galasso G. & Castronovo V., 1987, *Storia del movimento cooperativo in Italia*, Einaudi, Turin.

Zanone V., 2002, Il liberalismo di Franco Romani, *Biblioteca della libertà*, no. 164–5, May–August.

Zanotti A., 2016, *Cooperative e imprese di capitali: quanto sono diverse e quanto sono uguali?*, Rubettino, Soveria Mannelli, Catanzaro.

Zevi A., 1982, The Performance of Italian Producer Cooperatives, in Jones D.C. & Svejnar J., eds, *Participatory and Self-Managed Firms: Evaluating Economic Performance*, Heath, Lexington, MD.

Zolo D., 1974, *La teoria comunista dell'estinzione dello Stato*, De Donato, Bari.

Index